ISBN: 9781314714081

Published by:
HardPress Publishing
8345 NW 66TH ST #2561
MIAMI FL 33166-2626

Email: info@hardpress.net
Web: http://www.hardpress.net

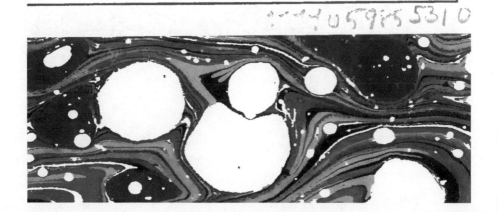

EX LIBRIS

RESONARE CHRISTUM

From the Library of

JEANNE D'ARC.

Engraved by J. Swaine.

From an Original Picture in
the Town House at Orleans.

MEMOIRS

OF

JEANNE D'ARC,

SURNAMED

LA PUCELLE D'ORLEANS;

WITH THE

HISTORY OF HER TIMES.

IN TWO VOLUMES.

VOL. I.

LONDON:

PRINTED FOR ROBERT TRIPHOOK,

OLD BOND STREET.

1824.

ADVERTISEMENT.

As the use of so many Roman numericals in paging these volumes may appear singular to the reader, we beg leave to state that they were adopted in consequence of an alteration having taken place in the original plan of the work after some sheets had been printed. In the first instance it was only intended to print the DIARY of the SIEGE OF ORLEANS, with Notes; but owing to the bulk of original matter in the Editor's possession, it was afterwards determined to extend the publication to two volumes, which led to this mode of paging. The writer having for some years made the subject of JEANNE D'ARC his particular study, and the major part of the documents comprised in these pages having never before appeared in print, it is hoped that circumstance will compensate for the irregularity thus alluded to.

ENGRAVINGS IN THE FIRST VOLUME.

CONTENTS

OF

THE FIRST VOLUME.

TITLE OF THE ORIGINAL MANUSCRIPT.

Historical Diary of the Siege of Orleans by the English; begun on Tuesday the 12th day of October, 1428: Charles VII., King of France, then reigning. With an account of all the Sallies, Assaults, Skirmishes, and other notable particulars, which occurred from day to day; with the arrival of Jeanne La Pucelle,

CONTENTS.

SUMMARY

OF THE

REVOLUTIONS OF FRANCE

DURING THE

REIGNS OF CHARLES VI. AND CHARLES VII.

WHICH IMMEDIATELY PRECEDED THE APPEARANCE OF

JEANNE D'ARC,

LA PUCELLE D'ORLEANS.

b

SUMMARY,

TOWARDS the close of the fourteenth century, Charles V., son of Jean le Bon and grandson of Philip de Valois, healed those accumulated evils which the first representatives of the race of Valois had heaped upon France by their imprudence and obstinate conduct, and had thus succeeded in rendering the kingdom more flourishing than at any former period.

In regard to her exterior relations, France boasted several allies, and scarcely any enemies; while the English, who had been masters of half the French territory, found themselves not only confined to the ports of Bordeaux, Bayonne, and Calais, but reduced to watch over their own country, on account of the fleets of France which incessantly menaced the safety of the British coast. The gallant Edward the Black Prince, victor at Cressy and Poitiers, and conqueror of Jean le Bon, had ceased to exist; and his son, Richard II., then only a child of eleven years of age, filled the throne of the belligerent Edward III.; while the reins of government were in the hands of the dukes of Lancaster, York, and Gloucester, princes divided in their political opinions, and more occupied in studying their private interests, than

striving to exert themselves for the benefit of the
state: in short, every thing appeared favourable to
the French government, and to preclude all idea
of invasion from beyond seas.

In the south, the house of Castile was indebted to
France for the crown; and although gratitude cannot
be ranked as a virtue appertaining to governments,
yet, that degree of modesty which sometimes
checks the too frequent and immoral proceedings
of policy, seemed to promise that the inheritors
of Henry Transtamare would not very speedily
forget the eminent services performed by the great
Duguesclin.

Italy and the East were not even in a state to
menace France; for the grand schism in respect to
the papacy had lulled the spiritual thunders to rest:
Genoa wished to become subject to the French, an
event that subsequently took place in 1395: the
queen of Naples claimed of France a successor, and
the duke of Milan was fearful of losing his chance:
the progress of the Turks, and the safeguard of its
commerce, completely occupied the states of Venice:
Savoy was too enfeebled to think of aggression:
Switzerland, occupied in checking the efforts of
Austria, and extending her confederation, served as
a boulevard for France against Germany: Burgundy
was in possession of a French prince of the blood
royal, to whom also several provinces of the Low
Countries had devolved: the prince of Lorraine

sought for a son-in-law and an heir in another
French house; and the whole power of Scotland
was at the disposal of the French government:
indeed, if the king of France had only sought, in
a proper manner, to unite Brittany to his empire,
the duke, satisfied with the recovery of his estates,
would have tendered the monarch every facility for
repairing his unjust and impolitic fault, without
incurring dishonour.

In the interior of the kingdom, sedition and
rebellion were at an end; a numerous and well disciplined army, experienced generals, a nobility
replete with valour, a marine already equal to that
of Castile, and superior to the maritime force of
England, (which had so much fallen to decay since
the death of Edward III., that the parliament com-
plained aloud on that head in 1377, the first year
of the reign of Richard II.,) all combined to ensure
tranquillity abroad as well as at home. In addition
to this, the revenues of France were prosperous,
though taxation was moderate; her finances were
well administered; the treasure was immense; the
magistrates and public functionaries of every class
were found by experience to do honour to their
respective employments; agriculture, freed from the
hordes of adventurers who had formerly oppressed
it, was pursued with redoubled energy; commerce
and industry were encouraged; arts and sciences
had awakened from the long dream of feudal

oppression ; the citizens, in short the whole population, became united in support of the government,
whose benefits and whose services were duly appre-
ciated, after twenty years of civil commotion, blood-
shed, and plunder. Such proved the state of France
about the year 1380.

This fortunate posture of affairs might, indeed, have
increased, since Charles V., to whom it was due, still
continued in the prime of life. — Alas ! the prosperity of millions is frequently dependent on the
life of one individual ! The king died ; * the administration of public affairs devolved to a regent ; †
and almost immediately a series of evils deluged re-
viving France, during a longer period of time than
that sedulously occupied by Charles in re-establishing her prosperity. The experience acquired from
the last regencies to which France was subjected,
rendered the then state of affairs so familiar to
the public mind, that the idea of a regency is, even
to the present day, obnoxious to a Frenchman's

* Charles V. was born on the 21st January, 1337 ; he ascended
the throne on the 8th of April, 1364 ; and died on the 16th
September, 1380. — See *Laboureur, Introduction*, page 3 and 4 ;
Villaret, xi. 101 ; *Thomassin*, 86.

† Charles VI. at this period was only eleven years old, being
born on the 3d December, 1368 ; and, from an ordinance issued
in 1374, it appears that the king did not enter into his majority
until the age of fourteen. — See *Laboureur, Introduction*,
pages 4 and 5.

ear : a sentiment, perhaps, better founded in justice
in the age of Charles VII., than at the present time.
According to the existing state of European government, a regent can only be regarded as the first
subject of the king ; but at the period on which we
are writing he was sometimes the monarch. At the
present day he may be tempted to increase his
fortune at the expense of the revenues of his prince ;
whereas, formerly, he was prompted to augment his
authority by the aid of his wealth and the forces
of the state. Charles V. had been fearful of the
first inconvenience ; but he was not sufficiently awake
to the danger of the second, or, perhaps, the generosity of his own heart had concealed from him the
extent of the danger : besides, are we now aware
whether the laws and public opinion, at that period,
might have sanctioned or tolerated those measures
that would have been necessary to prevent the evil ?
Be this, however, as it may, Charles had recourse only
to timid, and consequently inefficacious precautions.
He never made mention of the word *regency* in the
ordinance which he published concerning the future
government of the kingdom; all that he prescribed
on this subject was, fixing the data of his successor's
majority, such being the only act passed in regard
to his survivor. The first care of the regent duke of
Anjou, younger brother of the king, was to take
possession of the treasures of the monarchy, upon
which had been founded the hopes of future pro-

sperity; and with the greater semblance of reason, as the finances of all the neighbouring states were in a most impoverished condition. It would be futile to suppose that these riches were carefully hoarded up by a man whose boundless pride was solely bent on his own aggrandizement. The rank of first prince of the blood, and the eminent post of regent, did not satisfy his inordinate vanity, — a crown could alone satiate his ambition; and the hope of effecting the conquest of Naples, in his opinion, sanctioned the attempt to gain it. To accomplish this scheme, after having exhausted the royal treasures in the short space of two months; in order to make good the deficit, he became as cruel as rapacious in pillaging the people, rendering himself equally dreaded by his subjects as by the enemies of the state. New imposts were imperiously called for to augment the scanty supplies exacted from the public; these measures fomented revolts,* and forced

* Le Laboureur speaks positively respecting these popular tumults, at page 50 of his introductory matter; and in regard to the rigorous measures pursued, as well as for a detail of such commotions, see the same history, pages 6, 13, 15, 35, and 41. It was, above all, in the month of February, 1384, at the return from the expedition which had been undertaken to Flanders, that these coercive measures were in particular resorted to. Many of the Parisians, in easy circumstances, were punished with death, and thousands of the citizens condemned to pay penalties which ended in their complete ruin, without the public treasury being in any degree benefited.

the government to adopt those rigorous proceedings which very soon terminated in alienating the affection and respect of the citizens.

The regent had not yet completed the preparations for his expedition, when, as a just punishment for his crimes, he lost his life ; upon which Philip le Hardi, duke of Burgundy, one of his brothers, hastened the young king, Charles VI., into a fresh war, from motives of self-interest. Flanders, which was one day to become his territory, in right of his wife, only gave him a precarious power; because the Flemish, enriched by their commerce, were incessantly struggling against their sovereigns : and it was, therefore, upon this account that Philip le Hardi impelled the French monarch to march with a formidable force, for the purpose of reducing that people to subjection. The victory of Rosbecq, obtained by the French, on the 11th November, 1382,* inflicted a blow from the effects of which the Flemish could not recover: this event strengthened the au-

* The above date of the battle of Rosbecq, which is omitted by Villaret, is in the history of Laboureur, page 63.

Notwithstanding the Flemish revolted several times, this victory was certainly a decisive blow ; in proof of which, a conclusive authority may be found in the discourse delivered by the ambassadors of Louis XI. to Charles le Téméraire, great grandson of Philip, in 1470. " Never," said they, " would the dukes of Burgundy have enjoyed such uninterrupted good fortune, had not Charles VI. humbled the Flemish, and re-established your grandfather in the possession of his estates."—See *Villaret*, xvii. 387.

thority of the counts of Flanders, and subsequently that of the house of Burgundy. Thus, the revenues of the French monarchy, and the blood of the people, served to cement an empire, which, in less than thirty years afterwards, had very nearly overturned its own government. Philip was not destitute of virtues, or attachment to France ; but the pernicious impulse of ambition stifled every nobler sentiment : nor was he, when invested with authority, very scrupulous in his measures, provided he could by any means enrich his own family.*

Although the second brother of Charles V., John, duke of Berri, did not thirst after a diadem, he no less contributed to increase the public calamities.† His whole life was one tissue of such extravagant

* And it might also be said, to satisfy his own inclination for magnificence and ceremony ; since the attendants on Philip's court were far more numerous and splendid than those of the French king, as will be found from a list of such personages, which does not occupy less than 91 pages : this document is to be found in the continuation of the Journal de Paris, as well as in Choisy, page 222. The duke also caused every thing to be paid him, even to the expedition undertaken against Flanders for his own particular interest ; yet, notwithstanding these enormous exactions, he died insolvent. See the *Introduction of Laboureur*, page 90, &c., who recites a number of exactions of Philip le Hardi.

† John, duc de Berri, voluntarily renounced all idea of governing, that he might enjoy the right of pillaging the people. He pretended that the provinces were indebted to him in all that his

dissipation, that absolutely nothing remained from the rapine and the plunder of every description of which he was guilty, during a lapse of thirty-six years. The royal treasures were lavished in useless prodigality, excepting only such sums as were expended in erecting palaces and churches, and furnishing the latter with an immense number of reliques.*

Preparations had been made for an expedition against England, which, to all appearance, would have impeded for a length of time any war between the two countries.† The fleet was upon the point

deceased brother, the duke of Anjou, had wrested from them. The prodigality of this prince converted him into a complete tyrant, and the consequence was, that whole towns, subject to his government, emigrated to Spain.

* In the inventory of the goods of this prince, appears the following singular collection of saintly scraps, viz.:— 1. A rib of Saint Zacharias; 2. Another of Saint Barbe; 3. Half of a foot of Saint Cyprian; 4. Half of the sponge whereon the Holy Virgin wept the martyrdom of Saint Stephen; 5. Half of the gridiron of Saint Lawrence; 6. Half of the rib of Saint Anthony: (see *Laboureur's Introduction*, page 85,) independent of which he had given numerous other reliques to different churches. For instance, to the abbey of Saint Denis, a part of the skull and the arm of Saint Benedict; for which he obtained in return the chin of Saint Hilary, and subsequently the hand of Saint Thomas the Apostle. See the same history, pages 249, 327, and 436; *Juvenal des Ursins*, page 127.

† The arrangements for the accomplishment of this undertaking had been prodigious. Among other objects, at the beginning of

of sailing, and only waited for the duke of Berri, as first prince of the blood royal, to assume the command : he, however, did not think fit to join in due time, fearful lest Charles VI. should reap the honour of the enterprise ; and thus, the enormous preparations were rendered abortive.

To describe these princes, is to convey a faint idea of the sufferings which France experienced during the first eight years of the reign of Charles VI., which comprised the period of their administration: nor does it less tend to delineate what the country must have suffered even to the period of their deaths ; when the king's extraordinary delirium left them at liberty to re-assume the sovereign authority, or to struggle and intrigue in order to acquire it. Notwithstanding this, it will scarcely be credited that France would have fared much better had Philip and John lived as well as the monarch ; even supposing the latter had uniformly continued insane, and under their direction.

In the first place, the administration exercised immediately under the direction of Charles, during the four years that he estranged himself from them,

August, 1386, nine hundred transports were assembled at the port of Ecluse ; Smollett computes them at twelve hundred. The duke of Berri did not arrive until the middle of the equinox ; so that the tempestuous weather, conjoined with the English forces, destroyed the major part of this numerous fleet.

merely tended to place public affairs in the hands of new depredators ; since his ministers and courtiers proved more bold than the two princes who had preceded them ; for it was their policy to enrich themselves as fast as possible, whereas the former were satisfied with the more ordinary course of ministerial rapacity. Charles, on the other hand, fiery and impetuous, without either character or application, full of phantasies and caprices, gave himself up entirely to their counsels, merely requiring that they would ease him of the burdens of state affairs, furnish food for his wavering mind, pamper his prodigality, (for he was not less extravagant than the dukes of Berri and of Burgundy,) gratify his love of pleasure, and constantly amuse him with chimerical projects. One of these courtiers, Oliver de Clisson, the successor of Duguesclin, in some respects praiseworthy, although, on account of his cruelty, surnamed the *Butcher*, carried this abuse of his credit to such a pitch, that he took upon himself to declare war against the duke of Brittany, under the mere suggestion that that prince had accorded an asylum, not to an enemy of the king, but one of his own opponents.*

* This was Pierre de Craon, who had endeavoured to procure the assassination of the constable ; the duke, however, solemnly protested his ignorance respecting the retreat of Craon. See *Laboureur's History,* page 216; *Choisy,* page 162; *Villaret,* xii. 110, &c.

The dukes of Berri and of Burgundy, irritated at
finding that the spoil of France, which they had been
accustomed to regard as their own patrimony, had
been consigned by the monarch to other hands, waited
with impatience for the moment when they might
vent their rage and avenge themselves.

Too soon did the evil genius of France present
the favourable opportunity, — if, indeed, they themselves were not accessory to this event. The appearance of the pretended spectre * which first

* About the beginning of August, 1392, it was apparent that
Charles, in his words and actions, became somewhat changed, at
which period he expressed a desire of riding out armed in the open
country; and in consequence he mounted on horseback, when, after
proceeding some distance, there came to meet him an ill-looking
man, in wretched attire, poor, and of miserable appearance, (some
authors state he wore the garb of an hermit,) who, seizing the
bridle of his palfrey, thus addressed the monarch : " King, where
goest thou ? proceed no farther, thou art betrayed, and it is
intended to deliver thee into the hands of thine adversaries."
Upon this Charles VI. immediately became frantic, running
distractedly in all directions, and striking whomsoever he met;
whereby four men were killed. Every effort was diligently
pursued in order to secure the king, who was conducted to his
chamber, and placed upon a bed, where he continued, neither
moving hands nor feet, being apparently dead ; and, upon the
arrival of the physicians, they adjudged him to be gone past all
hopes of recovery; every one wept and lamented ; and in this
state he was exposed to the view of those who wished to behold
him. This singular occurrence took place in the forest of Mans,
which Charles was traversing, in order to go to the attack of the

occasioned the mental derangement of Charles—that
apparition which is said to have presented itself
just as the expedition against Brittany was completed,
a measure those princes had uniformly opposed,
because the duke was their ally ; the particular care
they took in making no inquiry into this singular affair ; the eagerness displayed in abandoning the expedition on resuming their authority ; the immediate and
active proceedings instituted against the ministers
who might have unveiled the machinations connected
with this apparition ; every thing leads to a conjecture of their having been the primary agents in
this mysterious occurrence.*

In whatsoever light, however, the event may be
regarded, from the character of these princes, no one

duke of Brittany. Charles, however, recovered, and lived for
twenty-two years afterwards, being frequently subject to these
strange attacks ; and died at the Hotel of Saint Pol, in the fifty-
third year of his age.—See the *History of Laboureur*, p. 219;
Choisy, p. 163; *Villaret*, xii. 117.

* Independent of this supposed spectre, history details the
account of a grand ball, at which the fire caught the habiliments
of the king, who wore the disguise of a satyr ; which circumstance again turned his brain, the event having occurred at the
end of the January following.—*Laboureur*, page 235; *Juvenal*,
page 115. Some writers, however, conjecture that these accidents
only tended to increase a disease which had its origin in the
debaucheries that took place during the youth of this unfortunate
prince.—*Laboureur*, page 326 ; *Choisy*, pages 165, 185.

will imagine that France acquired much additional prosperity; because, having to make good the time lost during the reign of ministers and courtiers, it is but natural to suppose they adopted with redoubled ardour the means most expedient to facilitate their depredations, and augment their power. This line of conduct they uniformly pursued for the period of six years, during which they disposed of the kingdom just as suited their own convenience. Yet, however incredible it may seem, so wretched a state of affairs was nevertheless to give place to a still more deplorable order of things.

During this interval, Louis, duke of Orleans, the king's brother, and the queen, acquired the age of maturity. Louis possessed a very engaging exterior; he was affable, endearing, eloquent; and by obliging and generous manners, usurped an ascendency over the mind, and riveted the affections, before his real character could be ascertained: his conduct, however, soon unmasked the hidden duplicity of his soul and the depravity of his heart. He was ostentatious from taste, addicted to uncontrolled dissipation, not less audacious in rapine than his uncles; totally divested of the military talents of the one, and the faculties as an administrator possessed by the other; in short, he carried to an excess the vice of concupiscence, which was not imputed to either of them. Sacrificing every thing to his predilection for debauchery, he even dared to pollute the bed of his own brother, — of his sovereign ; and that, too, at a period when he scrupulously observed the forms of the most degrading superstition.

From this statement, some opinion may be formed respecting the character of his accomplice in iniquity, Isabella of Bavaria. Her name is, indeed, a stain upon the page of history; nor have four centuries sufficed to wipe away from the recollection of the French nation the odium so justly attached to her memory.

This unnatural pair, so flagitious in crime, did not fail to thirst after power, which they soon obtained, at a period when Charles enjoyed a faint ray of reason ; * and it must be confessed that the office of regent did, by right, devolve upon Louis, as being first prince of the blood royal.† He, however, had

* For a long period a misunderstanding had taken place between Louis and his uncles, and their quarrel became manifest in 1401. The adverse parties set their forces in motion about the month of December ; subsequently, however, they became reconciled, and on the 14th of January, swore to maintain an inviolable friendship. During this interval of peace, Philip proposed to perform a journey to Arras, for the purpose of witnessing the nuptials of one of his sons. Scarcely, however, had he taken his departure, (the middle of April, 1402,) than Louis demanded and obtained the sovereign authority. See *Laboureur,* pages 441, 447. Juvenal states, at page 168, that their quarrels existed in 1398. See also *Choisy,* 234, 262 ; *Villaret,* xii. pages 328, 348.

† It is true that no positive law existed on this head, but, at all

not the art to exercise or to preserve his authority :
impost succeeded impost, and one concussion proved
only the forerunner of another, such constituting the
climax of his political science ; neither was he capable
of masking these odious measures, but by the most
ridiculous pretexts, which were abandoned as soon
as he had reaped the fruits of his flagrant injustice.
To this system there appeared to be no end; for
Louis, overburdened with debts,* was every day
borrowing; besides which, he was forced to supply
the insatiable cupidity of Isabella ; and this completed the ruin of his reputation, which had long
been sullied by his infamous connexion with that
perfidious woman.

The duke of Burgundy, taking advantage of the
crimes of his rival, set every engine on foot to blast
his character.† No blame would have been attachable

events, it appears that it was considered as a right belonging to
the first prince of the blood royal by the French people at large.
—*Laboureur*, page 44 ; *Villaret*, xii. page 143.

* He did not pay a farthing towards his household expenses,
which were enormous, the whole being procured on credit.—
Laboureur, page 515. Many other princes and noblemen followed
this example. See the same historian, page 621; and *Choisy*,
pages 296, 299.

† Louis had dared to assert that a general impost was established with the consent of his uncles; to this Philip gave
the lie, by a manifesto which he profusely disseminated, and
wherein he declaimed with great vehemence against imposts in
general.—See *Laboureur, History*, page 448.

to this prince, nay, even some share of praise might
have been due to him, had he contented himself with
thus paving the way to the disgrace of Louis; but
he established the credit of his own family on the
ruins of legitimate authority; and thirty years were
scarcely sufficient to open the eyes of the Parisians
in this respect, whose blindness had uniformly
continued, notwithstanding the evils into which
they had been thereby plunged, and the crimes
of the successor of Philip. A second lucid interval
which Charles experienced, replaced the government
in the hands of Philip, which Louis again strove
to acquire at subsequent periods of the monarch's
temporary convalescence. Charles was literally
nothing more than a puppet in the hands of the two
factions; as either reigning party, upon the return
of his reason, made him sanction all the acts which
had passed during their respective administrations;
and by this means the monarchy became one general
scene of desolation. Thus the king recovered a
temporary state of sanity only to perceive the horrors
of his situation, and to aggravate the evils wherewith he was surrounded; and when a relapse took
place, he was abandoned in a manner so cruel and
disgraceful, that humanity sickens at the recital.
Indeed, were it not for the ample and precise
account given by historians concerning this affair,
one might be led to doubt whether the heart of
man could harbour such deliberate baseness. So

absolutely absorbed in profligacy were the brother and wife of this unhappy monarch, as it is not only denied him the necessaries of life, but neglected to clothe his children, and sometimes left them in want of bread.

Five years rolled on, during which these troubles continued, when Philip died, at the beginning of 1404; and immediately Isabella and Louis, conceiving that from this time there would be no person to control their actions or give cause for apprehension, abandoned themselves to all the inebriety of their passions, paying no respect whatsoever to public opinion either in their depredations, or their unbridled licentiousness and debauchery.

It becomes a painful task to dwell upon the subject of two beings so entirely abandoned to immorality: it is, nevertheless, the duty of the historian to delineate truths still more aggravating; to depict, in short, one of the greatest villains that ever disgraced the records of history, who figured in the person of *Jean sans Peur*, the son of Philip, duke of Burgundy, who was more justly entitled to the appellation of *Jean sans Vertus,* had he not displayed very great talent in the art of war, and a rooted detestation for licentiousness and inordinate pleasures. It is much easier to recount the vices which this prince did not possess, than those wherewith his heart was gangrened: pride, ambition, impudence, hatred, cruelty, perfidy, and withal consummate hypocrisy, which last rendered him far more dangerous than all the rest of his vices combined.*

Scarcely were the ashes of Philip consigned to the tomb, when Jean, thus armed for iniquity at all points, appeared upon the great political scene. Charles had constituted Louis lieutenant-general of the kingdom of France; but he had also appointed a council composed of the leading characters in the state, whose decision was to constitute the law. Jean demanded and obtained a seat in this assembly, on account of his elevated rank, his real character being altogether unknown. Upon the very first occasion Louis was desirous of having recourse to his favourite object—a new impost; Jean opposed the measure ; on which occasion he depicted, in the most glowing language, the miseries endured by the people, and the misfortunes brought upon the state, by the malpractices of evil governors : his advice, as he had foreseen and desired it should be, was

* These complicated vices of Jean, duke of Burgundy, will be fully exemplified by the statements which follow, as well as from innumerable passages that might be quoted from the historians of his own time. Such verifications, however, are useless, as the character of Jean sans Peur is too well known to require any further elucidation.

not followed. The first step, then, was to give every degree of publicity to the result of this sitting of the council, and to recall to the public mind the various oppressive measures which the house of Orleans had sanctioned. The French, generally speaking, and especially the Parisians, were already too well disposed towards the Burgundian family; and in consequence, this seeming noble conduct rendered Jean sans Peur the idol of the people, in proportion as Louis and Isabella became the objects of their contempt and horror. Jean then devised every means to augment the predilection his late conduct had inspired, and to foment popular hatred against his rivals, by feigning the necessity of seeking an asylum in his own territories; but, in order that the populace might not have sufficient time to cool in these favourable sentiments towards him, he very shortly after returned with a body of troops; when Isabella and Louis fled, and proceeded also to collect an armed force. The reasoning portion of the nation immediately predicted a civil war: a reconciliation, however, was at length effected, or rather the opposite factions were appeased, by sharing the government.

One might have supposed that this check, and the lapse of time, would have operated to restrain the dissolute measures of this co-partnership in administration; but Isabella became more importunate for riches, and the dissipation of Louis increased, while the impudicity of his debauches was, if possible, redoubled. Emboldened on finding that his illicit connexion with the queen remained unpunished, he seduced, or flattered himself with the idea that he had also corrupted, the wife of his rival; nay, he even proceeded so far as to place before the eyes of the latter certain presents stated to have been received, which tended to manifest this triumph. Such unblushing effrontery deserved punishment, and, according to the reigning opinions and customs of that age, called aloud for vengeance. A true knight would have dared the defamer to single combat, and met him in the lists : Jean, however, dissembled; and, perhaps, delighted that his shame afforded him an excuse in the eyes of the Parisians, he caused Louis to be assassinated, although they had been reconciled three days previous, and had received the sacrament together.

Jean was not mistaken; the inhabitants of Paris compared the seeming virtue of the duke with the depravity of his victim; and the assassin was not only excused, but even found an advocate among the ministers of the gospel.*

* The person above alluded to was Jean Petit, a professed theologian, whose apology for the murder of Louis, duke of Orleans, was publicly disseminated in the presence of the king his brother, and the whole court, as well as in Laboureur's History,

Jean, having the populace at his disposal ; supported by the university, which at that period
exercised considerable influence; and by the troops
of many of the provinces ; nothing more was required,
in order to reign over France, than to crown his
enterprises with the sacred name of king.   He succeeded without difficulty in procuring this phantom,
which the heir to the crown, Louis the dauphin, then
in adolescency, and already despised on account of
his early profligacy, was not able to dispute.

The princes, and the majority of the nobles,
however, conspired against the duke of Burgundy;
some with a view to oppose his ambitious projects;
others, namely the children of the duke of Orleans,
to satiate their vengeance; and a third class, to
shake off the burdens of his tyrannical government;
while nearly the whole sought to increase their
own power, during the general overthrow which
would thus be occasioned.

Armaments in consequence took place on all
sides, and the legitimate authority was no longer

page 631.—Consult also *Juvenal des Ursins*, page 236; *Choisy*,
page 330; and *Villaret*, xiii. page 14.

These propositions were subsequently condemned, and burnt
on the 24th of February, 1413, when the Armagnac faction had
gained the upper hand; but they were again solemnly approved
in a sermon delivered in 1418, at which period the Burgundians
had in their turn acquired the ascendency.

deemed an object worthy consideration. The state was plunged in one chaos of anarchy; every mansion-house, castle, or dungeon, was converted into a fortress, wherein each petty officer who could collect a few soldiers established himself the feudal despot of the surrounding villages, the pillage of which became the wages of their troops, whensoever the leaders of the respective factions did not find it necessary to purchase their assistance.

Jean sans Peur was at the head of the most puissant party; and the count of Armagnac, father-in-law of the young duke of Orleans, commanded the other, which he nominated after himself. He certainly was not a member of the royal family; but, sovereign of a large territory, descended from the most ancient house of France, allied to all those possessing an illustrious name, being equal in personal bravery to any nobleman of that age, and superior to all for his talents and his genius, public opinion bestowed upon him that dignity, of which he proved himself worthy in every respect by his character, which was a tissue of egotism, ambition, hatred, pride, vindictiveness, and cruelty.

From this period, and for several succeeding years, the two factions were in constant motion, contending for the possession of the capital, the king, and the dauphin, in order to carry them off. The good and peaceable citizens, victims of the alternate fury of the Burgundians and the Armagnacs, used every effort to restore tranquillity: several truces as well as treaties of peace, signed and sworn to, were almost instantaneously violated; so that the soil of France presented a scene of devastation and blood-shed. Upon one of these occasions, when the duke of Burgundy had Paris at his disposal, in order to render his dominion permanent, he gave arms to the lowest and the most ferocious band he could collect together; the butchers,* and those employed to skin the slaughtered animals, became the satellites of a prince of the blood royal, and one of the first potentates of Europe. To this mob of plunderers the partisans of the Armagnacs were delivered up; † so that the proscriptions of a Marius

* This measure was effected by means of Saint Pol, governor of Paris, a most determined Burgundian. In the month of December, 1411, Jean, duke of Burgundy, assisted at the funeral of one Legoix, a leading man among the butchers, who was killed in a combat, and matters went so far that an inscription was placed upon his tomb.—See *Laboureur*, page 803; *Juvenal*, page 297; and *Villaret*, xiii. page 201.

† When the dauphin Louis succeeded in rescuing Paris from the butchers, there were found in the house of one of the sanguinary chiefs of this band, two lists of proscription, the first of which contained a catalogue of no less than fourteen hundred persons; and in the second were a great many having the letters T., B., and R. before them, meaning (*à tuer, &c.*) to be *killed, banished,* or *ransomed.*—See *Laboureur*, page 899; *Juvenal*, page 332; *Villaret*, xiii. page 274.

and a Sylla were almost exceeded by the atrocities then committed.

These excesses tended to infuse energy into the minds of moderate men, who were seconded by Louis the dauphin, a prince that could ill submit to the yoke of the duke of Burgundy, and who, therefore, strove to form a party. Consultations and assemblies were held; and at length Paris was taken, and surrendered up to the Armagnacs, who did not, it is true, arm the multitude, yet their administration was almost as insupportable. The Burgundians in their turn were pursued and oppressed; the slightest movement, the least expression in their favour, was magnified into a crime, punished by death as soon as suspected, and the sentence always pronounced without judgment.

Twenty years were already passed away since the first access of insanity had seized upon Charles VI.; yet during the troubles that uniformly desolated France for such a protracted period, England had not been in a situation to take advantage of her disasters. Richard II., the successor of Edward III., who was despised by his subjects, had already courted the assistance of the French king;* and subse-

* After some renewals and partial treaties entered into with France, particularly those of 1381, 1383, 1384, and 1392, Richard II., in 1393, ratified a treaty of five years with Charles VII., and on the 19th of March, 1395, he prolonged

quently Bolingbroke, the usurper of his throne, was sufficiently occupied in supporting and establishing his unjust tenure to the crown, and in defending his ill-acquired authority against the Scotch and the Welsh, to be empowered to hazard an attempt on the territory of France.† As Henry IV., however,

it for a period of twenty-eight years, so that it would not have terminated until 1426; and by 'a treaty of the 9th March, 1395, he also affianced Isabella, or Elizabeth, of France. — See *Laboureur's History*, pages 307, 320, where copies of these two treaties are inserted. Hume is guilty of error, when he ascribes their date to the year 1396; as well as in regard to the duration of this treaty, which he reduces to twenty-five years : and Smollett is equally faulty, giving the date as 1396, and the duration of the truce as for twenty-six years.—See *Juvenal des Ursins*, page 159. Richard, in 1396, ceded Brest to the duke of Brittany, and Cherbourg to the king of Navarre.

† The only enterprises attempted by England, were some trifling excursions, during which the French coast was plundered; and among others in 1402, 1403, 1404, and 1406. The French on their side likewise made descents on England in the years 1403, 1404, and 1405; the most considerable of those excursions having for object to forward succours to the Scotch and the Welsh, which occurred in 1384 and 1405. There were also some naval combats, for the most part fought by the natives of Brittany, namely in 1387, 1403, 1406, and 1410.

Treaties were also entered into with Henry IV. almost each succeeding year from 1400 until the period of his death; (see *Dutillet's Rec. des Traités*, page 335—339,) they did not, however, prevent this species of aggressions from taking place on either side.

towards the close of his reign enjoyed more tranquillity, the policy of that monarch led him to foment the divisions of the French, in order that he might reap the advantage when a favourable opportunity should present itself; and this policy succeeded, since by furnishing in turns sufficient succour to the two factions, he maintained the just equilibrium on either side.

We are now arrived at a period of our Summary, when it becomes necessary to detail the ignominy that marked the conduct of too many Frenchmen; and although their historians may have wept over their errors, they certainly have accorded no pity or even indulgence for their vices and their crimes. Such writers are more worthy commiseration than the judge, not being, like him, at liberty to express pity when pronouncing sentence on a relative, or a friend for whom he may feel interested; the historian, on the contrary, is compelled to steel his heart against every tender sentiment, in order to condemn those who have violated the precepts of virtue : it is not sufficient for him to exclaim, *Mihi Galba, Otho, Vitellius, nec beneficio nec injuriâ cogniti;* he must either abandon the pen, or adopt the maxim — *Amicus Plato, magis amica veritas.* Sovereigns, potentates, ministers, divines, soldiers, the learned, all in short, are desirous of having their memories honoured in futurity; and they are all equally well convinced that, sooner or

later, their characters will be subjected to this inflexible ordeal ; and there is little reason to doubt but a dread of the avenging pen of some new Tacitus, has stifled the hidden projects of many a youthful Nero.

Before we trace the name, the reader will no doubt feel a presentiment that the first who solicited and received aid from the English government, was the duke of Burgundy ; who, if culpable in using too much diligence in this respect, was a hundred times less criminal than were the Armagnacs, in respect to the conditions to which they subscribed, in order to deprive the duke of an alliance so disgraceful to his character as a native of France. No Englishman will even suppress his indignation when he is told that the first princes of the blood royal, the dukes of Orleans, of Berri, and of Bourbon, together with the count of Alençon, were content to own and qualify themselves the vassals and the subjects of the king of England, promising him their princely appendages and their fortresses ; in short, undertaking to surrender up every thing which Charles V. had recovered of the territory of Guienne from Edward III.

Upon this occasion, however, they did not reap the smallest personal benefit from their dishonourable conduct; France became the only victim ; for the politic Henry would not furnish any auxiliary troops until the ratification of the treaty at Bourges.* Finding, therefore, no enemies to encounter, the English proceeded to ravage several of the provinces; † nor could the progress of their spoliations be stopped but by the payment of a ransom, and by permitting them to re-occupy several towns of Guienne, with the assistance of the count of Armagnac, who, for the time being, rather preferred an adherence to the disgraceful alliance he had ratified, than to enter into a reconciliation with the duke of Burgundy.

---

* It appears from the statement of Rapin, that it was not until after their debarkation, and that they were proceeding on their march from Normandy to Blois, that the English got information of the peace being concluded; the contrary, however, results from consulting the acts of Rymer, which are given by Rapin himself. It was not until the first of July that the duke of Clarence was named commander in chief of the expedition, and, upon the eleventh, lieutenant-general of Guienne ; consequently, his departure must have been posterior. If after this we compute the time required for the embarkation and debarking of the troops and the crossing of the channel, it will appear evident, that they could not have arrived in Normandy till several days after the peace of Bourges, which occurred on the 13th of July, 1412.—See *Laboureur*, page 833, and following pages.

† Charles, duke of Orleans, undertook to liquidate half of the sum stipulated; and as a security for the performance of his promise delivered up his brother, the count of Angoulême, as an hostage.

This, however, was but a prelude to the ills which the French people were to endure from the policy pursued by the English monarch. About this time the death of Henry IV. took place, who was succeeded by an hero, equal in valour to any warrior of his time, while in every other requisite our fifth Henry surpassed them ; uniting firmness, prudence, sagacity, vigilance, and activity, both of mind and of body ; in short, every requisite seemed united in his person to constitute the greatest man of that time. Wholly divested of the title of usurper, which had been so prejudicial to his father, he took advantage of all the deep-laid policy of his predecessor : adored by his subjects, their lives and their fortunes were at his disposal ; wherefore, shielded from every internal disquietude, he was fully enabled to satisfy, with impunity, his thirst for conquest.

Notwithstanding all these flattering advantages, Henry might in all probability have failed in his ambitious projects, had it not been for the factions that divided France. There is indeed little reason to doubt this, if we calmly consider the small profit he derived from the glorious exploit which signalized the commencement of his martial career, and for which he had nevertheless been making preparations during two years with all the acumen of a skilful warrior and the most consummate negotiator. We of course allude to the battle, or rather the slaughter at Azincourt, in which conflict the flower of the French nobility perished or were made prisoners*. This signal victory, however, was productive of no beneficial consequences to the English, who were soon after obliged to return quietly to their own country, and did not further annoy their Gallic neighbours for the space of two years.

* It is well ascertained, that the English army, harassed by fatigue and weakened with sickness, would have been annihilated without beginning the contest, if the French generals had been guided by prudence. The memorable battle of Azincourt was fought on the 25th of October, 1415; the loss of the French being estimated at ten thousand men. *" Desquels dix mille,"* according to Monstrelet, ch. 149. vol. i. p. 226; *" on espérait y avoir environ seize cents varlets, et tout le surplus gentils-hommes."* From hence it is obvious, that Hume either did not comprehend Monstrelet, or consulted a very faulty edition of that historian; since, after estimating the same loss at ten thousand men, according to Saint Remi, lxiv. he adds, that Monstrelet computes the slaughter at eight thousand four hundred. Smollett, though almost a copyist of Monstrelet, in detailing this battle, has equally misunderstood his author. He certainly states, that the French lost many officers of distinction, some of whom he enumerates by name, and about ten thousand men.— Monstrelet, cxlix. gives a list of the principal gentlemen killed upon that occasion, and the catalogue occupies no less than two pages and a half grand-in-folio; he then proceeds to give a detail of the prisoners of note, such as Charles duke of Orleans, the son of Louis; the count of Richemont, &c. Le Laboureur also inserts copious details of the circumstances attending this disaster, at page 1005 and following. *Idem Juvenal,* 394, &c. *Chron. Manuscr.* 532 to 535; and *Choisy,* page 443.

Time was thereby given for the French to recruit themselves; and they might have been taught by their late reverse to unite against the common enemy; but there was no longer any love of country in their breasts; nothing but factions existed in every quarter. Independent of the two leading parties already described, a third had been formed by Louis the Dauphin : indeed, even the profligate Isabella had her adherents ; which circumstance furnished Voltaire, in his famous Essay,* with a reflection more ingenious than well-founded, which has so frequently been quoted, that *Le Roi seul n'avait point de parti.* It would, indeed, have been better that Charles VI. had not been seconded by any body; as in such case the factious who got possession of his person, would not have made use of his name and his authority in order to secure the neutrality of all the functionaries and citizens who continued faithful to the laws of duty and of honour. Indeed, we have merely mentioned the party of the Dauphin, which disappeared upon the demise of that prince, on the 18th of December, 1415, because, with a more worthy leader, and one possessing a proper capacity, he would have completely annihilated the other three, particularly at the period of the battle of Azincourt, when the heir to the monarchy had been named lieutenant-

* *Essai sur les Mœurs,* lxxix. This opinion is approved by *Villaret,* xiii. page 335.

general, being also master of the capital and of the king's person. On the contrary, both were placed under the dominion of the count of Armagnac, who was appointed Constable; when, in order to maintain his credit, he singly undertook to drive out the English by besieging Harfleur,* the sole but important conquest gained by the expedition of Henry V.

Two naval victories, one of which was gained by the duke of Bedford, completely annihilated the plans and the hopes of the Constable, and emboldened the duke of Burgundy to complete his dishonour and effect the ruin of France by ratifying a treaty so ignominious,† that he blushed at his own deed; and, whether owing to policy or a sentiment of shame, the details of this instrument

---

* Henry disembarked on the 14th of August, 1415, and immediately commenced the siege of that city, which undertook to surrender if it did not receive succour before the 18th September; and the place was accordingly given up, as no forces appeared to tender aid by the time stipulated.

† The contents of this document were not ascertained until the eighteenth century, when Rymer's collection appeared, where they may be found, as well as in Rapin. This instrument bears date in the month of October, 1416; and, very shortly after, the duke of Burgundy sought to enter into an alliance with the Dauphin Jean, whose ruin he had thus endeavoured to compass by signing the treaty in question.—See *Villaret*, xiii. 415, and the ensuing note.

were concealed with such scrupulous care, as to remain a secret for three succeeding centuries. The duke therein recognised Henry V. of England as king of France and his liege lord; and engaged to combat against Charles and his children in every possible way, until they should be dethroned — and this *upon the faith of his body, and the word of a prince!*

The reverses which he had experienced, and more especially this confederacy, would have opened the eyes of the Count of Armagnac in regard to his real interests, had the spirit of faction possessed less influence over his mind; but the sudden deaths of the king's elder sons * tended completely to blind him. Convinced of the support of the third heir (Charles VII.), he solely occupied himself in the preservation of power, and every means to maintain his own authority appeared justifiable. His grand effort was to continue master of Paris, and have the king at his disposal; which objects attained, he became indifferent about the English invading the

---

* Jean the Dauphin, who had succeeded to Louis, died on Monday the 5th of April, 1416, before Easter, and consequently about six months subsequent to the treaty of which we have spoken in the foregoing note. It may not be amiss to observe that the Count of Armagnac had been freed from another rival, powerful by reason of his rank and influence, in the death of the duke of Berri at the siege of Harfleur. (*Villaret*, xiii. page 407.)

territory, and gaining possession of the fortified
cities of Normandy, and quietly permitted the duke
of Burgundy to subjugate the north of the kingdom ; while France, a prey to the contending factions,
was sacked and plundered from one extremity to
the other.   Indeed, it appeared as if he only sought
to raise enemies against himself and the Dauphin.
Added to these circumstances, as if the king was
not sufficiently wretched, he selected this very juncture to produce evidence and render him a witness
of the profligate debauchery of Isabella his queen ;*
and what made the proceeding still more criminal
in the eyes of this second Fredegond, was, the
Count's taking possession, conjointly with her son
the Dauphin, of the immense treasures she had
accumulated notwithstanding the miseries to which
the people were reduced.   Hence originated that
implacable hatred which Isabella vowed against
her son Charles VII. — a sentiment so unworthy
the feelings of a mother, and which she nevertheless cherished with unabated acrimony to the
very moment of her death.

Far from repairing his fault, (and in the language
of policy a fault is more unpardonable than a crime,)
the Constable aggravated public calamities by his

* Louis Bourbon, the queen's favourite, underwent the question by torture, and was afterwards drowned by the king's
order; while Isabella, sent to Tours, was watched with rigorous
scrutiny.

shameful mismanagement of the affairs of the kingdom : burdensome taxes were increased ; executions
of every kind were tolerated ; and banishments,
and confiscations daily occurred : it appeared, indeed, as if the count of Armagnac was bent upon
his own ruin and that of the heir to the throne, who
implicitly gave himself up to his direction.

These coercive measures did not produce the
end proposed ; for the chains of despotism, however
strong, must still be severed, when the yoke im-
posed becomes too heavy. Some Parisians succeeded in introducing the Burgundian faction into
their city, and in an instant the Constable's power
faded into nothingness. To recite the horrors that
accompanied the triumph of the victors, would be
shocking to humanity. On the 12th of June, 1418,
the massacre of all the Armagnacs in the prisons
took place.* It is a scene recorded in such sanguinary
characters, that neither the hand of time nor the
pen of the historian, charged with recapitulating
a modern transaction of the same nature, can obli-
terate the horrors of the past. Let us cast a veil
over these disgusting atrocities, and content our-

* The corpse of the Count of Armagnac was dragged through
the streets during the space of three days ; and his body having
been shamefully disfigured, was covered with a scarf formed of the
strips of his mutilated flesh. (See *Villaret*, xiii. page 469; *Monstrelet, ib.*) These horrors were sanctioned by the leaders of the Burgundian faction. (See *Monstrelet, Choisy,* and *Villaret.*)

selves with stating, that the duke of Burgundy sanctioned other scenes of a similar description by his presence, over which an assassin presided, whom he treated with friendship, regarding him almost as an equal; the person alluded to being Capeluche, the public executioner. Nor did these measures terminate, until the plans of the duke no longer required such cruelties; when assured of the possession of Paris and of the queen, (who, burning with a thirst for vengeance, had voluntarily united herself to him,) after disposing of the royal authority, he was at full liberty to indulge in all the dreams of ambition which occupied his mind.

This prince, however, found himself much perplexed as to the conduct he should pursue. In some measure the master of France, it no longer was his interest to favour the English, since, having in their turn the ascendency, they might have oppressed the kingdom; while in another direction the Dauphin seemed to claim his assistance, who, through the devotion of a faithful adherent,*

---

* This individual was Tanneguy du Châtel, who wrapped Charles VII., then asleep, in one of his sheets, causing him to be transported to the Bastille, and from thence removed to Melun. This important service, recorded in the Journal of Paris, at page 37, is also detailed at length by two other cotemporary writers. (*Saint Remi*, page 120; and *Juvenal des Ursins*, at fol. 349.) Notwithstanding this, *Dutillet*, in his Collection of Treaties, page 319, attributes this action to the

had been rescued from the capital at the moment the revolution was effected. Had the duke acted in concert with the prince, the English party might have been subjected ; for the real friends of France immediately came forward for the purpose of bringing about a proper understanding between the other factions. The English were consequently intimidated, and France seemed to breathe more freely ; when, at an appointed interview agreed upon for the purpose of rendering the bonds of alliance more permanent, the duke of Burgundy was assassinated in presence of the Dauphin upon the bridge of Montereau.

A difference of opinion exists even to the present day in regard to the authors and the circumstances attending this flagitious deed ; since the murder even of a villain was no less a crime, than if the victim had been the most exemplary character. It is equally a mystery whether it was premeditated or the effect of chance : be the fact, however, as it may, notwithstanding the contradictions and the impenetrable obscurity that characterise the numerous recitals, whether of the witnesses, or the historians *

chancellor Robert le Maçon, who, says he, had conspicuously stood forward in support of Charles : and at page 340, in proof of this assertion, he quotes letters of the 7th of November, 1420, by which Charles makes a grant to Robert le Maçon in consequence *of his life having been saved by him, when Paris was taken.*

* Mademoiselle de Lussan, viii. pages 333 and 390, gives a

of the time, it is obvious that Charles VII. did not
participate in the act; * and the repugnance which
he uniformly manifested during the residue of
his life to the commission of any species of violence
is an additional proof. But nevertheless it is
scarcely to be imagined but that the king approved
of the deed, at least tacitly; since he was thereby
delivered from his most dangerous enemy, and
continued to countenance those who had perpe-

pretty copious detail of this affair. One of her accounts is to
be found with a great number of other documents at the end of
the *Journal de Paris.* Lastly, Fathers Griffet and Saint-Foix
have written long dissertations respecting this singular point in
the history of France, so very important, and yet so difficult to
unravel. (See *Daniel,* vi. pages 557 to 574; *Essais sur Paris,*
iii. pages 303 to 340.)

* Hume states that the tender age of Charles VII. leaves every
reason to doubt his having been in the secret of this plot.

Mademoiselle de Lussan, viii. page 391, states decidedly,
that the plot must have been communicated to the monarch;
but she founds her assertion upon mere conjectures, in reply to
which others equally feasible may be adduced. Among various queries, what answer can be given to the following statement? Charles had nothing to gain by this murder, while he
risked the loss of every thing, in tolerating the deed.

Father Griffet appears to coincide with Mad. Lussan; Saint
Foix and the editors of Voltaire support the opinion most
strenuously, that the murder of Jean sans Peur was merely
the effect of chance, and it is difficult to refute some of their
observations.

trated the act, or seized the favourable opportunity to inflict the blow.

In whatsoever light we are led to regard this occurrence, it certainly seems to have been one of the retributive dispensations of divine justice: and if the murder of the duke of Orleans had been avenged only by remorse and fear, that of his assassin was expiated by the almost entire ruin of the party of Charles VII. Philip le Bon, successor to Jean sans Peur, was a very potent enemy in a different point of view; Jean had entered upon the scene covered by crimes, whereas Philip was only rendered conspicuous by his virtues. The French estranged themselves from the one because he made war against his prince and his country; and they excused the conduct of the other from the duty that devolved to him of avenging the death of his father. Independent of this, Philip, possessing the military talents of Jean, was soon placed at the head of a more formidable power, by the acquisition of the inheritance of the sovereigns of Brabant and of Hainault.

United with Henry V. and Isabella, having in their hands the ensigns of royalty in the person of Charles VI., the Dauphin became a very feeble enemy. Eight months after the assassination of Jean, Charles VII. was adjudged guilty of the act; he was in consequence disinherited, banished,*

* On the third of January, 1420, the act of banishment (in case

and the hand of his sister Catherine, together with the crown of France, was bestowed upon the king of England.

Fortunately for the Dauphin, Henry was compelled to repair to London; standing in need of money and reinforcements; * besides which, he sought to deprive France of the alliance of the Scots, who had just sent troops to her assistance.

During the absence of Henry, which lasted between four and five months,† the partisans of

of non-appearance within three days) was proclaimed by sound of trumpet at the *marble table* against Charles VII., by order of Desmartes, solicitor-general to his father Charles VI., for the alleged murder of the duke of Burgundy.

* Prior to his departure, Henry took several strong places, namely, Sens, Montereau, and Melun; and he also concluded a treaty with the house of Albret, which shielded Guienne from all danger of invasion. The taking of Melun deprived Charles of one of his most experienced and valiant captains, in the person of Barbasan, who had the command of that place, and was not delivered from captivity until 1429, during the expedition to the Isle of France, and subsequent to the affair of Orleans.

† Henry V. took his departure at the end of January, and returned in the month of June. Monstrelet, fol. 303, fixes his return on the eve of Saint Barbe. Villaret, vol. xiv. page 115, erroneously fixes his departure in the year 1421.

This point of history being of some importance, we have carefully examined the acts published by Rymer, which tend to clear up the point. The last instrument executed by Henry in France is dated Rouen, the 30th January 1420, (or 1421, new style), and the first of the council after his departure is of the

the Dauphin took courage, especially after the trifling battle at Baugé,* which terminated in favour of the French, not so much on account of the wise plans they had pursued, as of the imprudent conduct of the duke of Clarence, who was general upon that occasion; after which reverse, several fortresses fell into the hands of the French.

The return, however, of Henry, with subsidies, ammunition, and an army of more than forty thousand men,† put an end to these trifling successes.

8th of February; and on the 12th of the same month is an act of Henry, dated from Westminster. The last acts during his stay in England are dated from Dover, the 9th and 10th of June, and the first after his return to France is dated Rouen, the 17th June; from whence it appears that on the 31st of January, or one of the first days of February, 1420, he quitted France, and returned between the 10th and 16th of June, 1421; having been absent about four months and a half.

* Baugé, which was invested by the English, is about eight leagues east of Angers: the siege was raised after the battle.

According to a document published in Rymer, bearing date the 3d of April, it appears that this conflict took place on the eve of Easter; the words are : *Ante diem Paschæ proximo præteritæ.*

The French army then proceeded to Normandy, and laid siege to Alençon; but after the lapse of some days, the earl of Salisbury caused it to be raised; when the French forces retired, partly in the direction of Anjou, and the residue to the territory of Chartrain. (See *Monstrelet,* i. fol. 303.)

† Hume states, after Monstrelet, twenty-four thousand archers and four thousand cavalry; whereas the latter says, "*quatre mille*

In a few days he regulated the affairs of the interior ;
and then opened the campaign, making himself
master of several places, and among others of Meaux,
one of the most important in the kingdom, as well
for its fortifications as for the situation it occupied upon the Marne, some leagues from Paris ;
the supplies for which he was thus enabled to intercept, and render the situation of its garrison precarious. He then took possession of many small
towns ; the inhabitants of which, for the most part,
yielding to the terror excited by his arms and the
influence of his genius, freely tendered to him their
keys. The duke of Burgundy, on his side, desirous
of showing that he was worthy of seconding these
efforts of his ally, obtained a victory near Saint
Riquier, in Picardy ; and thus deprived the adherents of Charles of all that remained to them in the
environs of that province.* The allies already
began to direct their efforts towards the south of
the kingdom,† then the only remaining asylum of

hommes d'armes," which implies a greater number ; Smollett, who
had also consulted the same authority, estimates the army of Henry
at thirty thousand men.

* From Paris to Boulogne. (See *Monstrelet*, i. fol. 317.)

† In August, 1422, Charles raised the siege of Cosne without
awaiting the arrival of the enemy. Villaret, vol. xiv. page 153,
on the contrary, says, without however mentioning his authority,
that Charles was desirous of giving his adversary battle notwithstanding the inequality of their numbers ; and that it was with

the Dauphin; in which direction he had undertaken the siege of Cosne, when suddenly the death of the king of England took place. If the supposition of various writers is true, that Henry died of the attacks of a fistula,* the cure of which disorder was then unknown, Charles and his subjects were certainly indebted for their salvation to the ignorance of that age. It is merely necessary to compare the two rivals and their opposing forces,

difficulty that he was prevailed upon to abandon this courageous, but imprudent resolution, &c. This romantic assertion is, however, destroyed by the uniform testimonies of *Saint Remi*, 162; *Monstrelet*, i. fol. 320; *Chron. Manuscr.* 553; *Chron. of France*, 328; *Pierre Defenin, in the fol. edit. of Juvenal*, p. 493; and *Choisy*, 555.

* Villaret, xiv. page 157, follows the statement of the secretary of Henry V., who says that the king died of a pleurisy: an opinion that would not be very feasible unless the disorder was only of a few days' duration; whereas, on the contrary, we are well informed, that the malady continued for a month at least, because Henry was attacked a short time after his departure with the army, and died on the 31st of August; whereas he did not commence his route until the middle of July. On the 27th of July, as soon as he felt the attack, the duke of Bedford, whom he had sent forward, arrived with a powerful body of troops at Auxerre; from whence he proceeded on the 4th of August to Vezelay, which place had been appointed the general *rendezvous* of the army of the allies. Rapin and Smollett both speak of a dysentery; without, however, referring to any authority.

together with their respective auxiliaries of every description, to become fully convinced, that but for the sudden demise of Henry, France must have become a province of his empire.

Such a termination of affairs seemed highly probable; but the English cause was weakened by the loss of its most able leader, and obliged to confide the administration of France and that of England to two different rulers.* This circumstance gave rise to divisions; but although the allies were soon after deprived, by the death of Charles VI., of the semblance of regal authority which had marked their usurpations, still the affairs of Charles VII. did not assume a more favourable aspect: on the contrary, the king experienced additional defection and fresh reverses, and was ultimately saved by what may be almost regarded as a miracle.†

---

* Bedford was regent under the title of *Protector ;* but during his absence, his brother the duke of Gloucester enjoyed the same title and authority in England, being, however, regulated in his proceedings by a council chosen by the parliament. The duke of Bedford when in France enjoyed the title of *Regent.*

† The allies opposed to Charles VII. conceived their triumph so certain, that by way of derision they designated him *The King of Bourges,* at which place he then resided, that being one of the few cities remaining subject to his authority. (See *Thomassin,* xci.; *Daniel,* vii. page 7 ; *Lussan,* ix. page 435 ; and *Chron. of France,* fol. 328.)

We should not feel surprised, if when reflecting upon the prodigious resources that France has of late years displayed, the question should be asked, how it was possible that the affairs of Charles VII. could become so desperate, especially as he had only the infant Henry VI. as a competitor? To this query, a very brief detail of the situation of both parties shall be our answer; and that will also serve to throw some light on the events that subsequently occurred.

Charles, it is true, was in possession of a part of the provinces of Orleans and Touraine,* the territory situated to the south of the Loire as well as Dauphiny; but Provence, Roussillon, and the counties of Foix and Navarre, had their distinct sovereigns. Guienne and Gascony belonged to the English. In the provinces subject to Charles there were many fortresses which had become the property of those adventurers of whom we have previously spoken, and the safeguard of which devolved to him who could afford to pay them the best. Numerous dependents of the Burgundian faction,†

---

* The province of Anjou belonged to the king of Sicily; that of Maine to his brother Charles of Anjou : the county of Etampes was the property of Jean of Burgundy, count of Nevers, son of the third male heir of Philip le Hardi, and cousin-german of Philip le Bon.

† Such also was the case with the duke of Savoy. Charles, on

such as the prince of Orange, had vassals of some importance in their territories ; and all that had been exacted on the part of Brittany, was the maintenance of a species of neutrality.*

The English, independent of Guienne and Gascony, had conquered all the northern provinces ;† to the east, their ally reigned over Burgundy and Franche Compté, and to the north the Low Countries were at his disposal; thus it is clearly demonstrated that the enemies of Charles, as respects territory, had the balance greatly in their favour.

The posture of affairs was the same in regard to the riches of their territory. The commerce of

the contrary, had been deprived, two years before, of the assistance of his most powerful supporter, Louis III., count of Provence, duke of Anjou, and king of Sicily. This prince, who had marched nearly all his forces to Naples, in 1420, did not return to France until 1429, after the expedition to Orleans had taken place, and during the coronation of Charles VII.—See *Monstrelet*, vol. i. folio 294; *Villaret*, xiv. page 114 and 412.

* The duke of Brittany had certainly entered into an alliance with Charles VII. in 1421 ; but he only furnished a very mediocre supply after the ratification of the treaty, because he asserted that Charles had failed in fulfilling the stipulations.—See *Morrice, History of Brittany*, vol. i. page 486.

† Among these provinces, Normandy, in regard to the resources which it furnished, was considered, even under Louis XI., as equivalent to one-third of the whole monarchy.—See *Villaret*, xvii. page 170.

VOL. I.   e

Belgium had long ranked as the most flourishing throughout Western Europe; the traffic of the cities belonging to Charles, with the exception of Lyons, might be considered as nothing. And, without taking the above city into the scale, he did not possess a single place that boasted great population, or was at all to be compared, in that respect, with Lille, Rouen, Bordeaux, Paris,* &c. Nearly the whole length of the coast was in possession of the allies; Charles having but one or two ports, through the medium of which he could receive succours, and he was bereft of a fleet to intercept such reinforcements as arrived from England.

In a military point of view, the opponents of the

---

* The possession of the capital alone placed a great preponderance in the hands of the allies, because its population and its riches procured them continual resources, both in men and in money. Besides, the vast efforts uniformly made, during the lapse of thirty years, by the Armagnacs, the Burgundians, the English and the French, to occupy Paris, afford so many incontestible proofs of the vast importance attached to that city.—See also *Journal de Paris*, page 170.

De la possession de cette ville, says the duke of Bedford, *despend ceste seignourie.*

During the period of the war carried on, for *Le bien Public,* as it was termed, in the year 1465, Louis XI. used to remark, that, " if he could enter the first, (into Paris,) he would save himself with his crown upon his head; but that if the enemy entered the first, he should find himself in danger." — See *Villaret,* xvii. page 82.

French king were not less powerful. Charles had no army, properly speaking, but merely some straggling bands and militia forces that were with difficulty collected together, and never amounted to any great effective body, being also without order, and void of discipline ; added to this, upon receiving the least check, and above all, when pay and pillage were wanting, they returned without opposition to their respective homes; so that it was scarcely possible to enter upon a campaign, until the Scotch had supplied their auxiliary troops.*

* James I., king of Scotland, was captured on board a vessel, in 1407, and detained against the law of nations, (for a truce then existed,) being conveyed to England, and there kept a prisoner until the year 1423 ; but the regency of his kingdom was not less zealous in espousing the cause of France. It was certainly the interest of Scotland to prevent France from becoming subject to England ; besides, Charles loaded the Scotchmen with honours and benefits. These assertions are fully confirmed by referring to the treasury of Charters, (*Melanges*, vol. ix. *Art. Scotland*,) where are found : — 1st. Two confirmations of ancient treaties between Scotland and France, dated from Perth and Stirling, the 6th January, 1407, and the 6th October, 1428 (*ibid*. Nos. 19 and 20, page 392).—2d. Two procurations for their renewal, dated from St. Jean, the 12th July, 1428 (*ibid*. Nos. 22 and 23). —3d. A treaty concluded at Chinon, the 10th November, 1428, whereby Charles VII., in the event of *his recovering his kingdom*, through the means of James I., solemnly bound himself to give that prince the duchy of Berri and the county of Evreaux (*ibid*.

The English, on the contrary, possessed a numerous
and well disciplined army; desertion was of little
detriment to their cause, since the sea served as a
barrier to prevent deserters from regaining their
country. If Charles had to boast some captains of
tried valour and experience, the English were by no
means deficient in that respect; and what tended
still more to give advantage to the latter, were those
distinguished and able generals intrusted with the
command of the army, the duke of Bedford, the
earls of Salisbury, Suffolk, Somerset, Warwick,
Arundel, and the lord Talbot; while Charles had
only Santrailles, La Hire, and the bastard Dunois,
to oppose them.

It will be obvious from the statement made of
the situation of France, and particularly of the
southern provinces, that what is esteemed the very
nerve of governments, did not exist to establish the
equilibrium in favour of Charles VII. Some imposts badly collected, a portion of which was retained by those exacting payment; together with
the precarious benefit derived from raising and
depreciating the value of money, were the only

No. 27, page 393). Finally, Dutillet, in his *Rec. des Traités*,
pages 358, 359, 361, and 362, inserts a number of treaties, acts,
gifts, &c. that passed between the same monarchs from 1422
until 1428.

sources for enriching the treasury.* It was certainly difficult for the allies to derive more benefit from the north of that kingdom, equally drained and plundered; but Great Britain and the Low Countries, sheltered from the scourge of war, and the two states of Burgundy, the frontiers of which had scarcely been approached, afforded sources of abundant succours in every point of view.

The necessaries thus furnished to the enemies of Charles, as well as their forces and their finances, were managed by very skilful hands. The duke of Burgundy was accounted one of the most able, and the duke of Bedford one of the greatest generals of his time. Nor was the latter less conspicuous as an active, enterprising, and indefatigable statesman: he was never absent, whether in the council or the field; upon all occasions where the presence of the chief was requisite, Bedford never failed to show himself.

From this cursory view of the situation of affairs,

* Many very striking instances are extant of the distress to which Charles VII. was reduced. The chaplain who assisted at the baptism of Louis XI., in July, 1423, was obliged to procure the silver vases employed upon that occasion; *forty livres*, however, which had been borrowed upon these articles, were not paid until the end of the year.—See *Villaret*, xiv. p. 285. In 1429, when it was found necessary to victual the city of Orleans, the treasurer of the queen had only *four crowns* left in the money chest.—See *Laverdy*, page 314.

it is apparent how powerful were the enemies of
the French king; and yet we have not mentioned
his most dangerous opponent, which was no other
than — himself. At the very dawn of adolescence,
Charles had manifested symptoms of personal
energy, and displayed some interest in regard to
his own affairs; he also assisted frequently at
political conferences, and attended expeditions in
person;* but having attained the age of twenty, and
being invested with the regal dignity, he became
estranged, as it were, to every thing but his pleasures, his mistresses, and his favourites. While
his warriors were prodigal of their blood and their
fortunes, in order to maintain him on his throne,
he was only occupied with banquetings, masque-
rades, and balls. He abandoned the revenues of his
provinces to the plunder of his ministers and con-
fidential favourites, permitting them to impoverish
and persecute his most loyal subjects, to make use of
the forces he possessed against his own generals,

---

* In 1418, at the sieges of Tours and the town of Azay, near
that city; in 1419 and 1420, (see *Chronicle of France*, pages 324
and 325,) at those of Nismes and St. Esprit; and in 1421, at the
attacks of Beziers and of Sommière, near Nismes; as well as at
the siege of Chartres, and some other places in Perche and its
environs; and also at the investment of Cosne, in 1422. From the
latter period, however, until the expedition for the purpose of the
coronation, in 1429, it does not appear that Charles ever showed
himself to his army.

and even sometimes approving of their crimes. He almost uniformly selected his friends from among those who were conspicuous for their vices* and paucity of talent; and he was so deficient in that species of firmness which should be the most prominent virtue in a king, particularly when troubles oppress the state, that he permitted the murder of his own friends, within the confines of his palace, and even in his presence, without undertaking either to defend or to avenge them.

Such, however, is a correct portrait of the monarch to whom historians have given the surname of *The Victorious*. If he proved triumphant, it was owing to the devotion of his warriors and his subjects, as well as to propitious and unexpected occurrences, but never to his own labours or individual exploits; in fact, he recovered his kingdom in opposition to himself, and in despite of his own insensate mode of proceeding.

* During ten years, Charles VII. had for superintendent of the province of Languedoc, from whence he derived the greater part of his resources, one Guillaume de Champeaux, bishop of Laon, whom he was obliged to displace on the 31st December, 1441. This ecclesiastic appropriated for his own benefit *from six to seven hundred thousand crowns*, a most enormous sum for that period; and not contented with these pilferings, he committed various other crimes, even conspiring against the king; and notwithstanding the royal commands several times reiterated, he nevertheless retained his functions for a considerable period. —See *Lettres de Destitution*, in *Vaissette*, vol. iv. page 461.

It must be confessed that Charles was much improved by the experience of twenty years, after which his conduct seemed happily to coincide with the posture of his affairs; yet, this acknowledgment cannot justify his extraordinary mode of administration at a time when it was necessary that he should have conducted himself even with more than ordinary prudence, and displayed the utmost stretch of penetration; when it was requisite for him to act as a skilful statesman struggling against his enemies and adverse fortune, and to display the courage of a hero in his country's cause.

It is, above all, essential that a king, at the commencement of his reign, should give proofs of his courage, his activity, his equitable administration of public affairs, and all those qualifications which are the essentials of royalty. The conduct of Charles VII. formed a complete contrast. Towards the close of 1422, scarcely three months after the demise of his father, one of his partisans, having scaled the walls, and surprised the small town of Meulan, was therein besieged by the duke of Bedford and the earl of Salisbury; in consequence this captain applied for succour; the post was of importance; and six thousand men were despatched to his assistance. Instead of accompanying this force in person, Charles thought fit to remain sixty leagues distant from the scene of action. An apathy even more unpardonable was displayed in respect to the funds appropriated for the main-enance of these troops; for a favourite courtier charged by the king to distribute the same, con-sumed the whole amount in purchasing silver vessels, trinkets, and precious stones. In conse-quence of this, the army, on arriving within six leagues of Meulan, disbanded for want of pay; and the result was, that the besieged, rendered furious on finding themselves betrayed to such men, and for such ignoble purposes, tore the standards of Charles into pieces, trampled them under foot, entered into an immediate capitulation, and the garrison forthwith passed into the service of the enemy.

The duke of Brittany, who had hitherto continued neuter, at length joined the English, and after this alliance, took possession of numerous places. Charles, in the spring, received reinforcements from Scotland and from Spain, when an army of ten thousand men was collected, and employed to lay the siege before Crévant. The allies, under the command of the earl of Suffolk, marched to their rencounter; but the positions occupied by the French were impregnable; the army, therefore, without any risk, might have continued the siege and braved the English forces — but the French stood in need of experienced commanders; and Charles, whose presence on this occasion might have served to make them act with circumspection,

and stifle those divisions that existed among the
principal corps, did not make his appearance in
the field.   Under these circumstances, the French
abandoned their strong position, and marched towards the enemy, without having previously adopted
any of those necessary precautions prescribed by
the rules of war; the consequence was, as might
have been expected, a complete victory obtained
over the French, three thousand of whom were
killed or made prisoners,* together with a number
of generals and officers : the raising of the siege of
Crévant followed, together with many other places
that voluntarily surrendered to the victors.

However fortunate the result of this conflict was
to the English, the consequences did not prove
decisive, owing to the following circumstances.
The duke of Bedford was entirely occupied for
two years in smoothing the difficulties connected

---

* Berry, at page 270, states from 800 to 1,000: the Parlia-
mentary Registers of France (in *Villaret, ibid.*) compute the
loss at more than 3,000 killed : the Journal of Paris, page 94,
says, 6,500 killed, captured, or drowned : Claude de Chastellux,
governor of Crevant, affirms that there were from 4,000 to 5,000
killed, taken, or marched away.   See the two Acts of the 6th of
August, 1413, six days after the battle.—*Lebœuf's History of the
Diocese of Auxerre,* vol. ii. Nos. 383 and 384, page 315.

The loss of this battle led to the surrender of Mâcon, of
which town the French had recently obtained possession.—See
Villaret, xiv. pages 281 and 284.

with the establishment of a regency; in gaining over the duke of Brittany; in rendering the link more firm that bound him to the duke of Burgundy by a marriage with his sister;* and in appeasing the differences that existed between his brother, the duke of Gloucester, and the duke of Burgundy. Shortly after, the victories of Gravelle in the Maine,† and Bassière in the Mâconnais, gained by the French, procured some respite, and enabled them at the opening of the second campaign to receive another army furnished by the king's allies the Scotch, and a small reinforcement sent by the duke of Milan.‡

* By the treaty of the 17th April, 1423.—See *Monstrelet*, vol. ii. folio 4; *Dutillet, Rec. des Traités*, page 343. She was asked in marriage in the month of February, 1422, affianced in May, and married in October.

† L'Abrégé Chronologique, page 328, and Monstrelet, vol. ii. folio 4, places this battle towards the end of 1422; and, consequently, prior to that of Crevant. Chartier, page 4—6, Berry, page 370, Histoire de la Pucelle, page 483, the Cronique de France, folio 330, and Dom Plancher, vol. iv. page 78, ascribe it subsequently to the affair of Crevant, and this opinion we have adopted. Chartier, and the biographer of La Pucelle, seem to have been much better informed than the other historians respecting the detail of this action, and Berry positively affirms that it took place after that of Crevant.

‡ According to Berry, page 370, this force consisted of six hundred horsemen bearing lances, and one thousand foot. The duke of Milan above adverted to, was Philippe Marie Visconti, brother of Valentina, who died in 1408, four months after the

The adherents of Charles, being encouraged,
made a considerable effort; and, in consequence,
an army of about eighteen thousand men was
assembled,* destined to succour the city of Ivry,
then closely besieged by the duke of Bedford.
The two armies came in face of each other in
the month of August, 1424, near the town of
Verneuil, when the superiority of the English
commanders, as at Cressy, Poitiers, Azincourt, and
Crévant, crowned the arms of the allies with
victory. The French upon this occasion, though
displaying prodigies of valour, were entirely defeated, sustaining a loss of five thousand men,† with
the greater part of the nobility, besides a multitude
of prisoners : while the rest of the army dispersed.
The immediate results of the victory at Verneuil
were, the capture of the equipage and the treasures
of the army; the surrender of Verneuil and the
whole province of Maine ; with the plunder of Anjou
and all the surrounding territory.

assassination of her husband Louis, duke of Orleans.   Philippe
was uniformly attached to the cause of Charles VII.

* Hume states, after Monstrelet, vol. ii. page 14, and Grafton,
that the army amounted to fourteen thousand troops, half of
whom were Scotchmen.   Villaret computes the force at twenty
thousand.

† In regard to the number of killed at this encounter, Hume
states four thousand, Berry four thousand five hundred, while
the Journal de Paris estimates the loss at nine thousand men.

More disastrous consequences were anticipated, when the good fortune of Charles once more intervened to rescue him from total destruction, at least during a certain period of time. Jacquelina, of Hainault,* heiress of the western districts of Belgium, had separated from her husband, the duke of Brabant, in 1421, to seek refuge at the court of Henry V. for the purpose of annulling her marriage, through the aid and protection of the English monarch. The duke of Gloucester, who had now become regent of England, flattered by the hope of receiving a crown, gave Jacquelina his hand in marriage; which circumstance produced a breach with the duke of Burgundy, who was very nearly related to the duke of Brabant, and had calculated upon inheriting the joint territories of the separated couple. The endeavours and crafty conduct of the duke of Gloucester only tended to

---

* Or Jacquelina of Bavaria, widow of the dauphin Jean, and wife of the duke of Brabant, cousin-german of Philip. Consult, in respect to this misstatement, *St. Remi,* page 123 and 152; *Monstrelet,* vol. i. folio 236, &c. &c. ; *Daniel,* vii. page 22, and various other authorities.

Jean of Burgundy, duke of Brabant, was the son of Anthony, second male heir of Philip le Hardi. A maternal great aunt of Anthony had bequeathed to him, in 1406, the duchies of Brabant and of Limbourg, and at the death of Jean, in 1427, they descended to his brother, Philip le Bon, their cousin.—See *Anselme, Généalogies,* vol. i. page 248.

lull the quarrel for a certain period ; when, throwing aside the mask, he appropriated to himself the subsidies destined for the regent his brother, raised an army and invaded Hainault, two months after the battle of Verneuil, at the very moment when the allies were preparing to complete the subjugation and the ruin of France.*

Philip le Bon, duke of Burgundy, immediately separated his forces from those of Bedford, and marched to the assistance of Hainault. This individual state of warfare, which continued four years,† deprived the English of the support of Philip, and thus disabled them from profiting by the signal victories they had obtained. Another circumstance

---

* All the historians coincide in opinion that without this timely diversion, Charles VII. must have been irretrievably lost.

† By the treaty of Delft, bearing date the 3d July, 1428, entered into by Philip and Jacquelina, (see the document in *Dumont*, vol. ii. part ii. page 218,) it appears that Villaret, xiv. page 338, was not aware of this instrument, since he is undecided as to the period when the war terminated.

By the third article of this treaty, Philip is denominated the heir, and from that period had the control of the possessions of Jacquelina, that is to say, of Hainault, of Holland, of Zealand, and of Friesland.

In the same year, 1428, he purchased the counties of Namur and of Zutphen.—See *Anselme*, vol. i. page 240.

From these statements, it is obvious how powerful such an enemy must have proved to Charles VII.

likewise concurred to keep the regent passive during a length of time. The duke was not only deprived of his subsidies, but compelled to interfere in a quarrel that arose, after the invasion of Hainault, between the duke of Gloucester and the bishop of Winchester, their uncle, and a member of the English council; for which purpose the duke of Bedford visited England, and there remained until the year 1427.*

* Hume and Daniel fix the departure of the duke of Bedford in 1425, and his return (after an absence of eight months) in the ensuing year; by which it is apparent that they both followed the statement of Monstrelet, vol. ii. folios 27 and 29; but the chronicles of the latter historians, from 1423 until 1428, abound in errors as regards dates; added to which, many events are confounded together. For instance, under the date 1427, at folio 35, he says that Richemont had been *very recently (tout nouvellement)* invested with the dignity of constable, whereas that promotion had taken place three years before. The Journal de Paris, page 108, positively fixes the return of Bedford on Saturday the 5th of April, 1427, after an absence of sixteen months, which necessarily places his departure in the month of November, 1425.

We have since used every endeavour to clear up this important point of history; and, among other things, have verified all the letters patent inserted in the Treasury of Charters. The last which bears reference to the duke of Bedford, was given at Paris, on the 30th November, 1425. From that period until the 8th April, 1426, before Easter, (that is to say, to the 8th April, 1427, according to the present mode of calculating,) they all relate to the council; and during that interval several are found to

The court of Charles seemed anxious, in the first instance, to profit by these favourable circumstances; a general was required, and the count of Richemont was appointed to command the army. In order to induce him to accept this appointment it was necessary to bestow on him the sword of Constable, and other precious gifts. However, in acquiring the aid of the count, the duke of Brittany his brother became separated from the English faction: and beside this, auxiliary troops were obtained, of which Charles stood in the greatest need.

No sooner, however, were these succours procured, through the medium of negotiations, than

have been given in England, relating to the duke of Bedford, namely, at Sandwich on the 20th December, 1425, (No. 402;) at Worcester on the 9th March, 1425, (No. 488;) on the 12th *idem* at Leicester, (No. 636;) and at Westminster on the 5th of December, 1425, (No. 631.) The first letters patent subsequently given at Paris, bear date the 8th, 11th, and the 12th of April, 1426, before Easter, (Nos. 628, 630, 632, 647, 634, and 645.)

All these statements tend to confirm the assertion of the Journalist of Paris; and from hence it certainly does appear that the regent quitted that city at the commencement of December, 1425, (according to the present mode of calculating,) and that he returned the beginning of April, 1427, having been absent for the space of sixteen months. Villaret, vol. xiv. page 344, certainly ascribes the return of Bedford to the year 1427, but he is guilty of the same error as Hume and Daniel, in curtailing the period of his absence to eight months.

it appeared as if the court was wearied with the trouble which had been taken. One of the stipulations in the treaty had for its object the dismissal of several of the ministers or favourites of Charles, who were implicated in a conspiracy against the duke of Burgundy. The ministers refused to fulfil this condition, in which determination they were supported by the mistresses * and most of the

* Although Charles VII. was surrounded by a worthless set of courtiers, he could boast a queen and a mistress who were possessed of many noble qualifications. Mary of Anjou, the wife of Charles, used every effort to raise her pusillanimous husband above himself; while Agnes Sorel, surnamed *La Dame de Beauté*, exerted all the influence she possessed over the king, to convert her royal lover into a heroic monarch; regarding the noble allurements of glory as far superior to the frivolous blandishments of pleasure. The queen, fully sensible of the merits possessed by Agnes, not only admired her rival, but extended her generosity so far as to unite with her in striving to rouse the king to a sense of what was due to himself and his persecuted subjects. So truly exalted was Mary of Anjou, that she disdained the idea of jealousy; and while her magnanimity of soul equalled that of Agnes, she possessed a greater fund of virtue. Both united their prudent counsels and intrepid minds, to keep the crown upon the head of their master.

It seems to have been the fate of Charles to grant all to females, to whom he was indebted for every thing. In fact, four women appear to have been of more service to him than all his ministers and generals combined. Jacquelina of Hainault disunited his enemies, Mary of Anjou and Agnes Sorel invigorated his courage, and Jeanne d'Arc led him on to glory and to triumph. It is

courtiers of Charles ; one of whom carried his auda-
city so far as to assassinate an adversary in open
council—and under the very eyes of his sovereign.*

generally acknowledged that Agnes died from the effects of
poison, in 1449, administered, as is strongly surmised, at the
instigation of Louis the dauphin, eldest son of Charles VII.

At the period of Agnes Sorel's death, Charles was at Jumieges,
where he consoled himself for his loss by taking to mistress
Antoinetta de Maiguelais, dame de Villequier, a cousin of
Agnes Sorel ; besides whom he had many other damsels to please
his eye.—See *Mezeray,* page 462.

Agnes Sorel was interred in the centre of the collegiate church
of Loches ; her effigy was represented in white marble, with
two angels supporting a slab upon which her head reposed, while
two lambs lay recumbent at her feet.   She had bestowed considerable gifts upon this church ; notwithstanding which, the
prebends, conceiving that Louis XI. entertained the same
hatred towards the beautiful Agnes after her death as he had
cherished during her life, requested permission of that monarch to
remove the tomb from the choir of the church ; to which the
prince consented, if the fathers were willing to restore all the
riches which they had received at her hands.

The following couplets were penned by Francis I., on contemplating a portrait of Agnes Sorel : —

> " Gentille Agnès, plus d'honneur tu mérites,
>   La cause étant de France recouvrer,
>   Que ce que peut dans un cloitre ouvrer
>   Close nonnain, ou bien dévot hermite."

* The Dauphin d'Auvergne was thus murdered by Tanneguy
Duchâtel.—See *Villaret,* vol. xiv. page 315.

A scene unprecedented in the records of history then presented itself; the constable Richemont advanced towards the court at the head of a small army which he had raised by his personal influence. The king then fled from town to town in order to protect those ministers who were precipitating him to ruin, and he thus evaded the warrior who furnished him the means of preserving his crown. Nothing more was wanting than the retreat of the princes of the blood royal, and the surrender of some cities to the enemy, when Charles would probably have listened to the voice of reason; yet such was his infatuation, that even then he might have remained blind to his own interests, if Tanneguy Duchâtel had not set the example to his colleagues by voluntarily retiring from the court.*

Ultimately, however, Richemont, having overcome every obstacle, assembled an army of twenty thousand men in Brittany: and thus, at the be-

---

* The famous president Louvet was desirous, on retiring, to preserve all his influence, or rather, to be well assured that the same disorganized state of affairs should continue, although he could no longer participate in the spoil. For this purpose he left Giac, one of his creatures, at court, and advised Charles to select him as his favourite. Louvet had arrived to such a pitch of power, that count Dunois did not disdain to court an alliance with his family. — See *Daniel,* vii. page 31; *Villaret,* xiv. page 316.

ginning of 1426, he found himself enabled to invade Normandy, and attack the English in the very heart of their possessions.   After taking Pontorson, he laid siege to Saint James de Beuvron, which was the barrier of that province.   The enterprise would, doubtless, have been crowned with success ; but Giac, a favourite of Charles, aided by one of the ministers, a native of Brittany, * prevented the fortunate result of the expedition by with-holding the sums reserved for the payment of the soldiers.   The army in consequence disbanded ; when Richemont, in despair, boldly attempted an assault with the few forces that remained ; in which effort, however, he was completely beaten.

What a lesson this for Charles !   Any other being but himself would have degraded and severely punished the author of this disaster ; but a flatterer is more esteemed by a weak prince than the posses-sion of a kingdom, and the welfare of a courtier dearer than the happiness of a whole people.   Giac now became audacious in his measures ; and it

---

* The chancellor of Brittany, (see the *History of Richemont*, page 749 ; *Daniel*, vii. page 33 ; *Villaret*, xiv. page 321.)

In November 1425, Charles VII. had obtained of the clergy of Languedoc *two tenths ;* and of the commons the sum of 250,000 livres in support of the war, besides *twelve thousand for his private pleasures.* Giac, abusing the credit he had obtained over his master, *placed nearly the whole of these sums to his own account.* (See *D. Vaissette*, iv. page 467.)

was necessary to impede his course; the constable caused his arrest, then judged him by a commission, and delivered him over to be executed, in spite of the king. Richemont, however, did not deign to adopt that formality of justice in regard to Beaulieu, who had succeeded to the monarch's favour as well as to the insolence and extortionate proceedings of Giac, his predecessor; on this occasion he employed the hand of an assassin.

These acts of violence, so reprehensible in themselves, and so injurious to the sovereign, excited sentiments of pity towards Charles VII.; and some historians have sought to justify his conduct under an idea that his misfortunes made him require a confidant. A dissipation of the public treasure, and the consequent invasion and loss of provinces from a want of the means of defence, were the ordinary services of the pretended friends of Charles! Suppose even a defect of judgment could have prompted him to make so bad a choice: he could not adduce the common palliative of inexperience; for, when Richemont, perceiving that some favourite was absolutely necessary for his prince, proposed Trimouille as a person fit to replace Beaulieu: " *You will repent*," said Charles, " *I know him better than you.*" After such a reply any comment is unnecessary. It will be sufficient to observe, that the manœuvres of Giac and Beaulieu, and the effect produced by the operations resorted to in effecting their overthrow, completely exhausted for one year, (after the check experienced at Beuvron,) all the resources that remained to Charles, and thus prevented him from affording succour to many places which the English were besieging and ultimately conquered. *

The influence which Trimouille obtained over the king became even more fatal; he induced him to neglect the favourable opportunity of acting during the absence of the regent; and the duke of Bedford, after having arranged affairs in England, returned in 1427, with considerable subsidies and twenty thousand men. The king's partisans did not deign to trouble themselves respecting the movements of the regent, who marched unmolested into Brittany; forcing the duke to renounce his alliance with Charles,† and to sign a treaty by which the

* We must, however, except Montargis, which was besieged by Warwick and Suffolk, and succoured by Dunois—at least it appears from history, that about this time the expedition in question was undertaken. The French also surprised Mans about the same period; but Talbot and Suffolk drove them from thence, and afterwards got possession of Laval.—See *Villaret,* xiv. page 344.

† Hume makes mention of this expedition as at the end of the year 1426, and then immediately after passes on to 1428, without noticing any event of the intervening year. But the circumstance that tends to do away all uncertainty as to the precise period of the duke of Bedford's expedition, and demonstrates the error in Hume, is a letter of the 8th of September, 1427,

monarch would have been disinherited. Trimouille, seeking only his own aggrandisement and the acquisition of riches, did not interest himself about the welfare or ruin of the monarchy; and such was his shameful abuse of princely favour, that he at length forced the most zealous royalists and princes of the blood, in disgust, to declare themselves against the king, and forcibly take possession of Bourges, which then ranked as his capital. This civil war, through the exertions of the true friends of royalty, or, perhaps, because Trimouille perceived that it would be detrimental to his interests, was at length appeased; but, in the interim, no steps were taken against the English, who resorted to every measure which could render the opening campaign of 1428 successful.*

We are now arrived at the period when France

preserved in the Treasury of Charters, (see *Melanges*, v. iii. No.98, page 403,) wherein the duke of Brittany solemnly renounces all alliance to the prejudice of Henry, therein promising to obey him as well as the regent duke of Bedford, &c. (This document is quoted, with the oaths pronounced by the inhabitants of many towns, &c. of Brittany, in Dutillet, *Recueil des Traités*, 359 to 361.) The king of Navarre on the 16th of the same month tendered a similar oath for the duchy of Nemours. *Dutillet, ibid.* 345, 362.

* Hume, when speaking of the siege of Orleans, says that Bedford resolved upon attempting an enterprise, which, in case of success, would turn the balance completely in his favour, and pave a way for the entire subjection of France.

seemed verging upon her complete overthrow; for she was assailed by a most formidable enemy, and almost entirely divested of the means of defence. Intestine divisions and universal plunder had overwhelmed the state during the reign of Charles VI., and continued for the first six years of the administration of his son. France was a prey to a succession of evils, differing only in their nature, without the slightest alleviation; for the weakness and the dissipation of Charles VII. were as dangerous as the mental derangements to which his father had been subject.

The mode of warfare at the period of which we are speaking, was much more destructive than at present; for besides regular battles, simple combats, and the besieging of cities, incessant contests were carried on between the garrisons or the bands of adventurers, who occupied the castles or strong holds. France was in a state of convulsion from one extremity to the other; and when a temporary cessation of hostilities took place, the depredations committed by hordes of unlicensed freebooters rendered the state of the country equally deplorable.

The reader may inquire what became of the riches of France? The reply is, that during the long subversion of affairs, agriculture and commerce had dwindled into nothing: on the other hand, the essence of war, which consists in wasting many things without replacing any, necessarily caused

a vast dissipation of wealth; hence arose a con-
sumption far greater than in ordinary times, and a
produce infinitely inferior. Such annual deficit was,
in the first instance, made good by the aid of
capitals and accumulated wealth; but this succour
had necessarily a termination. Resources being
exhausted, universal misery was the result, with
the exception of some private fortunes made during
the troubles of the times. Let it also be remembered
that the English exported * all the produce of their
plunder; that the money gained by those who pro-
moted the universal disorders of the state was
forwarded to the Flemish or the Italians, who furnished articles of luxury in return; † while the expeditions to the kingdom of Naples, the Milanese,
and the river of Genoa, ‡ had served to expend a
large portion of the public treasure. Under these

---

* This may be easily conceived, and indeed many historians
of that period attest the fact; in proof of which, the following
statement will suffice for the rest: " *On the 18th of August,* 1427,
*the regent left Paris, always enriching his own country with spoils
from this kingdom, and never bringing any thing from thence,
upon his return, but a load of taxation.*" *Journal de Paris,* 111.

† Numerous statements are found in history, which equally
attest the pomp and magnificence displayed by those who had
enriched themselves at the public expense; among others, see
Villaret, xii. page 37; xiii. page 86.

‡ Under Charles VI. several distant expeditions were undertaken, either by his orders or on account of some illustrious

circumstances, was it surprising that France should have found herself in a complete state of exhaustion?

In such an afflicting posture of affairs, how was it possible not to tremble for the provinces that were preserved from the invasions of the English, not by the exploits or the policy of Charles, but from an unexpected chain of events, the recurrence of which could not reasonably be expected? At the commencement of 1428, the English were more powerful than ever. The peace ratified with Flanders guaranteed to England the alliance of the duke of Burgundy, and the last expedition equally secured the duke of Brittany. As no steps had been taken to enlighten or to gain over the good citizens of the ancient Burgundian faction, always inveterate against Charles on account of the assassination of Jean sans Peur, they continued to aid an enterprise which promised almost certain success. The English commenced this campaign with twenty-four thousand men, well paid, perfectly disciplined, animated with courage from the recollection of past victories, and led on by experienced

houses, such as those of Anjou and Armagnac, together with the following.

1382, Naples; 1383, Barbary; 1384, Scotland; 1388, Guelders; 1390, Barbary; 1395, the Milanese; 1396 and 1399, Turkey and Hungary; 1399, Naples; 1402, Constantinople; and 1415 and 1416, Italy.

and valiant captains, and at their head the regent
Bedford, who constituted the very soul of the enterprise, and had not lost any portion of that energy
or skill for which he had been so justly famed
upon all former occasions.

Charles, as we have before stated, had no treasures, except for his favourites and his mistresses; *
the number of his troops scarcely amounted to
one third of the forces led on by the allies, and
they were neither well equipped nor disciplined.
Every exertion, however, one might imagine, would
have been made to compensate for this want of nume-
rical strength, by activity and wisdom in the measures

---

* How widely different to this was the conduct adopted by
the politic Bedford, since in consulting the treasury of Charters,
preserved in France, we find a multitude of gifts, in rentals,
lands, and titles, accorded to the various English generals and our
allies; namely, to *Warwick* (Register 173, No. 220; Reg. 174,
Nos. 188 and 196.) to *Salisbury,* (Reg. 173, No. 645.) to *Talbot,*
(Reg. 174, No. 150; Reg. 175, No. 317.) to *Fastolf,* (Reg.
172, No. 345; Reg. 175, Nos. 203 and 287.) to *Arundel,* Reg.
175, Nos. 365 and 366.) to *Suffolk,* (Reg. 172, No. 571.) and
to *Luxemburg,* (Reg. 172. No. 9. Reg. 173, Nos. 646 and 686,
&c.)

It is certainly a fact, that these donations did not cost much,
because they consisted of confiscations on the possessions of
the adherents of Charles; nor did the Regent forget himself
in the distribution of such gifts. See the Registers 172, No. 487
and 518; Reg. 173, No. 319; Reg. 174, No. 330; and Reg.
175, No. 69.

resorted to.   Such, however, was not the case;
Charles, showed himself still more unworthy of
his station, constantly yielding to those pursuits
which had uniformly debased his character.   Instead
of marshalling his forces in order for battle, and
toiling to complete the preparations for an excur-
sion or a siege, he was studiously bent on making
arrangements for some ball or festivity. *   It is uniformly allowed, that the presence of a monarch
doubles the force of his troops; whereas all that
could be obtained of Charles at the commencement of the siege of Orleans, the capture of which
place might have produced his immediate ruin, was,
his attending at the distance of thirty leagues.   Experienced generals, it will be allowed on all hands,
are essential to ensure the success of military operations; yet at the period in question, Charles had
deprived himself of the assistance of Richemont,

* In the *Encyclopédie, Dict. d'Histoire,* under the article
Vignoles, as well as in other histories, we find that upon La
Hire's repairing to Charles VII. in order to communicate an
affair of the greatest importance, the king displayed to that brave
captain the preparations for a sumptuous feast, at the same
time demanding of the warrior what he thought of the gaudy
scene; to which La Hire made answer: " *Je pense qu'on ne
sauroit perdre son royaume plus gaiement.*"

N. B.   In Richer's manuscripts, note 1st, No. 28, page 107,
this anecdote is likewise given, from Egnatius and the chancellor
De l'Hôpital; the occurrence having taken place during the
hottest period of the siege of Orleans.

whom he sacrificed to the caprice of his new
favourite La Trimouille, refusing his services, and
causing the gates of his cities to be closed against
him as if he had been an enemy. The same
disorders prevailed in the administration of public
affairs : in every department the same overbearing
insolence and rapacity were shown. The ignorance
of the ministers and the courtiers was manifest
upon all occasions, and a state of discord prevailed
among the public functionaries of every description. The French, wearied with supporting
the yoke of such a vicious and impotent set of
panders, had lost all affection and esteem for their
prince, for whom they only retained some portion
of fidelity, on account of the hatred which they
bore to the dominion of the English.

The vast disproportion that existed between the
two powers, in every point of view, was rendered conspicuous in the opening of the campaign of 1428, which, fortunately for Charles, did
not take place until the month of July. * While
the Burgundians were occupied in taking some
places still subject to Charles on the borders of
Champaigne and of Lorraine, the English, in the
short lapse of two months, became masters of more

* According to Monstrelet, vol. ii. fol. 37, the earl of
Salisbury did not cross the channel until after the festival of
Saint John.

than fifteen towns. They subdued the whole territory of the Orleanais north of the Loire, as well
as some small places to the south,* necessary in
order to invest the capital of that province, which
might be considered the only boulevard of the
empire of Charles VII.

One half of the royal army, and nearly all the
most courageous captains,† shut themselves up
within the city (we need scarcely remark, that
such was not the post suited to La Trimouille, and
other courtly parasites) ; where they were nobly
seconded by the brave inhabitants, more enraged
than the generality of the French against their opponents, on account of the assassination of their

---

* From a variety of historians, we learn that among other
places northward, were, Nogent-le-Roi, Nogent-le-Rotrou, Jenville, Mehun-sur-Loire, Beaugenci, Marchenoir, Chartres, Ram-
bouillet, Rochefort, Pethivier, Puiset, Châteauneuf; and to
the south, Gergeau, Sully, and La Ferte-Hubert. All the cities
upon the river Loire, as far as Blois, and all those of Beauce,
except Châteaudun, belonged to the English, says *Chartier.*

† From the commencement of the siege there were present at
Orleans, Xaintrailles and his brother Guitry, Villars, and La-
chapelle. Gaucourt was governor of the city; but he was in fact
of little service, having broken his arm on the 21st of October,
when on his way to give directions for the defence of the Tournelles.

These captains were joined on the 25th of October, by Dunois,
Saint Severe, Beuil, Chabanes, Chaumont, and La Hire. (See
Tripaut, 4, 5, & 8.)

ancient duke, which still remained unpunished, while the abettor of the crime found protection among the English.

Having brought our Summary, occupying a space of forty-eight years, (from 1380 to 1428,) to the period when the English laid siege to the city of Orleans, we shall now proceed to give some account of Jeanne d'Arc from her birth to the day when she joined the garrison of that city. This we conceive to be required as a preliminary to the introduction of the Diary of the Siege ; the raising of which was certainly due to the perseverance and magnanimity of the heroine of our pages.

HISTORY

OF

JEANNE D'ARC,

LA PUCELLE D'ORLEANS,

FROM THE PERIOD OF HER BIRTH,

Supposed to have taken place in 1411,

TO THAT OF

HER ARRIVAL AT THE CITY OF ORLEANS, IN 1428.

HISTORY,

JEANNE D'ARC was the daughter of James d'Arc
and of Isabella Romée, labouring people, living
upon the produce of a small landed property
which they possessed at Domremy and its environs,
of which they were the cultivators. James d'Arc
was originally of Séfonds, near Montierender, being
descended from a good and ancient family of that
country, which is ascertained from several titles
and contracts still preserved at Saint Dizier. The
armorial bearings of this family were a bow armed with
three arrows, the remains of which are still apparent
upon some ancient tombs. Isabella Romée was
a native of Vouthon, situate about three miles from
Domremy. It appears that these villagers were
pious, unsophisticated, hospitable, and of the most
rigid probity, enjoying a spotless reputation. Besides the heroine of our memoir, they had four
children, three boys and a girl. The eldest son
was named Jacquemin; the second, John; the

third, Peter; and the sister of Jeanne was called
Catherine. Most of the biographers of the Maid
of Orleans have omitted to mention this female
relative, whose name was unknown to them; but,
from authentic documents which have been referred
to, there is no doubt of her having existed, and that
she was christened as above.

The whole of this family occupied a humble
cottage, still existing at the village of Domremy.
The chamber which is pointed out by tradition
as the birth-place of Jeanne, served to receive the
annual produce of the vineyard, that adjoining
was a stable for cows, and at the extremity of
the building is a cellar which formerly contained
the oven for baking. This homely edifice has,
however, undergone repairs, and is now carefully
preserved as an object of veneration for the French,
and of curiosity to the stranger.

The precise period of the birth of Jeanne d'Arc
has not been ascertained, but from what can be gathered in the course of her answers during the trial,
she was born at Domremy, in the month of February
or March, in the year 1411. Her baptism took place
in the church of Saint Remy, at this village, the
edifice being still in existence, and conveying testimonies of the veneration that the memory of Jeanne
d'Arc has inspired throughout the surrounding
country. On either side of the grand altar, are
placed two angels supporting the armorial bearings

of the family of Arc, the workmanship of which is rude, and does not appear to be of very ancient date.

The parents of Jeanne were only capable of giving her an education suitable to their rank in life; it is therefore sufficient to state that her mind was imbued with religious and moral principles. With reading and writing she was altogether unacquainted, having been taught only the *Pater Noster*, the *Ave Maria*, and the *Credo*, by her mother, which constituted the whole of her religious instruction. From every account handed down, it appears that Jeanne was chaste, modest, patient, very gentle and industrious, fearing God, dispensing charity, hospitable to the necessitous, and attentive to the sick.* Notwithstanding her poverty, she found means to succour the needy; being willing to relinquish her own bed

---

* According to history, we find that these qualities uniformly characterised Jeanne d'Arc at the period of her bearing arms, when she scrupulously attended to her fastings, which were principally every Friday during the year, unless the fatigues incidental upon military operations caused an infringement of this general rule. The priests, to whom she was in the habit of confessing, declared that they had never witnessed a female more pure of soul, more humble in spirit, or more resigned to the will of the Almighty. Although reared in rustic ignorance, she nevertheless knew how to conduct herself with extreme prudence when ushered into active life; and her piety supplied every defect resulting from a want of education. — *Lenglet*, vol. i. pages 4 and 5.

when the poor applied to her parents for relief. She was scrupulously obedient to her parents; she frequented the company of the most virtuous females of the village, and she was cherished by all the inhabitants of Domremy.

When her work was done, Jeanne would repair to the church, where, upon her knees, she offered up her prayers with a fervency that bespoke the devoutness of her mind.

In her thirteenth year, she displayed little taste for those amusements which are followed with avidity by girls of such an age; and when they commenced their pastimes, Jeanne retired to her secret devotions. She was particularly fond of conversing on the subject of the Almighty, and of the Virgin Mary, who was the object of her tenderest love and constant thoughts.

Jeanne did not frequent the church at mass only and vespers, but was equally fond of embracing all opportunities of religious worship. She often went to confession, and never failed to receive the sacrament at Easter. She was frequently discovered in the church alone, her looks stedfastly fixed upon the images of our Saviour and the Virgin; and when the sound of the bell summoned the rustics to devotion, Jeanne was uniformly among the first to repair to the village sanctuary for that purpose.

Not far from Domremy, was a small chapel con-

secrated to the Virgin, known by the name of the
Hermitage of Saint Mary, or, the Chapel of our
Lady of Bellemont.   The young men and maids of
Domremy and of Greux were accustomed to repair
thither, for prayer, on a certain day of every year.
Jeanne was in the habit of attending this spot
every Saturday to meditate upon God, and to de-
plore the calamities to which France was then subjected.   Thither, by way of offering, she carried
candles, which she burnt before the image of the
Virgin, to whom she addressed her prayers.   Sometimes, during the week, an irresistible desire would
prompt her to visit this chapel, while her parents
thought she was occupied in the fields, or pursuing
her usual labours.   The spot upon which this structure stood is still distinguishable by a mass of
stones, which are not, however, the remains of that
ancient building, but merely a heap of rubbish
collected in the fields, and regularly deposited
there by the labourers.

Not far from Domremy rose the venerable forest
of Chenu, which could be seen from the residence
of Jeanne d'Arc.   Beneath this wood, on the high
road leading from the village to Neufchateau'
was a majestic beech whose spreading foliage
afforded a welcome shade to the weary traveller.
So aged was this tree, that at the period of Jeanne's
infancy no one could ascertain the time at which
it had been planted, and it was known by the name

of the Fairies' Tree. Beneath the shade of this
beech the youth of both sexes were accustomed to
assemble, at certain times of the year, dancing to
their own songs, partaking of a rustic repast, and
tying crowns and garlands to its branches : of
which recreation Jeanne d'Arc partook in early
childhood ; but, at a riper age, she wholly abandoned these sports, dedicating her time to domestic occupations.   Sometimes she would assist in
conducting cattle to the meadows, as well as horses,
which formed part of the wealth of her father.   A
cotemporary author relates that Jeanne was well
versed in riding and managing steeds, so that she
contended with her companions at the race with as
much dexterity as any knight would have displayed. *

The fatal divisions which at that period reigned
in France had extended their baleful influence to
the remotest villages, and the names of the Burgundians and the Armagnacs were familiar to
their humblest inhabitants.   All the natives of
Donremy, with the exception of one solitary
individual, were determined Armagnacs, and con-

---

* Monstrelet, adverting to the prowess of Jeanne d'Arc in
managing a horse, thus expresses himself :— " *Elle estoit hardie
de chevaucher chevaux et les mener boire, et aussi de faire apper-
tises et autres habillitez que jeunes filles n'ont point accoutumé
de faire.*"

sequently devoted to the cause of Charles VII.
The inhabitants of Maxey, a neighbouring village,
situated between Domremy and Vaucouleurs, had,
on the contrary, pronounced themselves advocates
for the opposite faction. In consequence of this,
frequent battles were fought between the natives of
these respective places; and upon one occasion Jeanne
d'Arc is stated to have witnessed the return of
the boys of Domremy wounded and bleeding from
one of those affrays, which excited in her breast
such a rooted hatred for the Burgundian name, that
she openly avowed a wish, that the only inhabitant
of Domremy who had declared himself for that
party, might be decapitated, if such were the will
of the Lord. This circumstance, which shows to
what an extent these inimical feelings were excited,
might favour the supposition that Jeanne d'Arc was
naturally cruel, did not every subsequent action of
her life give evidence to the contrary.

It was about the year 1423 or 1424, that Jeanne
d'Arc for the first time conceived herself visited by
supernatural agents; at which period the battles of
Crevant and of Verneuil took place, which threatened
to annihilate the party of Charles VII. who had
been previously acknowledged king at Espali, near
Puy, the 28th of October, 1422, and then crowned
at Poitiers, after the lapse of a few days.

Jeanne d'Arc, then about thirteen years of age, (such
is her own account,) at twelve o'clock on a summer's

day, being in her father's garden, suddenly beheld, on the right side of the village church, a dazzling light, while an unknown voice echoed in her ear. These sounds breathed the wisest counsels, telling her to frequent the church, to be always good and virtuous, and to rely upon the protection of Heaven. " *La jeune fille oust moult paour de ce :* The young girl felt much afraid at this :" as appears from the statements of those who were present at the interrogatories during her trial : but she did not hesitate in believing it was sent from heaven, and in order to testify her gratitude, she voluntarily undertook to consecrate her virginity to the Lord.

Upon a subsequent occasion, when in the open country, the same voice was audible to Jean d'Arc, while an archangel presented itself to La Pucelle, accompanied by other celestial emissaries. This was Saint Michael, who expressed himself to the young girl to the following effect : " That the Almighty felt great pity towards France ; and that it was necessary she should go to the king's assistance : that she would cause the raising of the siege of Orleans, and deliver Charles from his enemies ; that it was necessary she should present herself to Baudricourt, captain of Vaucouleurs, who would cause her to be conducted to the king, where she would arrive without meeting any obstacle ; that Saint Catherine and Saint Marguerite would visit her, they having been chosen to guide and assist her with their advice; and that it was requisite for her to believe and obey them in all they should prescribe, such being the will of the Omnipotent." Jeanne confessed that in the first instance she could scarcely give credit to these apparitions, but that unknown beings again presented themselves at different times, and in particular she stated that the personage who addressed her, was " truly a comely man." The two Saints, above named, whose images Jeanne had been accustomed to decorate with flowers in the chapel of Domremy, accordingly visited her; and from whatsoever cause these appearances testified by the girl arose, they certainly elevated her mind, which was naturally prone to contemplation.*

In proportion as Jeanne increased in years, the

* In the progress of the interrogatories that took place during the trial, Jeanne affirmed that these revelations and apparitions began when she had attained the age of thirteen, (see *Laverdy*, 36.) She did not, however, communicate these circumstances to her neighbours. Her belief in such revelations is little to be wondered at, if we take into consideration the superstitious credulity which reigned in that part of the country, of which we will quote one example. It was currently believed that the fairies visited Domremy, assembling under a large tree; wherefore the curate, in order to drive them away, used to repair thither to chant one of the gospels, on the eve of the Ascension, being accompanied thither by the inhabitants; among whom Jeanne followed with the rest; but she was not observed to repair to that spot alone. — See *Laverdy*, 300; *Dartigny*, vii. 350.

injunctions of these heavenly emissaries became more importunate ; recommending her to set forward upon her mission and enter France. Notwithstanding the caution which Jeanne observed in not communicating her revelations to any one, she nevertheless found it impossible to execute her project without giving publicity to some circumstances; and it appears that in the course of a conversation which took place with a labouring man of Domremy, residing near her father, she went so far as to state * " that there was a girl residing between Compey and Vaucouleurs, who, before the expiration of a year, would cause the king of France to be crowned," which event certainly did take place within the period so stipulated. Assertions of this description being frequently made, caused considerable uneasiness to Jacques d'Arc and Isabella Romée, who became apprehensive lest their daughter should seek to accomplish her plan by joining some party of soldiers, many of which passed at

---

* Lenglet, vol. i. page 13, says, from the representations made during the interrogatories of Jeanne, that when conversing with the villagers concerning the misfortunes of the kingdom, she frequently affirmed that a young girl of the country would present herself to succour France and the oppressed blood royal, and that she would conduct the Dauphin to be crowned at Rheims ; but those to whom she thus addressed herself were far from conceiving that Jeanne intended any allusion to herself by these statements.

intervals through the village. In consequence of this, the proceedings of the girl were carefully watched by her parents, and upon one occasion, Jacques d'Arc said to his sons in the dialect of that period: " *Si je cuidoye que la chose advinsit que j'ai songié d'elle, je vouldroye que la noyissiez, et se vous ne le faisiez, je la noyeroie moi même:* If I thought that the circumstance would take place which I have imagined respecting her, I should wish you to drown her, and if you would not do so, I would drown her myself." Jacques d'Arc had previously a dream notifying to him that his daughter would quit her home with a band of armed men.

Such was the situation of Jeanne d'Arc with her family, when a troop of Burgundians suddenly appeared, ravaging the country, in order to punish the natives for their firm adherence to the cause of Charles VII. These troops advanced upon Domremy, and at their approach all the inhabitants took to flight, carrying with them their most valuable effects, and driving their flocks along the banks of the Meuse; seeking refuge within the walls of Neufchâteau. In this town Jeanne d'Arc and her family found an asylum in the dwelling of an honest labouring woman, named La Rousse, who kept a small inn;* and beneath her roof they

---

* It has been surmised that Jeanne d'Arc was for some time servant at an inn; but the most ancient, as well as all her

continued for five days, during which time Jeanne
was employed in superintending her father's flock
in the neighbouring fields.

In the midst of these domestic avocations, and
the embarrassments of her situation, Jeanne nevertheless scrupulously performed all her devotional
offices, and went to confess two or three times.
The residence, however, at Neufchâteau, became

modern biographers whose statements are worthy of credit,
make no mention of her having served in a house of public resort.
In the course of her trial it appeared from her own statement,
that she was resident at an inn at Neufchâteau for about
fifteen days, but that she never mounted horses to lead them to
the water, continuing, on the contrary, quiet within the house, and
solely occupied in attending to domestic concerns. If this residence at an inn for so short a period escaped the recollection of
the witnesses examined during the second process instituted for
the justification of Jeanne, it is not to be wondered at, as a
lapse of twenty-five years had transpired since her execution.
However, in order that the reader may be better enabled to
form an opinion as to the confidence that should be placed
in the testimony of the persons so examined, the following is an
account of the occupations they severally followed, extracted
from the lists of Laverdy, page 286, and Lenglet, vol. ii. page
166, &c.

One thatcher; nine labouring men; the wives of four labourers;
the wives of a notary, a clerk, and a draper ; two notaries; one
priest; two curates ; two canons who were curates; three
esquires; two lords, and one of them a knight ; the professions
of four other men and one woman are not recorded ; making
in the whole thirty-four witnesses.

insupportable to her, as she was thereby removed to a greater distance from Vaucouleurs, and consequently prevented from fulfilling the mission which she conceived herself delegated to perform. At length the Burgundian troops quitted the country, when Jacques d'Arc and his family, yielding to the strenuous remonstrances of the girl, were among the first to return to their native village. Upon this occasion Jeanne was led to contemplate the direful ravages which the country had sustained from the recent effects of warfare; she gazed on the profanation offered to that sacred spot where formerly she had been wont to offer up her fervent orisons to the Most High. The spectacle no doubt was afflicting to her heart, and tended to animate her mind with the noble idea of re-establishing the monarch upon the throne of his ancestors, and thereby terminating such a dreadful scene of crimes and impiety.

Jeanne d'Arc was incessantly occupied with the idea of her journey to Vaucouleurs, when a new incident occurred to retard the accomplishment of her ardent wishes. A young man, whose name has not reached posterity, captivated with the virtuous conduct and personal attractions of the maid, demanded her in marriage, but his proposals were rejected by Jeanne. It appears that Jacques d'Arc and Isabella Romée anxiously wished to bring about this union, which would have put a period to their uneasiness; and that they made unsuccess-

ful efforts to obtain the consent of their child.
The lover, however, was not so easily deterred
from his purpose; but in order to bring the maid
to an acquiescence with his wishes, he insisted
that she had promised to become united to him,
and in consequence cited her before the magis-
tracy of Toul. In this instance Jeanne displayed
the unalterable resolution of her conduct, and
appeared before the judge determined to defend her
own cause in person ; when she swore to pronounce
the truth, and declared she never had uttered such
promise to any man, much less to the individual
who had so summoned her ; upon which the magis-
trate, satisfied as to the veracity of her statement,
gave his decision in her favour.*

After this occurrence, Jeanne d'Arc, in all probability to escape the discontent of her parents,
testified a desire of visiting Durand Laxart,† her
maternal uncle, who resided at Petit Burey, a village
situated between Domremy and Vaucouleurs. In
consequence of this Laxart repaired to the family,
and requested permission of Jeanne's father that she
might spend some time with him, alleging as a
pretext, the services which his niece might afford
his wife, who was then in a state of pregnancy ; and

* This curious event in the life of Jeanne was made public
during the interrogatories that took place upon her trial at the
sitting of the 12th March, 1439.
† Some historians call him Jean-la-Part.

in consequence Jacques d'Arc gave his consent.
Scarcely had eight days elapsed, when Jeanne informed her uncle that it was necessary she should
go to Vaucouleurs, being desirous to proceed from
thence into France, to join the Dauphin (such was
the title she gave the king) for the purpose of effecting his coronation. Jeanne spoke to Laxart respecting her project with so much assurance, and insisted
with such perseverance, that in the end she persuaded him to acquiesce.

Durand Laxart, in the first instance, proceeded
alone to the lord de Baudricourt, in order to
explain the wishes and the projects of his niece;
but he met with a very bad reception. When
Jeanne ascertained the ill success which had attended his mission, she declared that it was her
intention to set out immediately for Vaucouleurs,
for which purpose she had already obtained possession of her uncle's attire, being desirous of wearing
man's apparel in order to facilitate her journey,
when Laxart, aware of this determined resolution,
resolved to accompany her.

Jeanne d'Arc arrived at Vaucouleurs on the
festival of the Ascension, being the 13th of May,
1428; and lodged with her uncle at the house of a
blacksmith named Henri, whose residence in that
town is still pointed out to the traveller: the
wife of this man, Catherine, imbibed a great
partiality for Jeanne d'Arc. The governor was

immediately apprized of her arrival, and the object
of her journey; but the only answer La Pucelle
received was a second refusal to send her to the
king. Notwithstanding this, however, she was
admitted to the presence of Baudricourt, to whom
she announced, " That she came on the part of
the Lord; who, through her, advised the Dauphin
to conduct himself virtuously; that he had not
given the battle to his enemies, because the Lord
would accord him succour towards the middle
of Lent." Jeanne stated, that the kingdom did
not belong to the Dauphin, but to the Almighty;
that nevertheless the Lord was willing that he
should become king, and receive the realm as a
deposit; adding, that in spite of his enemies he
should become king, and that she would conduct
him to be crowned. Robert then made inquiry
respecting this Lord to whom she so constantly
alluded, when Jeanne replied, " that it was the King
of heaven :" upon which, Baudricourt, not knowing
whether to regard the whole as a cheat, or if the
young girl was deranged in her mind, would listen
to no further statements, and so dismissed Jeanne
without acceding to any thing she required.

La Pucelle was sensibly touched at this ill success;
but she had recourse to her accustomed consolation,
repairing to confess and giving herself up to prayer;
a great portion of her time being spent in the
chapel of Saint Mary, at Vaucouleurs, where she

prostrated herself with the greatest humility before the image of the Virgin.

The uniform tenour of Jeanne's discourse was, that she must proceed to the presence of the Dauphin; and such was her impatience, that she with difficulty submitted to the long delays that occurred ere she found means of compassing her intention. " It is absolutely necessary that I should go thither," she incessantly cried, " for so wills my Lord. It is on the part of the King of heaven that this mission is confided to me; and were it necessary that I should repair thither on my knees, I would go." She exhorted all those whom she saw to conduct her to the Dauphin, adding, that it was for his special benefit.

At length public opinion, which was pronounced in favour of Jeanne from the incessant conversations and reiterated promises she made, began to produce some impression even on the mind of the lord de Baudricourt. Agitated by opposing interests and passions, he adopted a measure conformable to the prejudices of that period; and accompanied by the curate of Vaucouleurs, proceeded to the apartment of Jeanne, when the priest, carrying his stole, spread it out before the young girl, by way of an exorcism.*

* Lenglet, vol. i. p. 22, states that the priest thus addressed Jeanne : " If you come in behalf of the enemy of men, begone

At the sight of this priestly ornament, Jeanne humbly fell upon her knees before the curate, in token of respect to his sacred calling; after which she replied to all the interrogatories put to her by the governor, who, though unwilling to take any thing upon himself, conceived the affair of sufficient importance to warrant his addressing the king upon the subject.

Durand Laxart was under the necessity of returning home, and he conducted his niece to the village of Petit Burey. We are not informed from history whether Jacques d'Arc, at this period, had any knowledge of the journey undertaken by his daughter : it is, however, most probable that he was ignorant of the fact, since he permitted her to reside peaceably with her uncle.

Jeanne had completely succeeded in convincing Laxart of the truth of her mission, so that his faith was by no means shaken by the difficulties he had to surmount ; and at the beginning of Lent, in the same year, he again consented to accompany his niece to Vaucouleurs. Seeing how many impediments prevented the accomplishment of her

from our presence ; but if it is upon the part of God, then remain." See the depositions of Catherine, wife of Henri the blacksmith, at whose house Jeanne resided at Vaucouleurs, which statements were delivered during the revisal on Saturday, January 31, 1456.

views, Jeanne adopted the resolution of setting
forward on foot, accompanied by her uncle and
another individual named Jacques Alain, who offered
to follow her, for the fulfilment of the mission
wherewith she conceived herself to be charged.
But while on her route, Jeanne called to mind that
it would not be decorous thus to depart, and she
therefore retraced her steps to Vaucouleurs.

Jean Novelompont, surnamed of Metz, a gentleman of some consideration in that country, happening to call at the house of Jeanne's hostess,
and doubtless perceiving that, although clad in
mean red attire, the young maid carried something
in her appearance far above the common, made
inquiry respecting the business that had led her
to Vaucouleurs: " I am come," said she, " to
request of Robert de Baudricourt, that he will
cause me to be conducted to the king, either by
himself or some other person: but he does not
concern himself either about me or my representations. And yet it is absolutely necessary that
I should see the king before the middle of Lent,
even if I am compelled to wear my legs to the very
knees in the journey. For no living creature, nor
kings, nor dukes, nor the daughter of the king of
Scotland, nor any others, can retake the kingdom
of France, since there is no succour for him save
through myself; though I should much better like
to remain at home spinning by the side of my poor

mother ; for such is not a work fitted for me : * yet I
must go and do it, for such is the will of the Lord."
" And who is your Lord ? " inquired Jean de Metz :
" It is God," was Jeanne's reply.   Forcibly struck
with the words of the girl, and placing his hand
within hers, he declared upon his faith that he would
escort her to the king ; and then demanded when
she wished to set forwards : " Rather to-day than
to-morrow," she made answer : he further requested
to know if she was desirous of proceeding in the
clothes she then wore, to which she replied, she
would willingly accept of man's apparel, which he
caused to be brought, and Jeanne immediately
dressed herself in the same.

Bertrand de Poulengy, who had been present at
the interview between Jeanne d'Arc and the lord de
Baudricourt, speedily followed the example of Jean
de Metz, being anxious to share the honour of
conducting the maid on her journey.   Jeanne, however, still wished to procure the sanction of Baudricourt, in proportion as the fame of her alleged
mission increased throughout the country.

Charles, duke of Lorraine, weakened by a malady
which baffled the art of medicine, was desirous of
seeing Jeanne d'Arc for the purpose of consulting
her ; wherefore Laxart accompanied La Pucelle upon

* This deposition was made by Jean de Novelompont, gentleman, a resident of Vaucouleurs, on Saturday, January 31, 1456.

her journey which she undertook, to comply with the desire of that prince.* During this interview the duke proposed several questions relating to herself,

* According to the depositions made by the lady de Touroulde, at the revisal of Jeanne's sentence, we find that her uncle conducted her on a pilgrimage to St. Nicholas, near Nanci, when the duke of Lorraine, having heard statements respecting her, was desirous of seeing the maid; and for this purpose he despatched a passport for her safe conduct to Nanci, which event took place a short time prior to the feasts of Pentecost (Whitsuntide), of 1428. The prince was then labouring under a malady, and although his mind felt much more disquietude on that account than any other, he nevertheless proceeded to interrogate Jeanne about the reports that were disseminated concerning her. She immediately stated her desire to go and assist the Dauphin, and then supplicated the duke in the most urgent manner to issue his commands to his son, (René of Anjou, who had espoused his daughter,) that he would undertake to conduct her in safety to the Dauphin, Charles; and that she would offer up her prayers to the Lord for the recovery of his health. The duke then demanded what was her opinion respecting his illness; whereto she ingenuously replied, " that as he lived on bad terms with his wife, who was a very virtuous princess, he would not recover unless he changed his conduct in regard to her." The duke then dismissed Jeanne with a present of four francs, which she instantly confided to her uncle, who subsequently remitted the amount to her parents.— *Lenglet,* vol. i. p. 20, &c.; *Laverdy,* p. 301.

In a work written by M. Luchet, which we shall have occasion to quote, the author not only ridicules the idea of supernatural agency as being connected with Jeanne d'Arc, but also adduces arguments for the purpose of depreciating the merit so generally

and then proceeded to inquire if she could point out
any means for the recovery of his health; but
Jeanne answered that she was incapable of throwing
any light upon that subject. She, however, exhorted
him to live in peace with the duchess, his wife, who
was a good and virtuous princess, stating that he
would not recover unless he changed his conduct
in regard to her; and, lastly, she entreated that
the duke would furnish her with an escort under the
command of the prince, his son, for the purpose
of conducting her to Charles the Dauphin of
France.

The parents of Jeanne d'Arc could not long
remain ignorant of her departure from Petit-Burey,
of the ardent resolution she had formed of presenting herself to the king, and of the success attending
her visit to Vaucouleurs. When apprized of these
facts, they were completely paralyzed, and Jacques
d'Arc thus saw realized the dream he had had
some years before, by which he was forewarned
that his daughter would depart with men at arms.
In consequence of this, Jeanne's parents set out
with all expedition for Vaucouleurs, in order to

attached to La Pucelle. When speaking of this visit to the
duke of Lorraine, he states, "that the prince dismissed the
pilgrim, but did not think fit to change his conduct in regard to
the duchess; yet," adds M. Luchet, "the duke was subsequently cured of his malady, notwithstanding the menace of
the prophetess." Ed. 1776, page 5.

prevent the execution of their daughter's design; and it is by no means improbable that this journey was undertaken during the maid's absence to attend upon the duke of Lorraine. Jeanne caused a letter to be written, wherein she implored pardon of her parents for this disobedience, and received the forgiveness she had solicited. On a third interview with Baudricourt, to whom she was presented by Novelompont, she at length obtained the acquiescence of the governor, who consented to her journey for the purpose of joining the king. There appears some reason to believe that Baudricourt had then received an answer from the court to the letters which he had despatched, and that he had received orders to send the girl to Chinon; at all events her reiterated applications might have got the better of his reluctance in complying with her entreaties. Some historians have attributed the consent of Baudricourt to a supernatural cause; alleging, after the statements in ancient chronicles, that on the very day when the French were beaten at Rouvray Saint Denis, Jeanne d'Arc had announced to the governor the issue of that fatal encounter in the following words* : —

" *En mon Dieu, vous mettez trop à m'envoyer; car*

* Luchet, at page 6, speaking of this event, says : " This trait, which is the most singular in the life of this extraordinary girl, is

aujourd'hui le gentil Dauphin a eu assez près d'Orléans
un bien grand dommage, et sera-t-il encore taillé de
l'avoir plus grand si ne m'envoyez bientot vers lui:
In the name of God, you hesitate too long about
sending me; for this very day the handsome Dauphin has experienced a great discomfiture near
Orleans, and it shall so turn out that he will yet
suffer a greater, if you do not speedily send me
to join him."

The lord de Baudricourt having resolved on the
departure of Jeanne, preparations for the journey
were immediately made. The inhabitants of Vaucouleurs procured man's attire for the young woman;
and her uncle Durand Laxart, in conjunction with
Jacques Alain, purchased her a horse, for which

only guaranteed by the deposition of the wife of a blacksmith
of Vaucouleurs, named Henri. What renders the statement
suspicious, is, that Baudricourt did not alter his opinion respecting Jeanne d'Arc, saying to her when she departed: *Va, et advienne*
ce que tu pourras. If the prophecy had been really verified, the
people would have seen a miracle in all that transpired, and the
governor would not have conducted himself so cavalierly. The
major part of her panegyrists were ignorant of, or wilfully omitted
this occurrence, while others have contented themselves in relating
it with indifference. This would incontestably have proved the
most propitious moment of her life, the true sign which has been
so repeatedly and so fruitlessly demanded."

The deposition of Catherine, wife of Henri the blacksmith of
Vaucouleurs, was made on January 31, 1456, during the process
of revisal.

they paid twelve francs ; while Jean de Metz undertook to liquidate the expenses on the road. The registers of the Chamber of Accounts prove that the king did not order the disbursement of these sums until the 21st April, 1429,* which was subsequent to the examination of La Pucelle, and his having in consequence confided to her the. charge of conveying succour to Orleans.

The escort of Jeanne d'Arc consisted of seven persons ; Jean de Metz ; Bertrand de Poulengy, esq. ; Pierre d'Arc, third brother of La Pucelle ; Collet de Vienne, a messenger or emissary of the king ; Richard, a bow-man ; Julian, the valet of De Poulengy ; and Jean de Honnecourt, the attendant of Jean de Metz. Many of the inhabitants of Domremy proceeded to Vaucouleurs for the purpose of witnessing the departure of the young maid, who expressed to her their apprehensions on account of the numerous bands of armed men who scoured the country. *" Je ne crains pas les hommes d'armes,* I do not fear the men at arms," she boldly replied : *" j'ai Dieu mon Seigneur, que me fera mon chemin jusqu'à mon seigneur le Dauphin :* I have God for my Lord, who will make clear for me the road even unto my lord the Dauphin."

* In the notes to the manuscripts of Fontanieu, in the Royal Library at Paris, is a copy of the receipt for one hundred francs, the sum that was paid by order of the king.

Baudricourt administered an oath to those who had undertaken to conduct La Pucelle, whereby they swore to escort her in safety to the king; but he was far from sharing in the general enthusiasm which the maid had inspired. In thus forwarding Jeanne, the governor complied with the orders of the court; he merely presented a sword to Jeanne d'Arc, and took his leave of her in these words : " *Va, et advienne ce que tu pourras:* Go, and let come what thou canst accomplish."

La Pucelle and her companions began their journey the first Sunday in Lent, being the 13th of February, 1429 ; but she did not inspire the same confidence in all her escort. Notwithstanding this, after the commencement of the expedition the party became rather more emboldened, and proceeded during the first day through a country occupied by the Burgundians and the English, where they apprehended much danger, and therefore determined not to halt, but continue the march during the night. It is evident from all the accounts extant, that they were subjected to imminent dangers in the progress of the journey, so that a part of the escort, affrighted at the enterprise, had it in contemplation to abandon La Pucelle; and although De Metz and Poulengy had no idea of falsifying their oaths, they were nevertheless intimidated.* Jeanne d'Arc,

* In the deposition made by the Lady de Touroulde, it appears that Jean de Metz and Poulengy, during the first days

however, a stranger to fear, encouraged her companions by her dauntless bravery and her inflexible
resolution. " *Ne craignez rien*, fear nothing," she
exclaimed; " *tout ce que je fais m'est commandé. Il
y a quatre ou cinq ans mes frères de Paradis m'ont dit
qu'il fallait que j'allasse à la guerre, pour recouvrer le
royaume de France.* I am commanded to execute
all I do. Four or five years ago, my brethren in
Paradise told me, that it was requisite I should go
to the war, to rescue the kingdom of France :" and
in order to give them encouragement, she then promised, that upon their arrival at Chinon, the king
would look kindly on them.

The danger to which Jeanne d'Arc was exposed
in undertaking such a journey through the territory
of an enemy, was not the only peril wherewith she
was threatened; for as there is every reason to
conjecture that she possessed great personal charms,
she might have excited criminal desires in the
minds of her conductors. But on consulting the
depositions made during the process of revisal by
those of her party, it will be found that such was
not the case. The unbounded goodness that characterized the young maiden, and the unaffected and
sincere piety with which she was animated, tended

of their march, had an idea of throwing La Pucelle into some
quarry as a girl out of her mind; but at length they resolved to
obey her in every thing.

to conciliate every heart, and impressed all those who surrounded her with respectful admiration.

De Metz and Poulengy proceeded by the most unfrequented routes, avoiding the public roads, and all towns of consequence. They passed near Auxerre, and soon arrived at Gien, the first city under the dominion of Charles VII. which they had as yet gained in the course of their march.

The news of the arrival of Jeanne d'Arc spread with rapidity even to the city of Orleans, for the succour of which place she was so speedily to march.*

* Some popular reports were spread in favour of Jeanne d'Arc even prior to her arrival at Chinon; which gained considerably upon the public mind from the following circumstance. One of the doctors named to examine La Pucelle, stated before witnesses, that a woman named *Marie d'Avignon* had previously presented herself to Charles VII., who pretended it had been revealed to her that the kingdom of France would still suffer great misery, (which was by no means surprising under existing circumstances,) and that it would be precipitated into a state of universal desolation. She then added, that in a vision, arms had been presented to her, at which she was greatly terrified, under the apprehension that they were intended for herself; but she was told to be under no apprehension, for that it was not her who was to use them, but a certain *Maiden* who would appear to rescue France from its enemies.

To this first tale may be subjoined what had been stated by Jeanne herself; that it was rumoured abroad, a girl would come from the wood of Chenu, which was situated near the dwelling of her parents, who was to rescue the country. It was

La Pucelle then passed the Loire, and proceeding on her road towards Chinon, arrived at the town of Fierbois, containing a church dedicated to Saint Catherine. Meeting with an edifice consecrated to one of her celestial protectors, did not fail to make a strong impression upon her mind. Being then only five or six leagues from Chinon, she might consider herself as arrived at the end of her journey, and from thence she addressed a letter to the king, which was in substance as follows : That she was desirous of knowing whether or not she should enter the city wherein his majesty then sojourned ; that she had performed a tedious and a perilous journey of one hundred and fifty leagues for the express purpose of rendering him assistance ; and that she was acquainted with many things that would be agreeable to him.

Jeanne d'Arc carried her devotion to such a length that she attended the celebration of three masses in one day, in the church of Saint Catherine de

in consequence of this popular tale, that one of the assessors at the process of revisal stated, that he had read it in the book of Merlin ; and another witness pretended that the circumstance was mentioned to the lord Talbot, after he was captured at the battle of Patay. It is not surprising that circumstances of this nature should have forcibly operated on the public mind ; particularly as a prediction had long existed purporting that a girl from the marshes of Lorraine would prove the saviour of France. It may be conceived what an impression the arrival of La Pucelle in the neighbourhood of Chinon must have created.

Fierbois.*   It is most probable that the king's answer to her letter was favourable; for she very soon left Fierbois, and arrived at Chinon the same day, taking up her abode at an inn, kept by a female, near the castle of Chinon.

The arrival of Jeanne d'Arc was at a favourable juncture for giving publicity to the wonderful promises which she conveyed to the king. Orleans, the only remaining rampart of the monarchy, was reduced to the last extremity, and there appeared no possibility of yielding assistance to that determined and faithful city. Money and troops were both wanting—all was despair; and the only assistance to be hoped for, was from Heaven.

Jeanne d'Arc was not admitted to Charles VII. without much precaution being observed; since the court manifested great irresolution as to the steps that should be taken in regard to her, and many were of opinion that she ought to be dismissed without having an audience.† After deliberating

---

* Novelompont testifies how much he was edified by the piety and the charity of Jeanne d'Arc, who, notwithstanding all the difficulties incidental to the journey, uniformly sought every opportunity of attending mass, and never failed to distribute charity.

† Charles does not appear to have been biassed by the first impulses of his mind; but was, on the contrary, particularly reserved, having refused to see Jeanne until after he had consulted the council.

for two days, it was decided that Jeanne should be admitted; but she underwent an examination before the commissioners previous to her interview with the king. In the first instance she refused to make any answers to interrogatories, merely stating that her desire was to communicate with the Dauphin.*

The maid, being lodged at the castle Ducoudray, was visited by such persons as the king deputed. The members of the council were divided in their opinions, some being adverse to, and others in favour of Jeanne's admittance to the king. The former, in particular, advised Charles not to pay attention to the phantasies of a bewildered girl, who was very probably suborned by the enemy; and that he should, above all, take heed not to be made the dupe of the English.

Jeanne was in the first instance examined by the bishop of Meaux and Jean Morin, to whom La Pucelle stated, as usual, that she came from *Le Roi du ciel*, that she had heard celestial voices which gave her advice, and that she was to be guided by those supernatural emissaries.

Charles, having compared the contents of Baudricourt's letter with the statements made by Jeanne at this preliminary examination, and being in particular struck with the account of her dangerous journey, so miraculously effected, was led to wish for an interview with the maid. These circumstances being equally made known to the council, the major part acquiesced, and her introduction to the royal presence was in consequence decided upon.—*Chaussard, part first, pages* 10, 11, & 12.

* It was particularly asked of Jeanne, why she did not apply the title of King, in lieu of Dauphin, to Charles VII.; to which she made answer, that he would not be king and the absolute possessor of his kingdom until he had been crowned at Rheims; after which event his affairs would continue to prosper, in

At length, being pressed to reply on the part of the monarch, she stated: " *Qu'elle avait deux choses à accomplir de la part du Roi des cieux; la première de faire lever le siége d'Orléans, et la deuxième de conduire le Roi à Rheims, et de l'y faire sacrer et couronner.* That she had two things to accomplish on the part of the King of heaven; first, to cause the siege of Orleans to be raised; and secondly, to conduct the king to Rheims, there to be anointed and crowned."

Charles VII. feeling dissatisfied with the report made by the first commissioners appointed for that purpose,* ordered a second examination of Jeanne

proportion as those of the English declined.—*Lenglet*, vol. i. page 41.

* The persons deputed to examine La Pucelle, were, Regnaut de Chartres, archbishop of Rheims, who had been three months nominated chancellor of France; Christophe de Harcourt, bishop of Castres, the king's confessor; Guillaume Charpentier, bishop of Poitiers; Nicolas le Grand, bishop of Senlis; the bishop of Montpellier; Jean Jourdain, a doctor in theology of Paris, together with many other doctors. Jeanne d'Arc was interrogated in presence of Jean II. duke d'Alençon, a prince of the blood, who was bound upon his faith and his religion.—*Lenglet*, vol. i. page 33.

Luchet, at page 9, speaking of this examination, says, that the ambiguous answers of La Pucelle gave rise to fresh doubts; that a second commission was nominated; and the following five questions addressed to Jacques Gelu, archbishop of Tours, for the purpose of ascertaining his opinion upon each.

Ques. Does it appertain to the Supreme Being to concern him-

d'Arc; and resolved upon sending into her native
country to ascertain the life she had led, her character, and her morals. During this interval, a

self with the actions of a simple individual, or even with the
concerns of a kingdom?

Ans. Sometimes, and always for the good of the concern in
question.

Ques. Is it not more fitting for God to employ his angels in
accomplishing his will than to have recourse to man?

Ans. If God in ancient times thought fit to depute a crow, in
order to give sustenance to Paul and Anthony the hermits,
with much more semblance of reason might he resort to the
agency of men.

Ques. Is it more fitting that the Almighty should employ a
woman than a man?

Ans. The Virgin knew the mystery of the Incarnation, and
the Sibyls taught men secrets which they acquired from the
Divinity.

Ques. May it not be an artifice of the devil?

Ans. That will be ascertained by the good that results.

Ques. In such case is it not necessary to employ prudence
and wisdom?

Ans. That costs nothing.

M. Luchet then continues to state, " that notwithstanding
these answers of archbishop Gelu, and the revelations made to
the king respecting the prayer addressed to the Divinity in his
oratory at Loches, *where he was not at the time she specified,*
Jeanne acquired no great reputation. The kind of insensate rapture with which we frequently hail momentous occurrences failed to denote any grand success that might accrue to
our heroine in future, as the only conclusion was, that Jeanne
should undergo a second interrogatory."

lodging was assigned for her in the castle Ducoudray.   Many noblemen went thither to see the
maid, who were astonished at her natural eloquence,
the tone of inspiration that reigned throughout her
discourse, and the extraordinary piety she manifested. It appears that Jeanne spent nearly the
whole of the day in prayers, and was frequently
found upon her knees bathed in tears. After watching all her actions with scrupulous care, no symptoms of imposture were discoverable ; every thing
on her part announced a self-conviction of supernatural agency, which she insensibly infused into
the minds of all those who approached her.

The king, still undecided, nevertheless wished to
see Jeanne before the return of the agents whom he
had forwarded to Domremy ; but at the very time
when she approached his residence, being overcome
by fresh doubts, he was not prevailed upon to admit
her until the journey she had so recently performed
was represented to him as miraculous. This expedition, which, on account of the circuitous
routes that were traversed to avoid the enemy,
had extended to a hundred and fifty leagues, was
accomplished in eleven days.   In the course of this
march it was found necessary to cross the rivers
Ornain, Marne, Aube, Armançon, Yonne, Loire,
Cher, Indre, and many other streams, rendered
dangerous on account of the inundations which
regularly occur at the season when this journey

was undertaken. The individuals who had served
as an escort to Jeanne were astonished at finding
no obstacle in traversing an enemy's country in the
depth of winter, and along such difficult roads.

An audience with the king was at length accorded
to Jeanne, on the third day after her arrival. Fifty
torches illumined the apartments of the prince;
many lords more sumptuously dressed than the king
were present, and upwards of three hundred knights
had assembled in the audience chamber.

On the same day a singular event took place, as
if for the express purpose of bringing the most
incredulous minds to believe in the heavenly mission
of Jeanne d'Arc. At the precise moment when she
entered the royal residence, a man on horseback
who had seen her pass, made inquiry of a by-
stander, whether that was not La Pucelle? who
being answered in the affirmative, exclaimed, blas-
pheming the name of the Lord, that if he had her
in his possession she should not long continue a
virgin. Jeanne, having overheard these words,
turned her head and cried: " *Ha, en mon Dieu, tu
le renies, et se es si près de ta mort:* Ah! by my God,
thou blasphemest him; and yet thou art so nigh
unto thy death!" About an hour after, this man fell
into the water and was drowned.

As soon as the king understood that Jeanne was
coming, he stepped aside, in order to ascertain
whether she would not mistake some other person

for himself. La Pucelle, however, distinguished the
monarch in the crowd ; stating that her *supernatural
voices* had made him known to her.*

* Jeanne d'Arc was presented to the king by the Count de
Vendôme, and without hesitation recognised the monarch at
first sight, although there was nothing particular in his attire,
or exterior appearance, and he was indiscriminately mingled
with the crowd : she immediately made a profound reverence,
and thus addressed him : " *Gentil Dauphin, j'ai nom Jeanne la
Pucelle, et vous mande le Roi des cieux, par moi, que vous serez
sacré et couronné à Rheims ; vous serez le lieutenant du Roi
des cieux, qui est roi de France.*" Charles, removing from those
that surrounded him, conversed with Jeanne in their presence,
but without being overheard ; which conference lasted for some
time, and all the courtiers perceived that a degree of satisfaction
was legibly depicted on the countenance of their sovereign during
this parley. The king afterwards declared to several persons,
that a revelation which she had made to him, of a secret known
only to himself, gave birth to the confidence with which she
inspired him.

Robertson, in his introduction to the History of Charles V.,
examines the mission of La Pucelle in a political point of view ;
and while rendering justice to her wisdom and courage, deplores
her misfortunes, and most eloquently inveighs against the superstition to which she was sacrificed : he however considers her
but as an instrument and a victim to party. Our countryman
is not the only writer who has raised objections against this
heavenly mission : we find that one Dr. Beaupère, who
acted as an assessor during the trial of Jeanne, was of opinion,
" that her alleged visions and apparitions were rather the effects
of human invention, than originating in divine inspiration ;" and
in the " Histoire Générale des Rois de France depuis Pharamond

" *Dieu vous doint* (donne) *bonne vie, gentil Roi*—God
give you a prosperous life, comely king," said Jeanne

jusqu'à Charles Sept," written by Bernard de Girard, Sieur du
Haillan, first historian of France, and genealogist of the Order of
the Holy Ghost, to Henry the Third, appears the following statement, given as nearly as possible verbatim.

"Some say that Jeanne was the mistress of Jean, Bastard
of Orleans; others, of the Lord of Baudricourt, who being wary
and cunning, and seeing that the king knew no longer what to
do or to say, and the people, on account of continual wars, so
much oppressed as not to be able to raise their courage, resolved to have recourse to a miracle, fabricated in false religion, being that which of all things most elevates the heart,
and makes men believe (even the most simple) that which
is not; and the people were very apt to imbibe such superstitions. Those who believe she was a maid sent by God, are
not damned; neither are those who did not believe. Many
esteem this last assertion an heresy; but we will not dwell too
much upon it, nor too much on the contrary belief. Wherefore these lords, for the space of some days, instructed her in all
she was to answer to the demands which should be made of
her by the king and themselves when in his presence; for they
were to interrogate her; and in order that she might recognise
the monarch when conducted into his presence, they caused
her to see his picture several times every day. On the day
appointed, when she was led to him in his chamber, which they
had already arranged, they did not fail to be present. Having
entered, the first persons who addressed her were the Bastard
of Orleans and Baudricourt, who demanded of her her business? She replied she wanted to speak to the king. They
presented to her another of the lords who was there, telling
her that he was the king; but she, instructed in all which

d'Arc, addressing Charles VII. *" Ce ne suis-je pas qui suis Roi, Jehanne;* It is not I who am the king, Jeanne,"* answered the monarch, at the same time pointing out a lord of his retinue, to which he added : *" Voici le Roi:* Here is the king." *" En mon Dieu,* By my God," answered Jeanne, *" gentil Prince, cestes vous et non aultre;* Handsome prince, it is you and no other." Charles, finding it was useless to dissemble any longer, felt more disposed to listen to the maid, who thus continued : *" Très noble seigneur Dauphin,* Right noble lord Dauphin, *je viens et suis envoyée de la part de Dieu pour porter secours à vous et à votre royaume, et vous mande le Roi des cieux par moi, que vous serez sacré et couronné en la ville de Rheims malgré vos ennemis, que sa volonté est*

should be done and said, as well as what she was to do and say, stated that it was not the king, and that he was hid in the alcove, containing the bed. This feigned invention, and appearance of religion, was of such profit to the kingdom that it raised the courage, lost and beaten down by despair * * * * * *   Wherefore the king caused horses and arms to be given to her, and an army with a number of great captains, in company of whom she carried succour to those of Orleans." It is extraordinary that Du Haillan, the writer of this account, who was historiographer of France, should have made these statements ; as every other narrative concurs in affirming, that at the period of Jeanne's introduction to Charles VII., the Bastard of Orleans in person commanded the garrison of that city, while Baudricourt continued at Vaucouleurs, nearly a hundred and fifty leagues from Chinon.

qu'ils se retirent en leur pays, et vous laissent paisible possesseur de votre royaume comme étant le vrai, unique, et légitime héritier de France, fils de roi : I come and am sent on the part of God to bring succour to you and to your kingdom; and the King of heaven through me makes known, that you shall be anointed and crowned in the city of Rheims in spite of your enemies; that his will is that they retire into their country and leave you peaceable possessor of your kingdom, as being the true, only, and legitimate heir of France, son of a king."

Charles VII. then took Jeanne aside, and conversed with her in private for a considerable time; during which intercourse, it appears, she stated circumstances that completely secured his good opinion. Contemporary authors differ very much in regard to this secret said to have existed between the king and La Pucelle. N. Sala, a writer of that period, states, that Charles VII., finding his affairs in a most desperate condition, one morning repaired alone to his oratory, and there offered up an internal prayer, devoutly supplicating the Almighty, that in case he was the lineal descendant of the noble house of France, and that the kingdom belonged to him of right, it would please him to guard and defend the same as his patrimony, or, at worst, that the Lord would accord him grace, so as to elude his enemies, save him from imprisonment or death, and permit him to escape into Spain

or Scotland, which powers had uniformly continued
brothers in arms, and friends and allies of the kings
of France.*   This prayer Sala states to have been

* The mysterious circumstance here alluded to, is thus detailed:
" The king, having taken Jeanne aside, demanded that she would
give him some assurance in order to dispel every doubt from his
mind. ' Sire,' said Jeanne, ' were I to communicate secrets
known only to God and yourself, would you then believe in
my celestial mission ?' To which Charles having replied in the
affirmative, La Pucelle continued : ' Sire, do you not call to
mind, that upon the last day of All Saints, being alone in your
private oratory at the chapel of Loches, you there supplicated
God respecting three things :—first, that if you were not the true
heir of the kingdom of France, it would so please him to deprive
you of the means of continuing the war which is productive of
so many evils: secondly, that if the sufferings of the people are
inflicted on account of your sins, that you alone may be punished:
and lastly, if they arise from the iniquity of your subjects, it
would please the Almighty to pardon them.' The king, very
much astonished at this answer, recollected that Jeanne had
spoken the truth, and consequently was led to infer that her
knowledge of his secret must have originated in divine revelation."

M. Luchet, at page 30, &c. states, that more reflections than
one may be made upon this passage; and that contemporary
authors do not allude to it. During the trial of Jeanne, when
she was made to repeat all that she had said to the king, no
mention occurs of this secret; while Charles VII. was absent
from Loches on All Saints' day, the time indicated by Jeanne.
" The king," continues M. Luchet, " was by no means devout;
and it appears very improbable that after the lapse of six months,

mentioned to the monarch by Jeanne d'Arc for the purpose of proving the reality of her mission. If La Pucelle is reproached for having afterwards stated to her almoner, that when she had replied to a variety of questions put to her by the king, she added, " *Je te dis de la part de Messire que tu es vrai héritier de France et fils de Roi; et il m'envoie à toi pour te conduire à Rheims, afin que tu y reçoives ton couronnement et ton sacre si tu le veux :* I tell thee on the part of Messire (the Lord) that thou art the true heir of France and son of the king; and he hath sent me to conduct thee to Rheims, in order that thou mayest be crowned and anointed if such be thy will :" it may easily be conjectured why Charles VII. and Jeanne d'Arc attached so much importance to the concealment of the secret that existed between them. Had this fact been known, it would have confirmed the doubts entertained by the Burgundians and the English in regard to the legitimacy of the king's birth; a doubt

he should remember what he said to God, when at the same time he forgot that he was absent from his oratory at Loches. It might be imagined, that the monarch would have confided in other promises of La Pucelle after this; but he did not; for Jeanne was sent to Poitiers, where the parliament was then sitting, in order to be examined; as if the interrogatories of judges and doctors of the university could tend to increase his confidence in a privileged person with whom Heaven had deigned to hold secret communication."

which they sedulously strove to promulgate, and which originated in the profligate course of life pursued by his mother queen Isabella, to which we have so frequently adverted in the course of our summary.

The king, having ended his discourse with Jeanne, advanced towards his courtiers, and stated, that the young girl had communicated to him certain secret affairs, which led him to place in her the greatest confidence.*

Charles VII. then deemed it expedient to commit Jeanne d'Arc to the care of Guillaume Bellier,

---

* Notwithstanding the favourable opinion which Jeanne had gained in the mind of the king, a very opposite sentiment prevailed among the princes and captains of the court, who conceived themselves dishonoured in yielding obedience to a mere country girl, devoid of experience and of education. It was in consequence represented to Charles that he would become the sport of Europe and the ridicule of the English, for relying upon the promises of a bewildered girl, as there did not exist a doubt but the French would be defeated by the enemy; that it was disgraceful in the extreme for a nation to be led by such a fanatic, and particularly the French people, who had never suffered a female to mount the throne; and that by permitting this girl to head the armies, the pretensions of Catherine of France, then queen of England, who aspired to the French crown, would be sanctioned. Such was the resolution of the council, which consisted of all the great and distinguished personages in the retinue of Charles VII.—*Lenglet,* vol. i. pages 31, 32.

superintendent of his household, and lieutenant governor of Chinon, whose wife was a woman of singular piety, and renowned for her praiseworthy actions.   La Pucelle was permitted to present herself at court, and attend the celebration of mass in the Chapel Royal ; she also accompanied the king on his excursions of pleasure ; and the duke of Alençon, astonished to see the skill and graceful manner with which she conducted her palfrey, made her a present of a horse.*   Every succeeding day increased the astonishment and admiration La Pucelle excited by her conduct, her conversation, and her

---

* No sooner had the duke d'Alençon learnt the arrival of Jeanne at Chinon, than he forthwith repaired to St. Florent, and on the following day saw her pass by : " *Une lance à la main, qu'elle portait et faisait mouvoir avec beaucoup de grace, et alors il lui fit don d'un beau cheval :* Bearing a lance in her hand, which she carried and wielded with much grace, and then he made her a present of a fine horse."

In addition to this, a contemporary historian, speaking of Jeanne's equestrian prowess, states : *A principio ætatis suæ* •••• *pascendo pecora* •••• *sæpius cursum exercebat ; et modo huc atque illuc illi frequens cursus erat ; et aliquando currendo hastam ut fortis eques manu capiebat, et arborum truncos* •••• *percutiebat, &c.* — See *Phillipe de Bergame in Hordal,* page 40, who, according to Moreri, under the head *Foresti,* was born in 1434.

The duke of Alençon was not at Chinon when Jeanne was presented, for the first time, to the king.   Upon his arrival some days after, on entering the royal chamber, Jeanne demanded who he was, to which the king replied : " the duke of

exemplary manners. Jamet de Tilloy and Villars had been despatched to the court by the count Dunois, who then acted as the intrepid defender of Orleans, for the purpose of verifying what was reported concerning this extraordinary female, and to ascertain if any reliance might be placed on the succours she had promised. These

Alençon." " You are right welcome," said La Pucelle : " the more princes of the blood there are, the more will our affairs prosper." The following day Jeanne was present at the king's mass, and on perceiving the duke she made a lowly reverence. At the conclusion of the ceremony Charles summoned her to his apartment, from whence he dismissed all the courtiers except the duke of Alençon and La Trimouille. Upon this occasion Jeanne proposed several things to the king, and among others advised him to offer up his kingdom to God, who would restore it to him in the same state his predecessors had enjoyed it.—*Lenglet*, vol. i. pp. 43 and 44.

The beauty of Jeanne d'Arc, according to the deposition of the duke of Alençon, was of no ordinary kind ; and accompanied by such extreme modesty, that *her very look cooled any lascivious desires* in the beholder. Jeanne, in order to avoid any surprise either during her journeys or when with the army, never slept without wearing a part of her martial attire, and care was taken to lodge her in the cities and towns with women of the most spotless reputation.—*Lenglet*, vol. i. p. 46.

M. Luchet, at page 11, speaking of the peculiar effect excited by the glance of Jeanne, says, " it is a singular proof of her beauty that she should cool desire in the beholder ; but," adds he, " whether handsome or ugly is nothing to the purpose, and her scrupulous attention to decency is still of less consequence."

individuals returned to Orleans, and there gave
an account of every thing they had witnessed at
Chinon.*

Measures were now adopted in order to proceed
in the examinations to which it was thought proper
La Pucelle should be subjected ; and, to give more
celebrity to these sittings, it was determined they
should be held at Poitiers,† in presence of the
king, the parliament, and an assembly of theologians.
Jeanne d'Arc was interrogated, and answered with an

* On receiving this intelligence, Dunois, according to his
deposition at the process of the revisal, made the 22d of
February, 1426, caused the citizens of Orleans to be assembled,
and related to them all that his emissaries had heard and seen.
This recital elevated the public mind ; every one made his own
comment; and some individuals went so far as to assert that
several ecclesiastics had beheld an angel behind Jeanne
d'Arc, who conducted her steps.   The first use which count
Dunois made of the celebrity of La Pucelle showed his sound
policy, and was a lively indication of the result of Jeanne's
interference.

† Jeanne was conducted to Poitiers, whither the king repaired
for the express purpose of subjecting her to fresh interrogatories.
During her residence in the above city she inhabited the house
of the advocate-general, whose wife invited many young and
elderly devout women to keep her company, and scrupulously
examine whether or not she would belie any of her former assertions.   Her conduct was uniformly found correct, and her conversation most exemplary, although she was allowed to speak and
to act as she thought proper.—*Lenglet*, vol. i. page 47.

admirable presence of mind to all the litigious questions that were put to her. Among other points it was observed to her, that if, according to her assertion, the Lord was desirous of rescuing France from its calamities, men at arms were quite unnecessary; to which Jeanne replied, without being in the least disconcerted : " *En mon Dieu, les gens d'armes batailleront, et Dieu donnera la victoire :* In the name of God, the men at arms will fight, and God will give the victory." On being pressed to give some certain proofs respecting her divine mission,* she made this dignified reply : " *Je ne suis pas venue à Poitiers pour faire des signes; mais conduisez-moi à Orléans, et je vous montrerai des signes pourquoi je suis envoyée:* I am not come to Poitiers to perform miracles; but conduct me to Orleans, and I will then give you proofs wherefore I am sent." Brother Seguin, a doctor of Limousin, who is styled in one of the old chronicles, " *un bien aigre homme* — a very captious man," having demanded of Jeanne d'Arc, in what language she was addressed by her supernatural agents? she replied with peculiar vivacity : " *Meilleur que le vôtre*—Better than yours."

---

* M. Luchet, at page 12, makes this sensible remark : " that Jeanne d'Arc, upon the present occasion, had only to prove the revelation stated to have been made by her to Baudricourt respecting the defeat of the French at the battle of Herrings, and then her judges must have remained mute."

Do you believe in God? then demanded the monk : " *Mieux que vous*—Better than you," was Jeanne's reply.

Quotations were very frequently made to her from sacred writers, for the purpose of invalidating her mission, when she contented herself by remarking : " *Il y a ès livre de Messire* (*Dieu*), *plus que ès vostres:* There is more in the book of God than in yours." As the interrogatories were prolonged, Jeanne remarked : " *Il est temps et besoin d'agir:* It is time, and there is a necessity for action." La Pucelle concluded by announcing to the assembly the several events which were subsequently realized : the overthrow of the English and the raising of the siege of Orleans ; the coronation of the king at Rheims ; the reduction of Paris to the obedience of Charles VII. ; and the return of the duke of Orleans from England, where he had been detained captive ever since the memorable battle of Azincourt.

After many sittings, the assembly of the doctors at length came to a decision that the king might lawfully accept the services of La Pucelle. It would appear from what is stated by Edmond Richer, who wrote the history of Jeanne d'Arc, that the parliament were less propitious ; but none of the original documents which might afford a satisfactory conclusion are now extant.

Jean de Metz and Bertrand de Poulengy, who had

escorted La Pucelle from Vaucouleurs, made known to the public all the marvellous circumstances attending their journey through a territory occupied by the enemy. The bishop of Castres fomented the general enthusiasm which was thus created, by affirming that he believed Jeanne d'Arc was a messenger from God, and that it was to her the prophecies alluded which were at that period current among the people. These prognostics, the origin of which was altogether unknown, went to state, that the kingdom of France, lost by a woman, (Isabella of Bavaria,) would be saved by a virgin of the marches (frontiers) of Lorraine.*

Before he placed implicit confidence in Jeanne, Charles deemed it expedient to subject her to a new trial. She was supposed to be inspired, and such she might be by the intervention of Lucifer. According to the absurd prejudices of those times, the devil could not enter into any compact with a

* " Qu'aussi, avant que La Pucelle d'Orléans arriva à Chinon, où estoit le roy Charles VII., il luy avoit esté prédit, que luy et son royaume seroient fort affligés, mais que devers luy il viendroit une Pucelle qui le délivreroit." — *Gerson, Pasquier, Hordal, Dupleix.*

" Auxquelles révélations estoient jointes les prophéties des Anglois, qui disoient qu'ils avoient une certaine prophétie de Merlin, leur prophète, qui leur prédisoit qu'ils devoient estre destruits en France par une Pucelle."—*Hist. et Antiq. de la Ville d'Orléans, par François le Mair*, 1648, fol. 187 et 188.

virgin; and, in consequence, Jeanne d'Arc was obliged to submit to an examination, at which the queen of Sicily, Jolande of Arragon, and the ladies de Gaucourt and·de Treves, presided. She was, in consequence, pronounced pure;* and it is stated, on this occasion, to have been ascertained that Jeanne, who was then between seventeen and eighteen years of age, had not been subject to the monthly appearances incidental to her sex; which', it is further said, she never experienced: a peculiarity worthy of being remarked. According to the deposition of Jeanne Pasquerel, it appears that previous to this inquiry respecting her virginity, Jeanne had been subjected to an examination as to her sex.

During these transactions, the agents who had been forwarded to Domremy returned to Chinon, having brought the most favourable testimonies in regard to La Pucelle, who having thus surmounted every impediment, was at length permitted to proceed to the city of Orleans. The fame of her mission was now disseminated far and wide; the men at arms, who had previously felt discouraged, voluntarily flocked around La Pucelle; and the oldest captains, nay, even princes, felt disposed to march under her ensign.

Charles despatched the duke of Alençon to Blois,

---

* See Notes to the Diary, pp. 156 and 159.

in order to prepare the convoy which was intended
for the succour of Orleans ; and he permitted Jeanne
to proceed as far as Tours, there to remain until
every thing should be in readiness for the expedition.   At this period a regular establishment was
accorded to La Pucelle, consisting of a guard for
her person, valets to attend her, and all the equipage
suitable for a chief of war.   Jean Daulon, who
was afterwards seneschal of Beaucaire, uniformly
served her in the capacity of esquire ; * and her
pages were Louis de Contes and Raymond ; besides whom she had two heralds at arms, the
one named Guienne and the other Ambleville.
Jeanne chose for almoner Jacques Pasquerel, of
the order of brother hermits of Saint Augustin.
According to the statement of Charles Dulys, a
descendant of the family of Arc, in his collection of
inscriptions published in honour of this famous woman,
Jeanne d'Arc had also for chaplain brother Nicolas
Romée, otherwise called Vauthon, a professed monk
of the abbey of Cheminon, for whom she procured
a dispensation and permission from the abbot, by
command of the king, in order that he might follow
her to the army.   Charles VII., either at Chinon or
at Tours, caused a complete suit of armour to be
prepared, that was made to fit the body of Jeanne.
The sword wherewith La Pucelle armed herself,

----

* See Notes to the Diary, p. 160.

bore the impression of five crosses;* this weapon
was found behind the grand altar of the church of
Saint Catherine de Fierbois, where it was discovered
from the instructions given by Jeanne herself.† The
ecclesiastics, whom she had requested to search
for this weapon, furnished a scabbard covered with
crimson velvet, and powdered with golden fleurs-
de-lis; Jeanne, however, would only carry the
sword in a plain leather scabbard. She likewise
ordered a standard,‡ and gave directions in what
manner it should be decorated; of which the following is a description, as given by herself: — On a
white ground, powdered with fleurs-de-lis, was re-

* The king had expressed his intention of presenting a sword
to Jeanne, when she signified her wish to have the weapon that
was concealed in the church of St. Catherine of Fierbois. She
was very closely interrogated respecting this sword during her
trial, and particularly concerning the crosses wherewith it
was impressed, as if any sorcery could be connected with the
marks in question. — *Lenglet,* vol. i. p. 51.

† For some curious information respecting this sword, see
Notes to the Diary, pp. 171—173.

‡ There is every reason to suppose that Jeanne d'Arc bore
in mind the famous *oriflamme,* borne by the kings of France
in battle, when she caused this flag to be prepared. This royal
standard, which derived its name from the golden flames wherewith it was embellished, was, according to historians, sent from
heaven to Clovis, or Charlemagne, and used by the French
monarchs in their wars against the infidels. — *Abbé le Gendre,*
page 74.

presented the Saviour of mankind, seated in his tribunal in the clouds of heaven, and supporting a globe in his hands. To the right and to the left were depicted two angels in the act of adoration. One of these held a fleur-de-lis in its hand, upon which God was apparently pronouncing a benediction; and on the side were inscribed these words: *Jhesus Maria.* The king having particularly questioned Jeanne d'Arc concerning this banner, she stated, although very reluctant to speak upon the subject, that " *Sainte Catherine et Sainte Marguérite lui avaient donné l'ordre de la prendre* : Saint Catherine and Saint Marguerite had commanded her to bear it." This ensign La Pucelle bore in her own hand as frequently as circumstances would admit; and on being asked the reason for so doing, she made answer: " *C'est qu'elle ne voulait pas se servir de son épée pour répandre le sang:* It was that she would not carry her sword to shed blood."

The duke d'Alençon used every effort to expedite the several preparations necessary for the convoy intended for Orleans. Nothing more was to be done in the first instance, for notwithstanding the reiterated promises of Jeanne d'Arc, little hope was entertained of any further success. The orders were at length completed; and were duly paid for, which was no very trifling difficulty to surmount in the critical position of the finances of Charles VII.

Jeanne d'Arc set out from Tours and arrived at
Blois, followed by her whole retinue, having compelled her chaplain to promise that he would never
quit her from that period. She had received
from the king the authority attached to a general
of the army; and he also especially commanded
that nothing should be undertaken without her
having been previously consulted.

The marshals de Raïs and Saint Severe, to whose
care the escort of the expedition had been confided,
soon arrived in safety at Blois. La Pucelle continued in that city for two or three days; during
which period she for the first time arrayed herself
in armour. Being desirous that a certain number
of priests should attend the convoy, she issued
orders to her almoner to have a banner prepared,
as a particular rallying point for those ecclesiastics;
which standard was to bear a representation of
Christ upon the cross. These commands were punctually executed. Assembled under this pacific
banner, the priests chanted anthems and sacred
hymns; while Jeanne d'Arc, prostrate in the midst
of them, mingled with their solemn strains the most
fervent prayers to Heaven. No warrior was permitted to have any rank in this saintly corps, if
he had not on that very day presented himself
before the tribunal of penitence. Jeanne strenuously exhorted the soldiers to render themselves
worthy of constituting a part of this holy battalion.
Every disposition thus made was conformable to

the spirit of that era, and could not fail to produce a very lively sensation among the troops; which soon became apparent, as the religious enthusiasm of La Pucelle infused into the soldiery a firm belief that it was impossible they could fail of the victory.

Florent d'Illiers, a very brave captain who commanded at Châteaudun, joined the forces with a certain number of intrepid warriors; who, accompanied by La Hire, made an attempt to enter Orleans with four hundred combatants, and succeeded in this enterprise on Thursday the 28th April, 1429.

At this juncture, as we have before stated, the inhabitants of Orleans were reduced to such cruel extremity that their only hope was in obtaining assistance from Heaven : the arrival, therefore, of Jeanne d'Arc, announced as the envoy of God, was ardently looked for. La Pucelle used every effort to set forward from Blois with the expedition, and it was from that city she in the first instance summoned the English to abandon the siege of Orleans, charging one of her heralds at arms to convey the following letter to the chiefs of the enemy's forces :

*✠ JHESUS MARIA. ✠

" Roy d'Angleterre, et vous, Duc de Bedford, qui vous dictes Regent le royaume de France ; vous

* A translation of this letter will be found at pages 46 to 48 of the Diary.

Guillaume de la Poule (Pole) conte de Sulford
(Suffolk,) Jehan, sire de Talebot (Talbot,) et vous,
Thomas, sire de Scales, qui vous dictes lieutenant
dudit duc de Bedford, faictes raison au Roy du
ciel ; rendez à La Pucelle * qui est cy envoyée de
par Dieu le Roy du ciel, les clefs de toutes les
bonnes villes que vous avez prises et violées en
France. Elle est cy venue de par Dieu pour
reclamer le sanc royal. Ellé est toute preste
de faire paix, si vous luy voulez faire raison, par
ainsi que France vous mectrez jus, et paierez ce
que vous l'avez tenu. Et entre vous, archiers, com-
paignons de guerre ; gentilz et autres, qui estes
devant la ville d'Orleans, alez vous en vostre païs de
par Dieu ; et se ainsi ne le faictes, attendez les
nouvelles de La Pucelle, qui vous ira veoir briefvement à vos bien grans dommaiges. Roy d'Angleterre, se ainsi ne le faictes, je suis chief de
guerre,† et en quelque lieu que je attaindrai voz
gens en France, je les en feray tous occire. Je suis
cy envoyée de par Dieu, le Roy du ciel, pour vous
bouter hors de toute France. Et si veullent obéir,

* Jeanne in the course of her interrogatories maintained, that
the words in her letter were, " *rendez au Roi*," and that the
English had falsified this sentence for the purpose of impeaching
her.—*See the Interrogatory of the* 22d *of February*, 1431.

† During the trial of Jeanne d'Arc, she affirmed that the
words " *Je suis chef de guerre*" had been added to the original
as dictated by herself.—*Interrogatory of* 22d *February*, 1431.

je les prendray à mercy.   Et n'ayez pas en vostre opinion, quar vous ne tendrez (tiendrez) point le royaume de Dieu, le Roy du ciel, filz de Saincte Marie : ains le tendra le Roy Charles, vray héritier ; car Dieu, le Roy du ciel, le veult, et lui est revelé par La Pucelle : lequel entrera à Paris à bonne compaignie.   Se ne le voulez croire les nouvelles de par Dieu et La Pucelle, en quelque lieu que vous trouverons, nous ferrons dedens, et y ferons un si grant hahay que encore a il mil ans que en France ne fu si grant, si vous ne faictes raison.   Et croiez fermement que le Roy du ciel envoiera plus de force à La Pucelle, que vous ne lui sariez mener de tous assaulz, à elle et à ses bonnes gens d'armes ; et aux horions verra on qui ara meilleur droit de Dieu du ciel.   Vous, duc de Bedford, La Pucelle vous prie et vous requiert, que vous ne vous faictes mie destruire.   Se vous lui faictes raison, encore pourrez vous venir en sa compaignie, l'où que les Franchois feront le plus bel fait que oncques fu fait pour la Xhrestpiente (Chrétienneté.)   Et faictes responce se vous voulez faire paix, en la cité d'Orleans.   Et se ainsi ne le faictes, de vos bien grans dommages vous souviegne briefvement.   Escrit ce Samedi, sepmaine sainte."   (26 *Mars*, 1428, Old Style.)*

---

* That is to say, beginning the year at Easter, or 1429, calculating from the first of January.—This letter, which is written in a very plain style, occasioned numerous interro-

Every thing being in readiness for the departure of the expedition, Jeanne d'Arc, accompanied by marshals Saint Severe, admiral de Culan, the lord de Gaucourt, La Hire, and many other captains of less celebrity, quitted Blois, and directed her march for Orleans, about the close of April, 1429. La Pucelle on this occasion caused the priests to assemble under the banner she had destined for their use, directing them to proceed at the head of the forces, which amounted to about six thousand men.* This small army was well

gatories during the process of condemnation, and the judges were desirous of construing into a crime the insertion of a cross before and after the words Jesus Maria. — *Lenglet*, vol. i. p. 56.

* To the present period we have witnessed nothing but promises made by Jeanne d'Arc ; we shall now proceed to make known the effects produced. She strenuously urged the French to expedite the convoy, previously to quitting Blois, obliging them also to confess and receive the sacrament, and then gave them assurances of celestial aid. It might be looked upon as a kind of prodigy to behold a girl of seventeen or eighteen years of age, without education, performing the functions of missionary and general at the same time ; and what is still more extraordinary, that the generals and officers should have been obedient to her command as if she had been their superior.—*Depositions of Simon de Beaucraix and the Count Dunois, of 22d February,* 1456. Vide *Lenglet*, vol. i. p. 57.

In front of the army were assembled the priests of the city,

disciplined, and marched in excellent order. La Pucelle had resolved that the troops should advance by the route of Beausse, where the principal forces of the enemy were garrisoned. The generals, who vainly expostulated with Jeanne on the rashness of such a proceeding, took advantage of her ignorance of the country to mislead her into the road of Sologne.

La Pucelle was desirous that the troops should enjoy repose during the first night. She suffered much from indisposition: but soon recovered her strength, and continued the march, uniformly exhorting the warriors to go to confession, herself setting the example, and receiving the Host in the midst of them.

On the third day the army arrived in the environs of Orleans, when Jeanne d'Arc found that she had been deceived, and conducted by a route contrary to that she had prescribed. The

---

with a cross and a banner, the procession being conducted by La Pucelle. This march converted into a spectacle was well calculated to reanimate the drooping courage of the soldiers.— *Luchet*, p. 13.

During this expedition the ecclesiastics chanted the *Veni Creator* and other prayers, the march continuing for three days. Two nights were spent in the open fields, and on the third day they approached Orleans near St. Loup, the vessels which contained the supplies coming up at the same time.—*Chaussard*, vol. i. p. 20.

convoy was upon the banks of the Loire; and at
the only spot where the vessels despatched from
Orleans to receive the provisions might have
passed, the English had constructed a fort. In
every other direction the water was too shallow to
permit the barks to approach for the removal of
the convoy; and much danger was to be apprehended upon that account. Jeanne d'Arc wished
that an attack should be immediately made on
the bastilles of the English; when Count Dunois,
who had the command of Orleans, having ascertained the arrival of La Pucelle, repaired to meet
her, crossing the Loire in a small boat, accompanied by some captains, and arriving at the spot
where the convoy was stationed.

No sooner was the Bastard in presence of Jeanne
than she exclaimed, " *Estes vous pas le Bâtard
d'Orleans?* * Are you not the Bastard of Orleans?"

* As soon as the convoy arrived in the vicinity of Orleans,
Jeanne on beholding Dunois exclaimed " *Vous êtes le Bâtard
d'Orleans*—You are the Bastard of Orleans:" to which the
count having answered in the affirmative, she immediately
uttered some reproaches in consequence of the convoy having
been conducted by the road of Sologne, instead of that of
Beausse as she had directed. The count Dunois, in reply, stated,
that this measure had been adopted by order of council, to
which Jeanne made answer: " *Eh quoi! le conseil de mon Dieu
n'est il pas plus sûr que le vôtre? Vous croyez m'avoir trompée,
mais vous-même vous êtes trompé; puisque je vous amene un
secours de sa part:* Ah, council, is not that of my God

to which he replied in the affirmative, adding that he felt overjoyed at her arrival. La Pucelle immediately demanded if it was by his direction that she had been conducted on the side of the river where she then was, instead of that occupied by Talbot and his Englishmen; when Dunois having made answer, that such measures had been resorted to by the advice of himself and other captains, Jeanne briskly retorted : " *En mon Dieu, le conseil de Dieu notre Seigneur est plus sûr et plus habile que le vôtre. Vous avez cru me decevoir, et vous êtes plus deçus que moi ; car je vous assure le meilleur secours qui ait jamais été envoyé à qui que ce soit, soit à chevalier, soit à ville, c'est le secours du Roi des cieux, non mie par amour pour moi, mais procède de Dieu même, qui, à la prière de Saint Louis et de Saint Charlemagne, a eu pitié de la ville d'Orleans; et ne veut pas souffrir que les ennemis ayent ensemble le corps du duc d'Orleans et*

more certain than yours? You think that you have deceived me, but you are yourself deceived ; because it is from him I bring you relief."—*Lenglet,* vol. i. page 60.

M. Luchet, p. 13. on referring to this statement, says: "If it was Jeanne who conducted this convoy, she was mistress of her own actions; in which case, why did she not follow the impulse of her inspiration?" And when adverting to her reply to count Dunois, respecting the advice of her God, he remarks, we may naturally suppose it was a matter of no consequence to the Omnipotent, whether the convoy in question arrived after traversing Sologne or Beausse.

sa ville. In the name of God, the counsel of God our Lord is surer and of more effect than yours. You have thought to deceive me, and you are more deceived than I am ; for I assure you, that the best assistance ever yet sent to any one, whether to knight or to city, is the succour of the King of heaven, not accorded through love for me, but proceeding from God himself, who, at the prayer of Saint Louis and Saint Charlemagne, has taken pity on the city of Orleans, and will not permit that the enemy should at the same time possess the body of the duke of Orleans * and his city." A council was then held, when after due consideration it was resolved, that to prevent the English from having time to collect their forces, the French should remount the banks of the Loire as far as Checy, about two leagues east of Orleans, at which place there was a port in every respect commodious for discharging the supplies into large vessels. The wind, which had till this period uniformly continued adverse to the arrival of the barks, became favourable ; the craft passed at no great distance from the enemy's forts, and gained the left bank of the river in safety at the same time with La Pucelle and the army. Dunois then proposed that Jeanne

* Charles, duke of Orleans, who was made prisoner at the battle of Agincourt in 1415, still remained a captive in England, and did not recover his liberty until 1440.

d'Arc should enter into Orleans,* but she continued very undecided upon this point; being averse
to quit the troops, who were well disposed, and
had still a march to perform in order to cross the
river at Blois, in consequence of the difficulty
there was of procuring a sufficient number of boats
to enable them to pass the Loire at the spot where
they had halted. La Pucelle, however, yielded at
length to the entreaties of the Bastard, and entered the
city, armed *cap-à-pied*, mounted on a white horse, and
causing her standard to be carried before her.   She
was accompanied by the count Dunois and many
other chieftains of war, and immediately proceeded
to the principal church to offer up her humble
thanks to the Almighty.   Upon this occasion the
enthusiasm of the inhabitants of Orleans had attained its acmè; there was not an individual who
did not feel animated; both men and women flocked

* Lenglet, vol. i. page 61, states, that count Dunois entreated
Jeanne to enter the city of Orleans, where she was so ardently
looked for, but that she refused to acquiesce, being desirous not
to abandon her people; all of whom, she said, were perfectly
obedient, and fortified with the sacraments of the church.—*Deposition of Count Dunois, 22d February*, 1456.

In the same page, Lenglet adds, " At her entrance into
Orleans, she dismounted at the cathedral to offer thanks to God
for the prosperous result of her expedition."—*Deposition of
Jaques Lesbahy, 16th March*, 1456.

M. Lenglet must have been guilty of an oversight, as the
latter statement contradicts the assertion previously made.

around her; she was welcomed as a tutelar angel descended from heaven; while she continued exhorting the people to place their confidence in God, assuring them that through the medium of faith they would escape the hatred and the fury of their enemies.*

On the following day La Pucelle conferred with Dunois as to the measures most expedient to be pursued; giving it as her opinion that immediate advantage should be taken of the ardour and willingness evinced by the Orleanese to attack the English bastilles; in which decision she was seconded by La Hire and Florent d'Illiers, while several other captains conceived it necessary to await the arrival of the army. These contrary sentiments gave rise to very warm debates, which terminated in opposition to Jeanne's desire: it was, however, decided, that several leaders should proceed to expedite the arrival of the forces.

---

* It was originally the editor's intention to have here introduced the Diary of the Siege. However, upon consulting the various authorities, and comparing them with the contents of that document, so many additional statements were found, of a most interesting nature, connected with the siege, that it was deemed absolutely necessary to present them to the public.

In the ensuing pages the several details alluded to are condensed; and as the matter occupies but a few leaves, there is reason to hope, that the nature of their contents will requite the reader for the trouble of their perusal.

Jeanne d'Arc, finding that nothing could as yet be undertaken, and by no means discouraged on account of the ill success of her epistolary communication to the English, took advantage of this delay to renew the application. She despatched her two heralds at arms with a letter addressed to the lord Talbot, the earl of Suffolk, and the lord Scales, with the contents of which historians have not made us acquainted, but it is probable that it contained nothing more than a repetition of the contents of her former letter. This document was received with every mark of opprobrium and contempt: and one of her heralds was detained, the other being despatched for the purpose of making known to her all that had transpired. La Pucelle on perceiving her messenger immediately exclaimed: " *Que dit Talbot?* What does Talbot say?" When the herald having recapitulated all the injurious epithets which the enemy had lavished upon her, and told her that if they could seize her person they would burn her at the stake, Jeanne instantly replied: " *Or t'en retourne, et ne fais doute que tu ameneras ton compagnon, et dis à Talbot, que s'il arme je m'armeray aussi, et qu'il se trouve en place devant la ville, et s'il me peut prendre, qu'il me face ardoir; et si je le deconfis, qu'il face lever les sieges et s'en aillent en leur pays.* Return then thy ways, and do not doubt that thou wilt bring back thy companion; and tell Talbot that if he arms I will also arm myself, and let him take his station before the city ; and if he can secure me, let him cause me to be burnt ; and if I discomfit him, let him raise the siege and go back to his own country." This singular challenge was not accepted by our English hero.

Notwithstanding the disdain with which the English affected to treat Jeanne d'Arc, it is certain that they already began to feel the fatal effects of her influence, as the ardour with which she inspired the French soldiery spread terror through the British ranks.

On the day when the convoy entered Orleans, Dunois, according to the deposition of Daulon, repaired to the residence of La Pucelle, and announced to her that Fastolf was conducting reinforcements to the English. Jeanne, rejoiced at the idea of having to combat that redoubted enemy, expressed herself in the following terms to the Bastard : " *Bastard, bastard, en nom de Dieu, je te commande que tantôt que tu sauras la venue dudit Fastolf, que tu me le fasses savoir ; car s'il passe sans que je le sache, je te promets que je te ferai ôter la tête.* Bastard, bastard, in the name of God, I command thee, that as soon as thou shalt ascertain the coming of the said Fastolf, that thou lettest me know; for if he passes without my knowledge, I promise thee that thy head shall be stricken off." It is obvious that this exclamation was the result of an enthusiastic feeling which prompted Jeanne to wish for an en-counter with that hardy English chieftain. Dunois entertained a similar opinion, as appears from the moderation manifested in his reply, which was to the following effect: " That she need have no doubt upon that head, as he would take care to give her the necessary information."

Thus was the promise made by Jeanne d'Arc to succour Orleans accomplished. The unexpected success of an enterprise attended with so much difficulty, during which none of the impediments that were apprehended had presented themselves, forcibly operated upon the multitude; and in conse-quence, the most incredulous no longer entertained doubts as to the celestial mission of La Pucelle. The English, on the other hand, who were already apprized of the harangues and the conduct of Jeanne, felt a disquietude they were unable to con-ceal. When they beheld the maid come to defy them at the head of an inferior force, they were completely paralyzed with fear; and it is ascertained beyond a doubt that they regarded as a sorceress *

* The truth of this assertion may be inferred from the following letter, written by the duke of Bedford after the raising of the siege of Orleans and the battle of Patay.

" All things here proved propitious for you (Henry VI.) until the period of the siege of Orleans, undertaken God only knows from what advice. About this period, after the mishap that occurred to my cousin of Salisbury, whom God absolve, the very person who was looked upon by the French as a messenger from God : nor could it indeed be otherwise, when we consider the ideas then prevalent, and the superstition so universally predominating over the public mind.

Jeanne speedily commenced an attack upon the bastilles of the English. Military discipline in the fifteenth century differed widely from that of the present age. Commanders, in the times of which we are speaking, formed enterprises according to the events that transpired, and were led to decide from casual circumstances. Some of the military leaders at Orleans, without having either consulted Dunois or apprized La Pucelle, made a sortie from the city, and attacked the bastille of Saint Loup, which had been strongly fortified and well garrisoned by lord Talbot. The assault, which had been undertaken at the spur of the moment, was in the first instance successful ; but on a sudden the

another terrible blow hath been struck, by the hands of God, as I feel persuaded, upon your people assembled there. This reverse in a great measure resulted, as I have well ascertained, from the unfortunate belief and superstitions dread inspired in them by a woman, the true disciple of Satan, formed from the excrement of hell, called La Pucelle, who made use of enchantments and sorcery. These disasters and this defeat have not only caused a great part of your troops to perish, but have at the same time discouraged in the most astonishing manner those who still remain; and what is more, have led your enemies to assemble in far greater numbers. *Rymer*, vol. x. page 408.

tide of fortune changed, and victory abandoned the
French standard.   Jeanne d'Arc was at her hotel
near Renard Gate; and to the present day the
chamber is pointed out which she occupied in the
residence of Jacques Boucher, treasurer of the
duke of Orleans, now known by the name of *La
Maison de l'Annonciade.*

Jeanne d'Arc had retired to rest, when suddenly
awaking, she cried aloud for her arms, saying
that the blood of Frenchmen was flowing, and
complaining that she had not been earlier aroused
from   sleep.   She instantly accoutred herself,
mounted the horse of her page, which she found
in the street, and ordered Louis de Contes to go
for her banner, which she had forgotten ; and so
much was she pressed, that she desired he would
hand it to her through the casement.   Having procured her standard, she spurred her horse, and rode
direct for the scene of danger, using such speed
that Daulon and Louis de Contes could not over-
take her until they arrived at Burgundy Gate.*

* Jeanne was lodged at the western gate of Orleans, whereas
that of Burgundy is to the east ; so that she traversed the whole
city before her squires overtook her, such being the rapidity of her
movements.

When La Pucelle gained Burgundy Gate, she met some
men bearing the wounded into the city ; upon which she
exclaimed, " I never behold the blood of Frenchmen flow, but my
hair stands erect upon my head."—*Chaussard*, vol. i. p. 24.

The presence of Jeanne gave confidence to the retreating French, whom she commanded to return to the assault; thus changing the posture of affairs by her presence of mind, celerity, and courage. Lord Talbot in vain gave orders that the English who garrisoned the other fortresses should repair to aid the bastille besieged. The French, who had hitherto continued within the city, flew to the scene of action, and repelled those English who sought to assist the besieged; even lord Talbot did not dare advance to the spot whither the heroine directed her steps,* so that the boulevard was at length taken by main force, and all that refused to surrender were put to the sword.†

On the fifth of May, being the festival of the Ascension, La Pucelle declared that nothing should be undertaken to disturb the solemnity of the day; and in the evening Jeanne once more had recourse

---

* Hume agrees in stating that Talbot, after having ordered the troops from the bastilles, did not dare appear in open country against so formidable an enemy.

† Such was the piety of Jeanne d'Arc, that she gave orders that no injury should be done to the chaplains or ecclesiastics who should be found within the forts, as they were stationed there only for spiritual purposes. These prisoners, after being humanely treated in the city, were suffered to return to the English camp; a mode of conduct La Pucelle uniformly pursued during the various attacks that took place. —*Deposition of Louis de Contes, Lenglet,* vol. i. 67.

to pacific measures, sending a third letter to the English, which was affixed to the end of an arrow, whereto she annexed the following sentence : " *C'est pour la troisième et dernière fois, et ne vous écrirai plus désormais :* It is for the third and last time, and I shall write to you no more in future."*

* La Pucelle attacked the bastille or fort of the Tournelles, having previously exhorted the officer (Glasdale), who commanded, to adopt peaceable measures with France and return to England, otherwise misfortune would attend him. To this Glasdale replied, by loading Jeanne with the most opprobrious epithets, which so affected her that she shed tears. The mode of sending this letter, according to the deposition of P. Jean Pasquerel, was somewhat singular; the document being tied to an arrow, which was shot from a bow, and lighted on the fort. In this letter she informed the English captains that she had adopted that means in consequence of the detention of her heralds, and at the same time she caused these words to be proclaimed aloud : " *Prenez et lisez, voici des nouvelles :* Take and read, here is news."—*Lenglet,* vol. i. p. 63.

Chaussard, referring to this letter, states the contents to have been as follow :

" Vous Anglais, qui n'avez aucun droit au royaume de Français, le Roi des cieux vous ordonne par moi, Jeanne la Pucelle, de remettre vos forts et de vous en aller chez vous ; si non, je vous ferez un tel Ah, Ah, qu'on en parlera toujours : c'est pour la troisième et dernière fois que je vous l'ecris. Signé Jesus Maria ; Jeanne la Pucelle.

" Je vous aurais envoyé ma lettre d'une manière plus honnète ; mais vous retenez Guienne mon héraut ; renvoyez-le moi, je vous renverrai des prisonniers de votre fort St. Loup.

" You English, who have no right to the kingdom of France,

After the French, uniformly headed by La Pucelle, had become masters of several fortresses, as will appear in the progress of the Diary, the English still kept possession of the bastille Saint Privé, and the boulevard of the Tournelles, on the left bank of the Loire. These Jeanne had equally proposed to besiege, when, having just terminated a very abstemious repast of which she uniformly partook, news was brought her respecting the

the King of heaven orders you, by me, Jeanne la Pucelle, to give up your forts, and to go back to your homes; if not, I will perform such an Ah, Ah, that it shall always be spoken of: it is for the third and last time that I write it. Signed Jesus Maria; Jeanne la Pucelle.

"I should have sent my letter in a more civil manner, but you retain Guienne, my herald; send him back to me, and I will restore you prisoners from your fort of Saint Loup."

The English, on receiving this paper attached to the end of an arrow, exclaimed: "Here is something new from the w ——— of the besiegers!" which expression made Jeanne sigh and weep. —*Chaussard*, vol. i. p. 26.

M. Luchet, at page 16, says, "The fourth day count Dunois attacked the English, La Pucelle being in his company, '*et moult encourageoit les assaillans*—and much encouraged the assailants.'" "The English then loaded her with such abuse that she shed tears," says M. Lenglet. "This excess of weakness and sensibility," adds Luchet, "strangely belies the character of a person gifted with inspiration." The last history of France states that the French were conducted by her; whereas the most ancient histories of the siege of Orleans affirm that she accompanied the Bastard Dunois.

council having resolved that nothing further should
be undertaken until the arrival of fresh succours
from the king.   La Pucelle instantly replied to
those who brought the ultimatum of this delibera-
tion : " *Vous avez été en votre conseil, et j'ai été
au mien, mais croyez que le conseil de mon Seigneur
tiendra et s'accomplira, et que celui des hommes périra :*
You have held your council, and I have been to
mine ; but believe me, the advice of my Lord shall
hold and be accomplished, and that of men shall
perish." Jeanne had indeed other designs to execute, and she commanded her chaplain to call
her very early the ensuing morning, and never
to quit her : " *Car,*" added she, " *j'aurai demain
beaucoup à faire ; il sortira du sang de mon corps au-
dessus du sein.   Je serai blessée devant la bastille du
bout du pont.* I shall have much to do to-morrow ;
blood will issue from my body above my bosom.
I shall be wounded in front of the bastille before
the end of the bridge."

Saturday the seventeenth of May, Jeanne being
completely armed, in opposition to the orders passed
in council, but seconded by the Orleanese, prepared to conduct the troops to attack the Tournelles.
Just as she was quitting the mansion of her host, a
man brought a shad which he had caught in the
Loire. Having eaten nothing, Jeanne was entreated
to stop, that the fish might be dressed, when she
made answer : " *Gardez la jusqu'à ce soir, car je vous*

amenerai un godon,* (a nickname then given to the English), *qui en mangera sa part ; je repasserai par-dessus le pont, après avoir pris les Tournelles :* Keep it until night, for I shall bring with me a *godon* who will eat his part ; I shall pass over the bridge after having taken the Tournelles."

The attack of these fortresses was so long and vigorously repelled by the English, that their assailants, about one in the day, began to feel dispirited and fatigued. Jeanne, at this critical juncture, animated by her courage, threw herself into the fosse, seized a ladder, and raising it with vigour, placed it against the boulevard. At this juncture an arrow from the enemy entered her neck and shoulder, and she instantly fell. Being immediately surrounded by the English, she drove them back sword in hand, defending herself with as much skill as personal bravery. A French force at length came to the rescue of Jeanne, when it was found necessary to carry her away, almost dying, although she obstinately persisted in desiring to be left within the fosse. The wound proved very deep, the arrow having passed completely through, projecting out at the back of the neck.†

* *Godon, godone,* means a *glutton,* a man of *voracious appetite.—Roquefort's Glossaire de la Langue Romaine.*

† Lenglet, vol. i. p. 70. says, " She was there wounded in the throat by an arrow, the aperture being more than a finger

She, in the first instance, testified symptoms of
fear, and could not refrain from weeping; but on
a sudden her wonted courage returned, when she
extracted the arrow with her own hand; after which
the blood flowed very copiously, and the wound
was dressed. This event struck consternation
among the troops and their leaders, and she strove
in vain to reanimate their drooping spirits. Count
Dunois was desirous of withdrawing the forces
and artillery within the city, and the trumpets
by his order had already sounded the retreat.
Jeanne d'Arc, sensibly touched at this conduct,
went in person to the Bastard, exclaiming: " *En
mon Dieu, vous entrerez bien brief dedans, n'ayez
doute. Quand vous verrez flotter mon étendard vers
la bastille, reprenez vos armes, elle sera vostre.* By
my God have no doubt, you will very speedily enter.
When you perceive my banner floating towards
the bastille, take up your arms again, it will then
be yours." Jeanne then gave the standard to one
of her people, called for her horse, and, lightly
vaulting into the saddle, retired to a neighbouring
vineyard, where she continued a quarter of an
hour in devout prayer. On returning to the

in width, and full half a foot in length. Some soldiers were
desirous of *charming* the wound, when Jeanne exclaimed : ' *God
forbid ; I would much rather die than do that which I conceive to
be a sin.*'"

Tournelles, La Pucelle, seizing the banner and brandishing it aloft, exclaimed, *"Ah! to my standard, to my standard!"* when she rushed precipitately to the brink of the fosse. The French, feeling invigorated by the conduct of Jeanne, returned to the assault, and began once more to scale the walls; the attack proved most determined, and the English opposed the impetuosity of their foes with equal valour.

Those warriors who had remained within Orleans for the purpose of guarding the city, could not resist the impulse they felt of joining their companions in arms. Actuated by this sentiment, they flew for the purpose of placing the enemy between two fires, but they were stopped by an impediment which appeared at first to be unsurmountable. Several arches of the bridge had been broken down, and it was absolutely necessary to pass that structure to effect the end required. The Orleanese for this purpose dragged some joists to the spot, and by this means formed a kind of flying bridge from one ruined pier to the other. Upon these weak timbers, amidst a shower of bullets, javelins, and arrows, the determined warriors ventured; and, flourishing their swords, passed the river and rushed to the assault. In vain did the English oppose a courage, the result of despair, to the efforts of their daring assailants;

the boulevard north of the Tournelles was carried,
and at the same time that to the south likewise
fell into the power of La Pucelle.

A universal panic now spread itself amongst the
English, who conceived that angels from on high contended for the French.   Even the haughty and daring
Glasdale, who had uniformly displayed his contempt
for Jeanne d'Arc, and had reviled her in the most
bitter and sarcastic terms, could not help feeling intimidated.   The heroine hailed him aloud to surrender;* but he continued deaf to her cries, seeking,
with the rest of the troops, to fly from the boulevard
of the Tournelles, and gain the interior of the
fort.   The bridge which kept up this communication was struck by a bomb, at the moment
when the English who followed Glasdale strove
to effect their passage : the arch gave way with
a tremendous crash, and every person upon it
was overwhelmed in immediate destruction.   Jeanne
d'Arc, banishing from her mind every thought
of resentment towards her brave but taunting

* At this juncture Jeanne cried out to Glasdale, who was
then in the tower, and most inveterately abusing her, " *Classi-
das, Clussidas,* (Glasdale), *rens ti au Roi des cieux ; tu m'as
appelé P—— et j'ai grand pitié de ton ame et de celle des
tiens.*   Glasdale, Glasdale, yield thyself up to the King of heaven ;
thou hast called me W—— and I have great pity for thy soul and
those of thine."—*Chaussard,* vol. i. p. 29.

foe, caused the body of Glasdale to be taken from the river and restored to the English, in order that it might be buried with those honours which were due to his warlike achievements.*

Jeanne d'Arc, after this final exploit, returned to the city over the bridge, as she had predicted on sallying forth to combat in the morning. She was hailed with enthusiasm; the populace in crowds rushed into the churches to render thanks to Heaven, and made the arches echo with their chants of praise.

* Jeanne could not refrain from shedding tears at witnessing the death of so many human creatures, whose souls, she conceived, were in greater danger than their bodies; and above all she mourned for the commander, Glasdale, who had heaped such injuries upon her. The French generals, namely, the duke d'Alençon and the count Dunois, at a subsequent period, candidly confessed that this fort seemed to have been taken by a species of miracle, as it was found, upon examination, to have been so strongly fortified.— *Deposition of Count Dunois. Lenglet,* vol. i. page 72.

Speaking of this attack of the Tournelles, Luchet says, " More than two hundred English perished on that occasion, the honour of which is not, however, accorded to La Pucelle, but to Saint Aignan and Saint Euverte, who received public thanks, by the performance of solemn processions. It is astonishing that the wound of Jeanne d'Arc excited so little notice, and that the populace, notwithstanding that event, yielded themselves up entirely to devotion."—*Luchet,* p. 17.

On returning to her dwelling, Daulon procured
the attendance of a surgeon, when the wound
Jeanne had received was again dressed, and she
partook of a very simple repast.   The English,
completely paralyzed at their sanguinary overthrow,
resolved on raising the siege.*   La Pucelle, being
informed that preparations were adopting for that
purpose, quitted her bed, and, having accoutred
herself in light armour, left the city with all the
captains of the garrison.   After ranging the French
in battle array, at a small distance from the English,
she commanded, as it was Sunday, that no hostile
operations should take place ; wherefore, if it was
the wish of the enemy to retreat, the will of the

---

* "The siege was raised," says Luchet ; " and, according to
both ancient and modern authors, it was to La Pucelle that
the city was indebted.   Is it likely that if the people had
entertained such an idea, they would have bestowed no mark
of gratitude on their deliverer ?   The populace celebrate a
procession in honour of Saint Aignan and Saint Euverte, at
whose intercession they conceive the victory had been obtained ; and yet they do nothing for the heroine, who is
regarded as a heavenly emissary despatched to repel the
enemy !   From the period of her being wounded, nothing
more is said respecting her.   No author makes mention of the
measures pursued to effect her cure.   Such a stroke from an
arrow above the breast, however, must have inflicted a wound
of no very trifling consequence."— *Luchet*, p. 18.

Lord was they should depart unmolested. Jeanne caused a table to be brought, whereon she spread many religious ornaments, and then prostrated herself, with all the army and the citizens of Orleans, before this altar, which was placed in the open field that separated the city from the enemy. Two masses were performed in succession, and, at the conclusion of the second, Jeanne inquired if the English had their faces turned towards the French. Being answered in the negative, and told that their faces were directed towards Meun, she exclaimed : " *En mon Dieu, ils s'en vont, laissez-les partir, et allons rendre grace à Dieu :* By my God, they are going ; suffer them to depart, and let us go and offer prayers to God."

All the bastilles were rased to the ground, and La Pucelle, with her escort, returned to the city, where the whole population renewed their contrite prayers to Heaven. After this a solemn procession of the ecclesiastics paraded the streets and ramparts of Orleans, making the air resound with hymns and canticles. This ceremony, which took place on the eighth of May, was regularly repeated every succeeding year until the stormy period of the revolution, when it was discontinued. In 1803 the procession was renewed, and has since been continued, according to the ancient forms adopted on this memorable occasion.

Thus in the short space of eight days from the arrival of Jeanne d'Arc at Orleans, only three of which had been devoted to combats, the face of things was completely reversed ; the standard of victory being transferred to the French, who had for so long a period bowed to the valour of the English arms.

DIARY

OF THE

SIEGE OF ORLEANS.

———

As the language of the following Diary may appear obsolete, it is necessary to acquaint the reader that this phraseology was purposely adopted, in order to convey the style of the Original Manuscript with the least possible variation.

D I A R Y,

THE earl of Salisbury, a great lord and the most renowned in feats of arms of all the English; and the which for Henry, king of England, to whom he was related, and as his lieutenant and chief of his army in this kingdom, had been present at many battles as well as divers rencounters and conquests against the French, where he had valiantly conducted himself; thinking to take the city of Orleans by force, which maintained the cause of the king, its sovereign lord Charles, seventh of that name, came to besiege it on Tuesday the twelfth day of October, one thousand four hundred and twenty-eight, with great host and army, which he encamped on the side of Sauloïgne, and near one of the suburbs called Portereau. In which host and army and in his company were, Messire William de la Pole, Earl of Suffolk, and Messire John de la Pole, his brother, the lord of *Escales* (Scales), the lord Faulconberg,

B

the bailiff of Evreux, the lord d'Egres, the lord de
Moulins, the lord de Pomus, Glacidas (William
Glasdale or Gladdisdale)* of high renown, Messire
Launcelot de l'Isle, Marshal of the host, and many
other lords and men of war as well English as others,
false French, maintaining their cause.   But the men
of war there in garrison, had, on the same day and
before the arrival of the English, by the advice and
aid of the citizens of Orleans, caused the church to be
destroyed, the convent of the Augustins of Orleans,
and all the houses which were then standing at the
foresaid Portereau, in order that their enemies
might not be lodged there, nor construct any fortification against the city.

On the ensuing Sunday the English threw into
the city two hundred and four bombarding stones
from large cannons, of which there were some stones
that weighed one hundred and sixteen pounds.
And among others was placed near to the Turcie
Sainct Jean le Blanc, between the wine-press of
Faviere and Portereau, a great cannon which they
named *Passe-rolant* (Beyond-flying); the which
threw stones weighing eighty pounds, doing much
damage to the houses and edifices of Orleans,
not however killing or wounding any one but a
woman named Belles, living near the postern
Chesneau.

* According to one of our Chroniclers.

This same week also did the cannons of the English beat down twelve windmills situated on the banks of the Loire, between the city and the new town. Therefore those of Orleans caused to be built, within the city, eleven mills for horses, which greatly comforted them. Notwithstanding the cannons and engines of the English, the French who were in Orleans made several sallies and skirmishes against them, between the Tournelles of the bridge of Saint Jean le Blanc, from the Sunday until Thursday the twenty-first day of the same month; upon which day the English attacked the boulevard, made of faggots and earth, placed in front of the Tournelles, which assault continued incessantly for four hours: for they began at ten in the morning and did not cease until two hours after mid-day, many valiant feats of arms being performed on either side. Of the principal French who defended the boulevard, were, the lord of Villars, captain of Montargis; Messire Matthïas, an Arragonese; the lord of Guitry; the lord de Couras, of Gascony; the lord of Sainctes Trailles and his brother Poton de Sainctes Trailles, also of Gascony; Peter de la Chapelle, a gentleman of Beausse, and many other knights and esquires, besides the citizens of Orleans, all of whom conducted themselves very valiantly. In like manner the women of Orleans afforded great succour; for they never ceased to furnish with diligence to those who defended the boulevard,

many necessary things; such as water, boiling oil
and grease, lime, cinders and *chausse-trapes*.*   At
the termination of the assault many were wounded
on either side; but mostly of the English, of whom
more than two hundred-and-forty died.   It so happened that during the assault, the lord of Gaucourt
rode by Orleans, for he was the governor; but, when
passing before Sainct Père Empont, he accidentally
fell from his horse, and broke his arm; and was
forthwith carried to the baths to have it set.

On the following Friday, the twenty-second day
of the said month of October, the alarm bell was
rung; the French believing that the English attacked
the boulevards of the Tournelles from the end of
the bridge, by the mine which they had dug, but
they retired at this period.   The same day the inhabitants of Orleans broke down an arch of the bridge,
and constructed a boulevard to the right of the
beautiful Cross which is upon the bridge.

The ensuing Saturday, the twenty-third day of the
month, the citizens of Orleans burned and broke
down the boulevard of the Tournelles, and abandoned
the same; because it was undermined and no longer
tenable by the said men at war.

On the following Sunday, the twenty-fourth day
of October, the English attacked and took the Tournelles at the end of the bridge; because they were

---

* This term is not found in any Dictionary of Old French.

completely demolished and broken down by the cannons and heavy artillery which they had discharged against them : and on this account no defence was attempted, because no one dared stand upright.

On the night of this day (Sunday), the earl of Salisbury, having with him captain Glacidas (Glasdale), and many others, wished to go into the Tournelles, after they had been taken, in order to examine the situation of Orleans. But no sooner had he arrived, and occupied himself with looking at the city through a window of the Tournelles, than he was struck by a ball from a cannon, said to have been fired from a tower, called the Tower of our Lady; but never positively known from whence discharged, so that it is said to have been an act of the Divinity. The blow from the said cannon struck him on the head, in such wise, that it carried away half of the cheek, and burst one of the eyes, which proved a signal benefit for this kingdom, for he was commander of the army, and the most renowned and dreaded of all the English. On this same day, when the Tournelles were lost, the French broke up another strong boulevard in the city ; and in another quarter the English destroyed two arches of the bridge in front of the Tournelles, after they had taken them, and there constructed a very large boulevard of earth and faggots.

The Monday following, being the twenty-fifth day of the month of October, arrived in Orleans for its comfort, succour and aid, many lords, knights, captains and esquires greatly renowned in war, the principal of whom were John, Bastard of Orleans; the lord of Saint Severe, Marshal of France; the lord of Bueil; Messire James of Chabanes, Seneschal of the Bourbonnois; the lord of Chaumont-sur-Loire; Messire Theaulde de Valpergne, Lombard knight; and a valiant captain of Gascony, called Stephen de Vignolles, otherwise La Hire, who, as well as the captains and those accompanying him, were all valiant and of high renown. And of these were captain de Vendosme, Messire Cerney, an Arragonese, and many others, accompanied by eight hundred armed combatants, such as archers, crossbowmen, with other Italian infantry bearing pointed stakes.

The Wednesday following, twenty-seventh of the month at night, died the earl of Salisbury at the city of Meung on the Loire, whither he had been carried from the siege, after receiving the wound from the cannon of which he died; whose death greatly stupified and discomfited the English carrying on the siege, for they mourned much thereat, wherefore they concealed the matter to the utmost of their power, fearing lest those of Orleans should become acquainted therewith. They caused his entrails to be taken out, and sent the body to England. The death of which Earl brought great harm to the English, and on the contrary, great profit to the French. Many since have said, that the earl of Salisbury thus met his end by divine judgment of God, and believe it: for that he had broken his promise to the duke of Orleans, held prisoner in England, to whom he had passed his word, that he would not injure any of his possessions; as well as, that he spared neither monasteries nor churches, all of which he pillaged when he could enter them. These are things sufficiently strong to make one believe that his days were abridged by the just vengeance of God. Among others was particularly pillaged the church of our Lady of Clery, as well as the town.

On Tuesday, the eighth day of November, was divided and removed the army of the English, the one part retiring to Meung on the Loire, and the other to Jargeau, leaving a strong garrison at the Tournelles and the boulevard of the bridge; amongst whom was captain Glacidas (Glasdale), and with him five hundred men to guard them.

This same Tuesday, the English burned and destroyed several houses, presses, and other edifices in the vale of the Loire; while at the same time the men of war and the citizens of Orleans acted with so much zeal, that they burned and threw down, by the end of the month of November, several churches which stood in the suburbs of the city; namely, the church of Saint Aignan, patron of Orleans, together with the cloisters appertaining thereto, which was

very seemly to behold; the churches of Saint
Michael and Saint Aux, the chapel of Martroy, the
church of Saint Victor, situated in the suburbs of
the gate of Burgundy; the church of Saint Michael
above the fosses, the Jacobins, the Cordeliers, the
Carmelites; Saint Mathurin, the Almonry of Saint
Povair and Saint Lawrence; besides these, they
burned and destroyed all the suburbs surrounding
the city, structures very rich and beautiful to behold
before they were beaten down.   For there were
sundry grand and rich edifices, insomuch so, that
they were esteemed the most beautiful suburbs in
the kingdom; notwithstanding which the French
garrison burned and threw them down.   All which
was done with the consent and aid of the citizens of
Orleans, in order that the English might not lodge
therein, which would have been very prejudicial to
the city.

The first day of December following, arrived at the
Tournelles of the bridge several English lords;
amongst whom of highest renown were, Messires
John Talbot, first Baron in England, and the lord of
Escalle (lord Scales), accompanied by three hundred
combatants; who conveyed thither provisions, cannon, bombs and other implements of war, from which
they fired against the walls and within Orleans, more
incessantly and strongly than had been done before,
during the lifetime of the earl of Salisbury; for, they
threw stones that weighed eighty-four pounds, which

did great evil and damage to the city, as well as to many houses and beautiful edifices of the same, without killing or wounding any one, which was regarded as a great marvel. For, among others, in the street of the *Petits Souliers* (Little Shoes) one fell in the hotel and upon the table of a man who was at dinner (he being the fifth person then present) without killing or hurting any one; which is said to have been a miracle performed by our Lord, at the request of *Monsieur* Saint Aignan, the patron of Orleans.

The following Tuesday, at three o'clock in the morning, was rung the alarm-bell in the belfry, because the French thought that the English wanted to attack the boulevard of the beautiful Cross on the bridge. And already had two scaled it, advancing as far as one of the cannoneers; but they presently returned back to their Tournelles. And while observing, they perceived that the English were upon the watch, having arranged all things, such as cannon, cross-bows, stick-slings, culverins, stones, and other implements of war, necessary for their defence, in case they were assailed.

On Thursday the twenty-third day of the month of December, began the bombarding by throwing of stones that weighed an hundred and twenty pounds, the bombs all newly made by one named William Duisy, a very subtle workman; the same being placed at the cross of the mills of the postern Chesneau, in order to fire against the Tournelles ; near which were posted two cannons, the one called Montargis, the other Rifflard, which, during the siege, played against the English, doing them much injury.

On the following Christmas-day, was a truce agreed upon on either side, lasting from nine in the morning till three in the evening: during this truce, Glacidas, (Glasdale) and other lords of England invited the Bastard of Orleans, and the lord of Saint Severe, Marshal of France, that they might play a tune of grand minstrelsy, with trumpets and clarions ; which was done accordingly ; so that they played on the instruments for a long space of time, producing great melody ; but no sooner was the truce ended, than every one took care of himself. During the festival of Christmas there were horrible discharges from bombs and cannon ; but above all was great injury done by a cannoneer, native of Loraine, being then of the garrison of Orleans, named Master John, who was said to be the most expert at the said business. And well did he show it ; for he had a large culverin, from which he often fired from between the pillars of the bridge near the boulevard of the beautiful Cross, in such wise, that he killed and wounded a multitude of English. And to scoff them, he often threw himself upon the ground, feigning to be dead or wounded, and caused himself to be borne into the city. But incontinent he returned to the skirmish, and so conducted himself, that the English knew him to be alive, to their great cost and displeasure.

Wednesday, the twenty-ninth day of the month of December, were burned and destroyed several other churches and houses which were still left standing near Orleans; namely, Saint Loup, Saint Marc, Saint Gervais, Saint Euverte, the chapel Saint Aignan, Saint Vincent of the Vines, Saint Lardre, Saint Povair, and also the Magdalen, in order that the English might not lodge there, or retreat and fortify themselves against the city. The last day of the said month arrived about two thousand five hundred English fighting men, at Saint Lawrence des Orgerilz, near Orleans, in order to invest the same; among whom were captains, the earls of Suffolk and Talbot, Messire John de la Pole, lord of Escalles, (lord Scales) Messire Launcelot de L'Isle, and many others. But, at their coming, great skirmishing took place; for the Bastard of Orleans, the lord of Saint Severe, Messire James de Chabanes, and many other knights, esquires and citizens of Orleans, who valiantly conducted themselves, went to meet them and receive them as their enemies. And there were enacted many noble feats of arms on either side. In these skirmishes was wounded in the foot by an arrow from the English, Messire James de Chabanes, and his horse killed, by a like adventure.

On the same day, were also performed many gallant feats of arms on either side, by the wooden cross near Saint Lawrence; and during the whole of this day, Master John did great damage with his culverin.

This Friday the last day of the year, at four o'clock in the evening, two Frenchmen so sagely defended themselves from the cannon and other warlike implements, that the English retired into the bastilles of Saint Lawrence.

The following Wednesday came Messire Louis Deculan, admiral of France, and with him two hundred combatants, repairing to the Portereau before the Tournelles, where was the garrison of the English; and in spite of them passed the Loire, at the gate of Saint Loup, himself and his men entering into the city to learn news concerning the government of the same and of the French therein; who, with his men, was much feasted and mightily extolled. For right valiantly had they conducted themselves against the English at the skirmish of the Portereau.

On the following Thursday, being the festival of Epiphany, that is of the kings, sallied forth from Orleans the lords of Saint Severe and Deculan, Messire Theaulde de Valpergne, and many other men at war and citizens; performing a great skirmish, where they conducted themselves right gallantly against the English; who also defended themselves well and stoutly. Many English lords were also there, as well as knights and esquires, but their names are not known. During this skirmish also did Master John gallantly conduct himself with his culverin.

About this period the English had worked so well, that they had raised two boulevards on the river Loire, the one being on a little island on the side, and to the right of Saint Lawrence, formed of faggots, sand, and wood. The second, was to the right of the former, in the field of Saint Privé, and on the bank of the river; which they traversed at this spot, conveying food the one to the other; and to guard them was appointed captain Messire Lancelot de L'Isle, Marshal of England.

Thursday, the tenth day of the said month, arrived in Orleans a great quantity of powder for cannon, and provisions which were conveyed from Bourges for its comfort and succour. On this same day, was a very hot and great skirmish as well with cannon as other culverins; so that those who fired them did their duty in a noble manner, insomuch, that many English were killed and a number taken prisoners.

The ensuing Tuesday, about nine at night, the whole of the roofings and walls of the Tournelles were destroyed and thrown down, and six English killed under them, by a cannon-ball of iron; which piece was planted on the boulevard of the beautiful Cross of the bridge, and fired off at that hour.

On the following Wednesday, the twelfth day of the said month of January, the alarm-bell of the belfry was rung, because the English uttered loud cries, and sounded their trumpets and their clarions

before the boulevard of Regnart gate; and on the
same day towards morning six hundred hogs were
driven into Orleans.

Next Saturday, fifteenth day of the said month,
about eight at night, sallied forth from the city,
the Bastard of Orleans, the lord of Saint Severe and
Messire James de Chabanes, accompanied by many
knights, esquires, captains and citizens of Orleans,
in order to make a charge upon part of the forces
at Saint Lawrence des Orgerilz; but the English
perceived them, and cried to arms throughout their
host; in consequence of which, they armed themselves in such wise, that there was a very great and
a violent skirmish. At length the French retired
to the boulevard of Regnart gate, for the English
sallied out in full force, so that the French were
well beaten.

The Sunday next ensuing, about two in the afternoon, came to the English army, twelve hundred
combatants commanded by Messire John Fascot,
(Fastolf) bringing with them food, bombs, cannon,
powder, arrows, and other implements of war,
whereof their army stood in great need.

The Monday following, the seventeenth of the
said month, happened a most marvellous occurrence;
for the English fired from a cannon on their boulevard of the wooden cross; the stone from which fell
before the boulevard of Banier gate, in the midst of
more than one hundred persons, without killing or

harming any one; only striking a Frenchman upon the foot, in such wise, that his shoe was carried away without doing him the least injury; a thing most marvellous to believe.

On the same day was to have been a pitched battle of six Frenchmen against six English, in the field close adjoining to Banier gate, at the spot where stands Turpin Dovecot; but there was no fight, which was not owing to any lack on the French side, for they presented themselves to meet their adversaries, who never arrived, not daring to sally forth.

Tuesday, the eighteenth of the said month of January, at the hour of nine at night, the English being in their tournelles, fired a cannon from the boulevards of the beautiful Cross, which struck a man named Le Gastelier, a native of Orleans, who was looking that way and bending his cross-bow, thinking to shoot at them.

The Tuesday following, arrived in Orleans, at the opening of the city gates, forty horned beasts and two hundred hogs.

On the same day, and immediately after the entrance of these beasts, the English possessed themselves at the tournelles of the road, two corner towers, and five hundred beasts, which the drovers thought to conduct for sale to Orleans; whereas the same were denounced by some traitors of a village called Sandillon, in order that they might have a part of the booty, but who were caught at L'Argeau, where the English were then stationed.

The same day, about three in the afternoon, was a great and bold skirmish in an island before the cross of the mills of Saint Aignan, because the English broke up the passage in order to secure the cross-road which they had taken at the gate of Saint Loup; and the French, as well soldiers as citizens, crossed the stream at this island, thinking to recover the cross-road which had been invested in the morning. At this rencounter, issued a strong force of the English lying in ambush behind the Turcie, a little farther than Saint John le Blanc, uttering loud cries against the French, who returned, and hastily retreated towards their boulevards; which they could not however effect with sufficient expedition to prevent twenty-two being killed. Independent of these, two gentlemen were taken, the one named the Little Briton, belonging to the retinue of the Bastard of Orleans; and the other called Raymonet, belonging to the Marshal of Saint Severe. In this skirmish was also lost a culverin, while that belonging to Master John, being long in great danger, was captured. For when he thought to retreat into his niche, others rushed in at the same time, in such wise, that he sunk into the river, wherefore he thought to regain his culverin by means of a large boat, but he could not succeed; he then laid fast hold of a beam whereto he clung, and, notwithstanding all these mishaps, swam upon the same till he gained the bank, and saved himself within the city, leaving his culverin to the English, who carried the same to their Tournelles.

The following Thursday, being the twenty-seventh of the same month of January, at three in the evening, a very great skirmish took place before the boulevard of the gate Regnart; because four and five hundred English combatants proceeded thither from their bastille, uttering great and marvellous cries. Against these, sallied forth those of Orleans by the same boulevard, making so much speed that they got into disorder, and in consequence the Marshal of Saint Severe caused them to return. Having once more marshalled them, he made them again sally forth, and so ably conducted himself, showing such prowess, that he compelled the English to return into their bastille of Saint Lawrence.

The following day, being Friday, arrived in Orleans, about eleven at night, certain ambassadors who had been despatched to the king from the city, in order to procure succour.

The Saturday ensuing, being the twenty-first day of January, at eight in the morning, the English raised great cries throughout their camp and in their bastilles, taking up arms in mighty force, and still continuing their shoutings, at the same time displaying signs of grand hardihood, approaching even to a barrier which was in the square before the

c

Tower of our Lady, as well as to the boulevard of
Regnart gate; but they were warmly received.
For the men at war and a multitude of the citizens
of Orleans sallied out forthwith against them, well
organized, in such sort, that there was a very bold
and grand skirmish, as well by hand as with cannons, culverins, and arrows; so that many people
were killed, wounded, and made prisoners on either
side.   And more especially there died an *English
Lord*, whom they mourned much, and whom they
carried to be interred at Jargeau.   And on this same
day towards the morning, arrived also in Orleans
the lord of Villars, the lord of Sainctes Trailles, and
Poton his brother, Messire Ternay, and other knights
and esquires coming to confer with the king.

The following Sunday, at night, the Bastard of
Orleans left the city, accompanied by several knights
and esquires, to repair to Blois, to Charles, Count
of Clermont, eldest son of the Duke of Bourbon.
Wherefore, the English hearing them speak, cried
to arms, and set a strong watch, doubtful whether
their intention was not to attack their bastilles.

The following day, being Monday, the twenty-
fourth of the month of January, about four in the
evening, arrived in Orleans La Hire, and with him
thirty men at arms; against whom the English discharged a cannon, the stone from which fell in the
midst of them, just as they had gained the spot
before Regnart gate, which neither killed nor hurt

any one, being a great marvel. So they entered *sains et saufs* into the city, and proceeded to render grace unto our Lord, who had preserved them from injury.

Wednesday, the twenty-sixth of the said January, was a great skirmish before the boulevard of Bannier gate; because the English cautiously thought that the sun shone in the faces of the French who were without the boulevard to skirmish. And there sallied from out their host a mighty power, showing great appearance of hardihood; and acted in such wise, that they caused the French to fall back to the edge of the fosse of the boulevard of the city; whereto they approached so near that they bore away one of their standards and a lance near the boulevard; but they continued only for a short space, because those of Orleans, and on the boulevard, thickly discharged against them cannons, bombs, culverins, and other arrows. And it was said, that in this skirmish were killed twenty English, not counting the wounded. But of the French died only one archer of the Marshal of Saint Severe, who fell by a shot from a cannon of Orleans itself, whereat his master, and the other lords, were mightily chagrined.

The day following, being Sunday the twenty-ninth of the said month of January, safeguard was accorded on either side to La Hire, and Messire Launcelot de l'Isle, to hold conference together. This took place about the hour of closing the gates.

But after they had spoken together, and that the
hour of safeguard was passed, as each of them returned towards his people, those of Orleans discharged a cannon, which struck Messire Launcelot,
in such wise, that his head was carried off, whereat
those of his party were very dolorous; for he was
their Marshal and a right valiant man.

The following, which was Sunday, a very great
skirmish took place; because the English carried
off the sticks, that is, vine stakes, from the vineyards
in the environs of Saint Lardre, and Saint John de la
Ruelle, near Orleans, and conveyed them to their
camp to warm themselves therewith.   Wherefore
the Marshal of Saint Severe, La Hire, Poton, Messire
Jacques de Chabanes, Messire Denis de Chailly,
Messire Gervais, Arragonese, and many others of
Orleans, sallied forth, rushing among them, and
valiantly assailing them, in such sort, that they
killed seven, and brought fourteen prisoners into the
city.   And this same day departed this world a
valiant citizen and a native, named Simon de Bau-
gener, who had been wounded in the throat by one
of the enemy's arrows.   And the following day,
being Monday the thirty-first and last of the said
month of January, arrived in Orleans, eight horses
charged with oil and grease.

Thursday following, the third day of February,
issued from Orleans, the Marshal of Saint Severe,
Messire James de Chabanes, La Hire, Couras, and

many other knights and esquires, proceeding as far as the boulevard of Saint Lawrence. Wherefore the English cried to arms, unfurling twelve of their banners, and placing themselves in battle array throughout their host, without coming forth from their boulevards and barriers. So that the French, perceiving they did not sally out, returned in good order into the city, without other thing being done.

Saturday, fifth of the said month, came to Orleans at night-fall, as the gates were closing, twenty-six combatants, very valiant men of war and well equipped ; who had journeyed from Sauloigne, belonging to the Marshal of Saint Severe; the which conducted themselves right gallantly, as long as they continued in the garrison.

The following day, being Sunday, about vesper time, sallied from Orleans the Marshal of Saint Severe, Chabanes, La Hire, Poton, and Chailly, with two hundred combatants, who ran as far as the Magdalen ; where they found the lord of Escalles (Scales), and thirty combatants with him, who retired in great haste to their camp and bastille of Saint Lawrence ; so that in the end were only killed and made prisoners, fourteen of the English.

The Monday, seventh of the said month, arrived in Orleans, Messire Theaulde de Valpergne, Messire Jean de Lescot, of Gascony, and other ambassadors, who came from having conference with the king,

bringing news of succour that was to arrive and cause
the raising of the siege.

The following Tuesday, entered into the city of
Orleans many very valiant men at war well armed,
and among others, Messire Guillaume Estuart
(Stewart), brother of the Constable of Scotland, the
lord de Saucourt, the lord de Verduran, with many
other knights and esquires, accompanied by one
thousand combatants, being in such sort clothed
for feats of war, that it was a right comely sight to
behold them.

This same day, towards night, came two hundred
combatants, belonging to Messire Guillaume d'Alebret, and shortly after six hundred others of the
suite of La Hire.

About these days, there was a young Pucelle named
Jeanne, native of a village in Barrois, called Dom-
prebemy, (Dom Remy) near unto another called Gras,
under the lordship of Vaucouleurs. To whom, while
formerly watching around the dwelling of her father
and her mother a few sheep which they had, and other
times sewing and spinning, appeared our Lord
several times in a vision. And he commanded, that
she should go and raise the siege of Orleans, and
cause the king to be anointed at Rheims: for that
he would be with her, and would cause her, by his
divine aid and by force of arms, to accomplish this
enterprise. Wherefore, she went before Messire
Robert de Baudricourt, then captain of the said place

of Vaucouleurs, and narrated to him her vision ; praying and requiring him, that for the great good and profit of the kingdom, he would cause her to be arrayed in the habiliments of a man, mounted on horseback, and after conducted to the king, according as God had commanded her to go. But, for that time, nor for many days, would he believe her; so that he only mocked and esteemed her vision as a fantasy and a bewildered imagination ; yet, thinking to use her in regard to his people, as a carnal sin, he retained her. To which none of them, nor any after, could in such sort make her turn. For, so soon as they fixedly looked upon her, they were all cooled of their luxury.

The Wednesday, ninth day of the said month, departed from Orleans Messire Jacques de Chabanes, Messire Regnault de Fratames, and le Bourg de Bar, accompanied by twenty or twenty-five combatants, in order to proceed to Blois to the Count de Clermont ; but they were met on the road by a power of English and Burgundians, who secured le Bourg de Bar, and carried him off prisoner to the tower of Marchesvoir, and the two other lords fled. On which day, arrived within the city of Orleans, Messire Gilbert de Faicte, native of Bourbonnois and Marshal of France, who conducted with him three hundred combatants.

The next day, which was Thursday, quitted Orleans, the Bastard of Orleans and two hundred

combatants with him, to go to Blois, to the Count
de Clermont and Messire John Estuart (Stewart),
Constable of Scotland ; the Lord de la Tour, baron of
Auvergne; the Viscount of Thouras, lord of Ambois,
and other knights and esquires, -accompanied, as it
was said, by full four thousand combatants, as well
of Auvergne, Bourbonnois, as of Scotland, in order
to know when it should please them to appoint a
day and an hour for the attacking the English,
and the false French conducting from Paris provisions and artillery, for their forces carrying on
the siege.

Friday, the ninth of the said month of February,
departed also from Orleans, Messire Guillaume
d'Alebret, Messire Guillaume Estuart (Stewart),
brother of the Constable of Scotland, the Marshal of
Saint Severe, the lord of Graville, the lord of Sainctes
Trailles, and La Hire, Poton, his brother, the lord
of Verduran, with many other knights and esquires,
accompanied by fifteen hundred combatants, intend-
ing to join them and assemble with the Count de
Clermont and the others already named, to meet the
supply of provisions and attack them.   And on this
day, also departed the said Count de Clermont, who
proceeded in such wise, that he arrived with all his
company in Beausse, at a village called Rouvray de
Sainct Denys, which is distant two leagues from
Yenville.   And when they were all assembled, there
were found from three to four thousand combatants,

and they did not depart from thence until the hour of three after mid-day.

The next day, which was Saturday, the twelfth of February, eve of *les Brandons* (Palm Sunday), Messire John Fascot (Fastolf), the bailiff of Evreux, who was of the English side, Messire Simon Morhier, Prevost of Paris, and many other knights and esquires of England and of France, accompanied by fifteen hundred combatants, as well English, Picards, Normands, as divers people of other countries, conducted about three hundred waggons and carts charged with provisions and different habiliments of war, such as cannon, bows, quivers, arrows, and other things, conveying them to the English then carrying on the siege before Orleans. But when, through means of their spies, they learned the force of the French, and ascertained that their intention was to assail them, they enclosed themselves, making a park of their convoy, and placing pointed stakes in form of barriers, leaving only one long and narrow issue and entry ; for, the hinder part of their park, so enclosed by the convoy, was large, and the inner part long and narrow ; whereto this issue or entry was such, that it was necessary to go in by that direction where it was intended it should be assailed. And, matters thus arranged in good order of battle, did they await there to live or to die ; for, to escape had they little hope, considering their small number, against the multitude of French, who all assembled

of one common accord; they concluded that no one
would dismount from his horse, unless it were the
archers and the arrow men, whose duty at their
coming was to shoot.   After such conclusion, in the
front took their stations La Hire, Poton, Saulten,
Canede, and many others from Orleans, making
about fifteen hundred combatants, who were advertised that the English conducting the provisions
marched in a line without order and having no
suspicion of being surprised; wherefore they were
all of one opinion that they should assail them thus
unawares as they approached.   But the Count de
Clermont sent word several times and by divers
messages to La Hire and the others so disposed to
attack their adversaries; stating, that he found in
them such great advantage, that they should not in
any wise assault until his coming up, and that he
would bring them from three to four thousand combatants equally as anxious as themselves to assemble
against the English.   For honour and for the love
of whom they abandoned their enterprise, to their
very great displeasure, and above all of La Hire,
who testified the appearance of their great chagrin,
for that a lapse was thus accorded to the English to
join and unite closely together; and with their
friends to fortify themselves with stakes and with
chariots.   And, in truth, La Hire, and those of his
company who had marched from Orleans, were halted
in a field in front, and so near to the English, that

very well had he seen them, as it is said, approach in
a line and fortify themselves, bewailing marvellously,
for that he did not dare attack, owing to the various commands sent by the Count de Clermont, who
still continued to advance as speedily as possible. No
less impatiently did the Constable of Scotland await
this attempt; the which had arrived there also, with
about four hundred combatants, among whom were
many valiant men.   And in this manner, between
the hours of two and three after mid-day, advanced
against the French archers and bowmen, some of their
adversaries, of whom none had before sallied forth;
these they constrained to fall back in haste, causing
them to retreat by force of arrows, with which they
charged so thickly that they killed many, while
those who could escape entered within their fortification with the others.   Wherefore, when the Constable of Scotland perceived that they kept themselves ranged in such close order without showing
any signs of separating, he was, from too much
warmth, so desirous of attacking, that he forgot
every order that had been issued; that no one should
dismount.   So he proceeded to attack, without
waiting the others, and following his example and for
the purpose of aiding him, dismounted also the
Bastard of Orleans, the Lord D'Orval, Messire Guillaume Estuart (Stewart), Messire John de Mailhac,
lord of Chasteaubrun, the Viscount de Bridiers, Messire John de Lesgot, the lord of Verduran, Messire

Loys de Rochechouart, lord de Monpipeau, and many
other knights and esquires, with about four hundred
combatants, not counting the bowmen, who were
already on foot and had driven back the English
most valiantly.   But little did this avail; for when
the English saw that the strong force, which was
then distant, approached in a cowardly way, and did
not join with the Constable and the others on foot,
then they hastily sallied from their park, striking
amidst the French on foot, and put them to route
and to flight, and not without great slaughter: for
there died of the French from three to four hundred
combatants.   And besides these the English, not
drunk with the butchery they had made in the
space before the park, spread themselves hastily
in the fields, pursuing those on foot in such manner,
that twelve of their standards were seen far removed
from each other in sundry places, not less than the
distance of a cross-bow shot from the principal place
of the discomfiture.   Wherefore La Hire, Poton,
and many other valiant men, who felt much pain in
flying thus disgracefully, having rallied near the
place of their first defeat, assembled from sixty to
eighty combatants, who followed from right and left,
and attacked the English, thus separated, in such
wise, that they killed many.   And certainly, if all
the other French had in like manner returned, the
honour and the profit of the day had remained on their
side: whereas, before were dead and killed many

great lords, knights, esquires, nobles, and valiant
captains and chieftains of war. And among others
were slain, Messire Guillaume D'Albret, Lord
D'Orval; Messire John Estuart (Stewart), Constable
of Scotland; Messire Guillaume Estuart (Stewart),
his brother, the lord de Verduran, the lord de
Chasteaubrun, Messire Loys de Roche-chouart, and
Messire John Chabot, together with many others,
who were all of high nobility and right renowned
for valour. The bodies of which lords were after
brought to Orleans, and interred in the grand church
called the Saint Cross; where was a divine funeral
service performed for them. From this conflict
escaped among others the Bastard of Orleans, only,
that from the commencement he had been wounded
by an arrow in the foot; in consequence of which,
two of his archers drew him with much difficulty
from the thick of the affray, placed him on horseback, and thus saved him. Neither the Count de
Clermont, who had been created a knight on this
day, nor all his great force, showed any desire to
succour their companions, as well from their being
dismounted, against the orders agreed upon, as also
beholding them almost all killed in front of him.
But, as soon as they perceived that the English were
masters, they took their road towards Orleans; in doing
which they did not act honourably, but disgracefully:
and plenty of time was accorded them to go; for
the English did not pursue them, in consequence of

the major part being on foot, and that they knew the
French to be in greater numbers than themselves.
Wherefore all the honour and the profit of the
victory remained to the English, the leader of whom
on this occasion was Messire John Fascot (Fastolf),
with whom also was Messire Thomas Rameston,
having equally a great command of men at arms.

On this same day, very late at night, arrived in
Orleans, the Count de Clermont, the Bastard of
Orleans, the lord de la Tour, the Viscount de Thouras, the Marshal of Saint Severe, the lord of Graville, La Hire, Poton, and many other French
knights and esquires, who returned from the battle
which had thus been lost from a want of due ordinance.
In such wise that La Hire, Poton, and Jamet de
Thilloy, were the last who entered.   For, according
to command, of all the rest they ever remained to
the last, at the tail of such as returned, to serve
as a counter-guard, in order that those in the
bastilles might not sally forth against them, should
they know of the discomfiture ; in which case they
might have still more harmed them than before, had
they not thus been upon their guard.

Upon this same day also, Jeanne la Pucelle knew
by Divine grace of this discomfiture ; and said to
Messire de Baudricourt, that the king had sustained
great evil before Orleans, and would still experience
more, in case she was not conducted into his presence.   Wherefore, Baudricourt, who had already

proved her and found her very circumspect, and as it were true, persevering always in her first request, caused her to be clothed in the attire of a man, according as she had demanded; and for her safe escort he awarded her two gentlemen of Champaine; the one named John of Mets (Metz), and the other Bertrand de Polongy, who greatly remonstrated, on account of the grand danger of the roads. But she strengthened them with assurances that no harm would befall them, and they began their journey with her, and two of her brothers, to go forward unto the king, who then was at Chinon.

The following Monday after this discomfiture, being the fourteenth of the month of February, was discharged a cannon by the English then garrisoned in the Tournelles, the stone from which fell into Orleans on the hotel of the Black head, in the street of Hosteleries, to which mansion it caused great injury, and fell into the said street and killed three persons of the city; one of whom, named John Turquoys, was walking.

The Thursday ensuing, being the seventeenth of the said month, were conducted into the camp and to the English besiegers, by Messire John Fascot (Fastolf), and his men, provisions and other accoutrements of war, which they had conducted from Paris, together with those which they had taken in the last discomfiture near Rouvray Sainct Denis; which many have since called the battle of Herrings.

Against whom sallied forth the French of the garrison and many citizens, in order to rush upon them and gain the provisions and the artillery which they conducted. But notwithstanding they neither the one touched the other, for that time.

At about this period arrived at Chinon, Jeanne la Pucelle, and those who escorted her, they wondering marvellously at their arriving thus in safety; considering the perilous passes they had found, the wide and the dangerous rivers they had forded, and the length of road they had been obliged to journey; in the course of which, they had passed many cities and villages taking part with the English, without naming those holding for France, who committed great evil and pillaging. Wherefore they rendered praise unto the Lord for the grace which he had shown them, according as the Pucelle had before promised. And all these feats they notified to the king; prior to which it had already been discussed in his council several times, that it would be best that he should retire into Dauphiny, and there be guarded by the countries of Lyonnois, Languedoc and Auvergne; at least, if they could be preserved; should the Englishmen possess themselves of Orleans. But all then present were mute; therefore the king demanded of the two gentlemen, and the lords of his grand council being there, did also interrogate them, in regard to the state of the Pucelle; of whom they spake the whole truth. And upon this occasion it became a question with the council whether they should cause her to speak with the king; when it was at last concluded in the affirmative; and forthwith she spake there, and bowed herself with reverence, and recognised him from amongst the others, notwith-standing that many of the number feigned (thinking to deceive her,) that they were the king; which wore a great appearance of truth; for she had never before seen him. Wherefore, among many other fine speeches, she told him, that God had sent her for his aid and succour, and that he must accord her men ; for that by Divine Grace and by force of arms, she would cause the siege of Orleans to be raised, and would afterwards conduct him to be anointed at Rheims, in such wise as God had commanded her, whose will it was, that the English should return into their country, and leave him his kingdom in peace, the which should remain unto him, or, that if they did not do so, evil would accrue to them.

These words having been thus spoken by Jeanne, the king caused her to be honourably conducted to his dwelling, and assembled his grand council, amongst whom were many prelates, knights, esquires, and chieftains at war, together with some doctors in theology, in laws, and in decretals, who altogether were of opinion, that she should be interrogated by the doctors, in order to ascertain whether there

appeared evident reason for her accomplishment of
what she said. But the doctors found her so honest
in appearance, and so sage in her speech, that
on delivering their relation the same was taken into
great account. Wherefore, and also because it was
found that she had truly known the day and the
period of the battle of Herrings, as it was proved by
the letters of the lord de Baudricourt, he having
written the very hour of the same which she had
stated unto him, being still at Vaucouleurs; as well
as in consequence of her since declaring unto the
king in secret, (there being then present his confessor and a few of his chosen counsellors) the
performance of a good action which he had done,
whereat he was much confounded, since no one
could know the same excepting God and himself.
It was in consequence resolved, that she should be
properly conducted to Poictiers, as well that she
might be anew interrogated and prove her perseverance, as also that money might be had to procure for her men, provisions, and artillery, for the
victualling of Orleans; the which determination she
knew by Divine Grace : for, being then in midway
of the route, she said unto many,

"In the name of God I know full well that I shall
have much to do at Poictiers, whither I am being
conducted; but Messires will aid me. Wherefore,
let us go by the order of God." For such was her
manner of speech.

Being arrived at the said Poictiers, where then the king's parliament was sitting, divers interrogatories were put to her by many doctors and other personages of high estate ; to the which she replied right ably.   And more especially unto a Jacobin doctor, who said to her, that if the will of God was that the English should depart, there was no need of arms.   To whom Jeanne replied, that she required but few fighting men, and that God would ensure to her the victory : on account of which answer, together with divers others made, and her firmness in maintaining the first promises given, it was by all concluded, that the king ought to place confidence in her, and accord her provisions and men, and send her to Orleans; the which he did accordingly, and besides, he also caused her to be well armed and gave her good horses.   And he also willed and commanded that she should have a standard, on the which, at her own desire, was painted and placed by way of device, *Jesus Maria,* and a *Majesty.*   The king being further desirous of giving her a beautiful sword, she desired that it might please him to send in quest of one, upon the blade whereof was engraven five crosses near unto the handle, the which was at Saint Katherine de Fierbois. Whereat the king was mightily astonished, and inquired of her if she had ever before seen it.   Whereto she made answer, that she had not, but that she nevertheless knew it to be there. The king in consequence sent, and the said sword was there found, together with others, which had been given in ancient times; and it was brought unto the king, who caused her to be dressed and adorned gallantly; and he gave to accompany her, a very valiant and sage gentleman named John Daulon; and for a page and to serve her with honour, he gave her another gentleman named Loys Decontes. In such sort that all these things declared in this same chapter, were enacted at several times, and upon divers days; but I have thus enumerated them for the sake of brevity.

Friday, the eighteenth day of February, the count de Clermont departed from Orleans, stating, that he wanted to go to the king at Chinon, who was then there, and in his company was the lord de la Tour, Messire Loys Deculan, admiral; Messire Regnault de Chartres, archbishop of Rheims and chancellor of France; Messire John de Saint Michel, bishop of Orleans, a native of Scotland; La Hire, and many other knights and esquires of Auvergne, of Bourbonnois and of Scotland, full two thousand combatants, whereat those of Orleans, seeing them depart, were not well contented. But to appease them, he promised that he would succour them with men and with victuals. After the which departure, there only remained within Orleans the Bastard of Orleans, the marshal of Saint Severe, and their people. And the count de Clermont, who after was duke of Bourbon, went away, and the lords and combatants above named with him, and retired into Blois. And when those of Orleans saw themselves thus left with a small number of men of war, and perceived the power and the siege of the English waxing stronger from day to day, they despatched Poton de Sainctes-trailles and other citizens unto Philip duke of Burgundy and Messire John de Luxembourg, count de Ligny, supporting the power of England, and caused them to be entreated and required that they should have care of them; and that for the love of their lord Charles duke of Orleans, being then a prisoner in England, and for the preservation of his lands; to secure which they could not for the present undertake; that it would please them to drive away the war of the English from them, and cause the siege to be raised until some light should be thrown upon the troubles of the kingdom, or that they might receive aid and succour in favour of their relation thus a prisoner.

The following Sunday was a very grand and sharp skirmish, for the English sallied forth from their camp and their bastilles, bearing seven standards, and conducted themselves after such sort, that they chased and caused the French to fall back, who had advanced to, and assailed them in Turpin field, which is the distance of a stone's throw from Orleans. But they were well received with cannons, culverins and other discharges, which were incontinently levelled against them from the city, so thickly, tha they returned in great haste within their camp as well as the bastilles of Saint Lawrence and others in the environs.

The Tuesday following, February the twenty-second, the earl of Suffolk and the lords Talbot and Escalles (Scales) sent by a herald, as a present to the Bastard of Orleans, a dish full of figs, raisins and dates; praying him at the same time, that he would be pleased to send to the said earl of Suffolk some black *Pane** wherewith to line a robe, the which he did most freely, for he sent him some by the same herald, whereat the earl felt much good will towards him.

Friday, the twenty-fifth day of the said month, arrived within Orleans nine horses laden with corn, herrings, and other provisions.

The Sunday immediately following, being the last day of the said month of February, the river increased in such wise, and so greatly, that the French within Orleans firmly believed that the two boulevards constructed by the English on the said river, to the right of Saint Lawrence, as well as that of the Tournelles, were undermined and beaten down; for it rose as high as the cannoneers on the boulevards, and the current was so strong and so rapid, that it was difficult to believe. But the

---

* The only explanation to be found of this word is, that it constituted a part of the ancient costume which covered the side from the girdle downwards; being derived from *Pannus*.

English applied themselves with so much diligence by day as well as by night, that the boulevards continued in the same state, and the river also in a short time went down. And notwithstanding this, the English threw several bombs and discharged cannons, which did much harm to the houses and the edifices of the city.

This same day, the bombarding machines of the city, which were placed at the cross of the mills at the Postern Chesneau to discharge against the Tournelles, fired so terribly against them, that they beat down a great portion of the wall.

The Thursday, being the third day of March, the French sallied forth in the morning against the English, constructing upon this occasion a fosse, for the purpose of proceeding under cover from their boulevard of the wooden cross to Saint Lardre of Orleans, in order that the English might not see them, nor plant cannon nor bombs. This sally caused great injury to the English ; for nine of them were there taken prisoners. And besides, there were killed by Master John five men by two discharges from his culverin. Of which five was the lord de Grez, nephew of the defunct earl of Salisbury, who was captain of Yenuville, and mightily regretted by the English, because he was of great hardihood and valour.

This same day was there also a very grand skirmish. For the French sallied out of Orleans, and advanced nigh unto the boulevard of the English, being at the wooden cross; and gained a cannon which discharged stones as large as a bowl. And besides, they conveyed into the city two silver cups, a robe furred with martern skins, and several hatchets, javelins, quivers, arrows, and other implements of war. But immediately afterwards sallied the English from their camp and their bastilles, bearing nine standards, which they unfurled, and drove the French until very near the boulevard of Banier gate; and this done they retired. But almost incontinent, they returned and charged so strongly and with such animosity upon the French, and so closely pursued them, that many of them precipitated themselves into the fosse of the aforesaid gate. Against them those of Orleans hurled stones in great quantities, wherefore among others who there fell, was one Stephen Fauveau, native of Orleans town, the which took place, because he could not run. In this skirmish did the English kill, wound, and take many prisoners; and in particular, they took a right valiant squire of Gascony, named Regnault Guillaume de Vernade, who was grievously wounded.

The ensuing day, which was Friday, departed about three hundred English combatants, who went to collect together vine-stakes in the vineyards that were in the neighbourhood of Saint Lardre and of Saint John de la Ruelle; wherefore the tocsin was sounded from the belfry. But, notwithstanding this, they seized and conducted as prisoners some poor labouring men who were cultivating their vines. And on this same day arrived within Orleans, twelve horses laden with corn, herrings, and other provisions.

The Saturday after, fifth of the said month of March, was fired off from a culverin of Orleans, a ball which killed a lord of England, for whom the English performed great mourning.

The ensuing day, which was Sunday, arrived within Orleans seven horses laden with herrings and other provisions.

Monday following, the seventh of the said month of March, arrived six horses charged with herrings. From another quarter the English discharged many bombs and fired off cannon, which fell in the street of Hostelleries, and did great injury in divers places. And there arrived also in their camp about forty Englishmen from England.

The ensuing Tuesday, sallied forth many French, and they met six tradesmen and a *demoisel*, conveying to the camp nine horses laden with provisions, which they seized and escorted into Orleans. This same day there came two hundred English who had left Jargeau; and in like manner arrived also in their camp and their bastilles many others coming from the garrison of Beausse. And upon this account did the French think that it was their intention to attack one of their boulevards. Therefore did they keep themselves upon their guard, getting all necessary things in readiness for their defence, according to the *ruse de guerre*.

The following day, which was Wednesday, and no Frenchman being there found, was an hole nearly pierced through the wall of the Almonry of Orleans, to the right of Paris gate, so that an opening had been made there to pass a man at arms. Besides this, there was found a wall all newly raised, where there were two cannoneers. And it was not known why it was so constructed; some presuming that it was for good, and others for evil. Nevertheless, be it as it may, the master of the said Almonry ran away, as soon as he perceived that it was discovered. For, in the first instance, he was in great peril from the popular commotion which happened on that day, as a great stir and noise in consequence took place in the said Almonry.

The following day, which was Thursday, the Bastard of Orleans caused to be hanged to a tree, in the suburbs and near the ruins of Burgundy gate, two Frenchmen at arms, being at Gallois de Villiers, because they had broken their *parole*. But as soon as they were dead, he caused them to be cut down and interred in the same suburbs.

In another direction the English proceeded this same day to Saint Loup of Orleans, and there began to erect a bastille, which they fortified; still determined to continue their siege against Orleans.

For the raising of the same, incontinent, proceeded

on her route Jeanne la Pucelle, accompanied by a great number of lords, knights, esquires, and men at war, supplied with provisions and with artillery : and she took her leave of the king, who expressly commanded the lords and the men at war, that they should be obedient unto her as to himself, and in such sort did they act.

The following Friday, the eleventh day of the said month of March, was rung the tocsin from the belfry; because the English being at Saint Loup ran as far as Saint Euverte; and there, near unto the vineyards, took several labourers at their vines, and led them away prisoners.

The ensuing day sallied forth several from the garrison of Orleans, and at their return brought in six prisoners.

Tuesday ensuing, the fifteenth of the said month, arrived at night, within the city, the Bastard de Lange, who brought with him six horses laden with powder for cannon. And on the same day thirty English quitted the bastille of Saint Loup, being disguised as women, pretending to come for the purpose of collecting wood and the faggots of vine branches, with many other women, who conveyed some into Orleans. But, when they perceived their advantage, they sallied forth hastily upon the labourers then cultivating the vines in the vicinity of Saint Marc and La Borde aux Mignons; and there acted in such sort, that they sent nine or ten prisoners into their bastille.

The following day, which was Wednesday, the marshal Saint Severe quitted Orleans, as well for the purpose of repairing to the king, as to go and take possession of several lands which had devolved to him by the death of the lord of Chasteau-Brun, his wife's brother. But he promised to those of the city, that he would continue but a short space absent, and they were right well content. For they loved and they prized him, because he had done them many good actions, and also for the great feats of arms which he and his people had enacted for their defence.

This same day, did the English of the bastille of Saint Loup convey many laden chariots to their bastille of Saint Lawrence. And when they were in front of Saint Ladre, they uttered a loud cry, in consequence whereof the tocsin of the belfry was rung. For the French of Orleans believed that they intended to attack some of their boulevards.

The following Thursday, seventeenth day of the said month, departed this life, Master Alain Dubey, Provost of Orleans; who died of a natural death. At which, those of the city were passing doleful, because he had always acted with justice.

The Saturday ensuing, the nineteenth of the same month, and upon Easter Even, did the English discharge into Orleans several large bombs, and fired off cannons, in such wise, that they had never done before, whereby they did great evil and damage. For the stone from one of the bombs as well killed as wounded seven persons, from the which died a tin-pot maker, named John Tonnau. And besides this, another stone from a cannon fell before the hotel of the late Berthault Mignon, from which were killed, as well as wounded, five persons.

The Monday following, the twenty-first of the said month of March, the appearance of the English caused the tocsin of the belfry to be rung, and there sallied forth from Orleans a great power, as well of men at war as of citizens and others of the surrounding country, who had retreated thither; so that they went and attacked the boulevards newly constructed by the English to the right of the Grange of Cuivret. But when those who guarded the same beheld them approach, they quitted the boulevards and took to flight, and acted in such sort, that they gained their bastille of Saint Lawrence, and carried away from thence whatsoever they could convey of their property and their artillery. And immediately after sallied forth the English from the said bastille, uttering marvellous cries, and in such power and hardihood, that they drove back the French even to the almonry of Saint Pouvair. But they did not pass beyond on account of the French returning against them, so charging them by the firing of cannons, culverins and other discharges, that they compelled them to stand still, and retreat in great haste to their bastilles. From this skirmish experienced the English a great loss in

one of their gentlemen, a native of England, named
Robin Heron; for he had shown himself a valiant
man at arms.

The ensuing day there was also a very smart
skirmish, and the tocsin from the belfry was rung;
because the English sallied out in great numbers
against the French, who had gone forth to the
environs of Saint Pouvair, beyond which they
were received by the English, who drove them back
to the almonry of Saint Povair and to Turpin field.
Till in the end, having recovered force, they struck
amidst the English host with such great hardihood,
that they forced them to fall back in the rear of their
bastilles. One of the which, not having sufficient
care of himself, fell into a well near unto the cross
Morin, within which he was killed by the French.

This same day, being Tuesday, the Pucelle being
at Blois, where she sojourned, awaiting a reinforcement of those that were to accompany her, but who
were not yet arrived, she despatched an herald to
the English lords and captains encamped before
Orleans; and by him wrote a letter, which she
herself dictated; having at the top, as principal
title:

"JESUS MARIA;"

and then commencing at the margin as followeth;

" King of England, account for yourself to the
" King of heaven concerning his blood royal.

" Give up the keys to the Pucelle of all the good
" cities which you have forced. She is come on
" the part of God to restore the blood royal, and
" is quite ready to make peace ; if you will act
" justly. Therefore put down your deposit, and
" pay for that which you have held from him.
" King of England, if thus you will not do, I am
" chieftain of war ; in every place where I shall find
" your people in France, if they will not obey, I
" will cause them to go out, willing or not. And
" if they will obey, I will take them in mercy.
" Believe that if they will not obey, the Pucelle
" comes to kill them ; she comes on the part of the
" King of heaven; body for body, you shall be driven
" out of France. And the Pucelle promises and
" certifies to you, that she will cause so great a
" ravage, that for a thousand years past has none
" so great been seen, if you do not act justly.
" And firmly believe, that the King of heaven will
" despatch more force to her and her good people
" at arms, than you could destroy in a hundred
" attacks. Between you archers companions in
" arms, who are before Orleans, in the name of God
" go back into your own country. And if thus you
" do not do, take you heed of the Pucelle, and call
" to mind your injuries done. Do not take much
" into your opinion, that you shall long hold France
" from the King of heaven and the son of *Sancta*
" *Maria ;* for king Charles, the true inheritor, will

" hold it, to whom God hath given it, who will
" enter into Paris in good company. If you do
" not believe the news of God and of the Pucelle,
" in whatsoever place we shall find you, we will
" fight you desperately, and then you shall see
" which of the two hath the best right, God or
" yourself. William de la Pole, earl of Suffolk,
" John, lord Talbot, Thomas, lord of Escalles (lord
" Scales) lieutenant of the duke of Bedford, calling
" himself regent of the kingdom of France for the
" king of England; return for answer, if you will
" conclude a peace or not, at the city of Orleans.
" If you do not do it, of your injuries you will have
" cause to remember.   Duke of Bedford, calling
" yourself regent of France for the king of England,
" the Pucelle requireth and prayeth you, that you
" do not cause great destruction. If you refuse
" justice, she will conduct herself in such sort that
" the French shall perform the greatest feat that
" ever yet was achieved in Christendom.   Written
" this Tuesday of the week.   Listen to the news
" from God and from the Pucelle."
    " To the duke of Bedford, calling himself regent of
" the kingdom of France for the king of England."
    When the English lords and captains had read
and understood this letter, they were marvellously
in choler; and in spite towards the Pucelle,
uttered concerning her many villanous words, especially calling her a strumpet, a cow-keeper, and

threatening to cause her to be burned. They kept as prisoner the carrier of the letter, regarding in derision every thing that she had written to them.

The next ensuing Thursday, the twenty-fourth of the same month of March, and the day of Holy Thursday, the English discharged a bomb within Orleans, the stone from which fell into the street *de la Charpenterie,* killing and wounding three persons : during the which day, a great report was spread, that some of the city intended traitorously to deliver the same into the hands of the English. Wherefore this same day and on the following, being the eve of Holy Lent, and upon the day itself, continued the men at war there in garrison, with the citizens and others having thither also retreated ; continually in arms, each being upon his guard, as well in the city and upon the walls, as on the surrounding boulevards.

The day of Holy Easter, which was the twenty-seventh of the said month of March, one thousand four hundred twenty and nine, was a truce ratified and given on either side between the French in Orleans, and the English carrying on the siege.

The Tuesday ensuing, twenty-ninth of the same month, arrived within the city a great number of cattle and other provisions.

The following Friday, which was the first day of the month of April, and in this same year one thousand four hundred twenty and nine, went forth the

E

French to skirmish with the English, near the boulevard, which they had newly constructed at the
Grange Cuyveret. Wherefore, they all sallied forth
against them, having two standards, and there continued for a long space of time, the one before the
other, and discharging of cannons the one against
the other, as well as culverins and other shots, so
that on either side there were many wounded.

The day following arrived within Orleans, nine
oxen and two horses laden with kids and other
provisions. And upon the same day after the hour
of twelve, did the French forthwith skirmish against
the boulevard of Grange Cuyveret, at which place
they were well received; for, from the bastille of
Saint Lawrence, sallied forth against them about
four hundred combatants, bearing with them two
standards, one of which was that of Saint George,
being the one half white and the other red, and
having in the middle a red cross; and they came as
far as Saint Maturin and to Turpin field, charging
strongly upon the French, the which were ranged
in good order of battle by the Bastard of Orleans,
the lord of Graville, La Hire, Poton, and Tilloy; so
that they behaved themselves right valiantly, and
there was a very hot and a strong skirmish. During
the which cannons, bombs, culverins, and other
shots, were marvellously discharged upon either side;
so that in the end there were several killed and
wounded as well of the French as of the English.

The Sunday following, named *Quasimodo*, which is the concluding day of Easter, sallied out many inhabitants from Orleans, and took possession of a barge near unto Saint Loup, wherein were nine tons of wine, a hog and venison, which were intended to be carried to the English, in the said bastille of Saint Loup; but those of Orleans drank the wine, and ate the hog and the venison. And upon the same day was a smart skirmish delivered by the pages of the French and those of the English between the two islands of Saint Lawrence, they having no shields, excepting small wicker baskets; and they threw stones and flints the one against the other. And in the end the French caused the English to fall back; to see the which was a multitude of people. And at this skirmish and others that often took place before Orleans with the French pages, was one of them their captain, a gentleman of Dauphiny, named Aymart de Puiseux; the which was afterwards named *gold-headed*, by La Hire, as well upon account of his being so fair, as also, that he was very enlightened and of great hardihood among the others; which was after showed in many feats of arms, not only in this kingdom, but in Germany and others.

The ensuing day, being Monday, just at the opening of the city gates, arrived a number of French, who had scoured the country as far as Meung, the captain of which they had killed, and brought with them forty-three heads of large cattle, many of the which had broken horns.

The same day, after twelve, another battle took place between the pages, who were attired as before; and there was killed by a blow from a stone, one of the English pages, and there were also many wounded on either side. So that, in the end, the English pages got possession of the standard from the French pages.

The Tuesday, fifth of the said month, at the opening of the gates, arrived within Orleans an hundred and one hogs and six fat oxen, which were conducted by dealers from Berry; the same passing to the right of Saint Aignan of Orleans. Against the which, very speedily, sallied out the English from their tournelles so soon as they had perceived them. But it was too late, for they lost their labour.

This same day, also, arrived two horses laden with butter and with cheese, and seventeen hogs which were brought from Chasteaudun. And there also arrived news that the French in garrison at the said city of Chasteaudun, had, as well killed and taken, as put to the route, from thirty to forty English, who were the bearers of much money and other things to the English camp.

The Thursday after, the seventh of the said month, arrived for the English at the bastille of Saint Lawrence, much provisions and other accoutrements for war, without finding any hindrance.

The following day, towards the morning, arrived within the city twenty-six horned cattle, which some French, forming part of the garrison, had gained in Normandy.

The Saturday ensuing, ninth of the same month, arrived also, towards the morning, seventeen hogs and eight horses; two of which were laden with kids and hogs, and the other six with corn; the same being brought from Chasteaudun. In another quarter the English about this period raised another boulevard, and made a fosse to the right of the Ars Press, in order to prevent which sallied out the French, proceeding as far as the boulevard. But a dreadful rain began to fall, and most marvellous weather, which lasted during a length of time; wherefore they could not accomplish their intention, and so returned within the city without doing any thing.

The Tuesday next following, the twelfth of the said month, many French took their departure from Orleans by night, and proceeded to Saint Marceau or Val de Loire, and demolished and broke open the church, in the which they found twenty English, whom they took and brought prisoners within the city; in which affair they lost two of their companions. And on the ensuing day was conveyed great quantity of money into Orleans for the paying of the garrison, who had acted gallantly.

Friday, the fifteenth of the said month of April,

was built and finished a very handsome and a strong
bastille, very well made, between Saint Povair and
Saint Lardre, in a spot which comprised a great space,
wherein were placed and remained many lords and
English gentlemen, together with numerous other
men at war, who were desirous of guarding on that
side, to prevent any provisions from being conveyed
into Orleans, as they had before witnessed upon
divers occasions, in spite of the forces which were
in their other bastilles.

On the following day, came from Blois to Orleans,
by the road of Fleury aux Choux, a quantity of
cattle and other provisions, which the English
thought to take possession of, and therefore advanced
accordingly, but too late, for the tocsin of the belfry
was rung to afford succour for the provisions; which
was done, in such sort that they arrived in safety
within the city.

This same day, came running before the tournelles
about fifty French men at arms, being part of the
garrison of Sauloigne, and they brought full fifteen
English prisoners. And on the night after this
same day, some French departed from the city, who
had killed three English that were keeping watch
near L'Orbecte.

The following Sunday, being the seventeenth of the
same month of April, arrived within Orleans, Poton
de Sainctestrailles and other ambassadors, who had
repaired to the duke of Burgundy and the Count de

Ligny, bringing with them the trumpeter of the said duke of Burgundy. The which, as soon as he had learned the request of those of Orleans, took his departure, and with him Messire John de Luxembourg, to join the duke of Bedford, calling himself Regent of this kingdom for the king of England; then making known unto him, what sorrow it was to the duke of Orleans; and required and prayed of him very earnestly, that it would please him to raise and cause the siege to be removed from before his principal city of Orleans; to the which would not acquiesce in any sort, to either of them, the duke of Bedford. Wherefore the duke of Burgundy was not content; and upon this occasion sent with the ambassadors his trumpeter, who, on his part, commanded all those of his lands and cities subject unto him, and being at the said siege, that they would go and take their departure, and that they should in nowise do evil unto those of Orleans. In obedience to the which commandment in great haste went away and departed many Burgundians, Picards, Champenois, and numerous others of the countries and under obedience to the said duke of Burgundy.

The following day in the morning, about four of the clock after midnight, sallied out the French against the camp of the English, and so conducted themselves, that at their entrance they killed a part of their watch and gained one of their standards,

and there continued for a long space of time ; during
which they did great injury to their adversaries,
the which cried, much affrighted, to arms, and
ranged themselves in order of battle the best they
could, turning against the French ; who knowing
that they were preparing to arm in great force,
issued forth from their camp, where they had gained
several silver cups, many robes of martern skins, and
a great number of bows, quivers, arrows and other
accoutrements of war.   Nevertheless the English
followed them, and came up so near that a very
great and smart skirmish took place, wherein many
were killed and wounded, as well on the one side as
on the other.   And specially was killed, from the
discharge of a culverin, him who carried the standard
of the English ; notwithstanding those of the city
were not without sustaining great injury, the which
was fully apparent upon their return, by the mourning performed by the women of Orleans, crying
and lamenting their fathers, husbands, brothers, and
relations, killed and wounded in this skirmish.   And
this same day were given up the bodies upon either
side, the which were interred in holy ground.

The Tuesday following, and the nineteenth day
of the month of April, about the hour of vespers,
arrived in the camp and bastilles of the English,
a great quantity of provisions and other necessaries
for war, and with them many men at arms who
escorted them.

The ensuing day, about the fourth hour of the morning, departed from Orleans a captain named Amadie, and sixteen men at arms on horseback accompanying him, who went in the direction of Fleury aux Choux, at which place the English were stationed, who had conducted the last provisions, and they acted in such wise, that they escorted six English prisoners, whom they took, with several horses, bows, quivers, and other accoutrements for war.

About this same period, the English fortified Sainct John le Blanc ou Val de Loire, and there stationed a watch to guard the passage.

The Thursday next ensuing, arrived within Orleans, three horses laden with powder for cannon, and many other things. In another direction, on this same day, those of Orleans pointed several cannon in order to fire against the English; because they thought that it was their duty to prepare a smart skirmish, for their welcome; and they discharged marvellously against them, being assailed, wherefore they returned back into their camp; but many of them departed on the following night, to go to the rencounter of provisions transporting towards the city, wishing to conquer and to seize them.

The Saturday, being the twenty-third of the same month of April, arrived within Orleans, four horses charged with powder for cannon and provisions.

And upon the ensuing day, entered Le Bourg de Mascaran, accompanied by forty combatants. And the next approaching day, which was Tuesday the twenty-sixth day of the same month, entered also Alain Degiron, accompanied by one hundred combatants.

The following Wednesday, the French sallied forth, and proceeded in mighty great haste and in comely array as far as the Cross of Fleury, to render assistance to any dealers, bringing provisions from the environs of Blois for victualling the city; because they had received news of their having hindrance; but they did not proceed further, on account of their having been there before, and it was told them that they would do nothing there, for that the English had already unburthened them. However, from another part, there came to them a reinforcement of sixty combatants advancing from Beaune in Gastinois, who brought them other hogs.

The day following, being Thursday the twenty-eighth day of the said month of April, arrived within Orleans after mid-day, a very renowned captain, named Messire Fleurentin d'Illiers, and with him the brother of La Hire, accompanied by four hundred combatants, who came from Chasteaudun. And upon this same day was a strong and a smart skirmish; because that the English came to skirmish before the boulevards of Orleans. But the men at war, and many citizens of Orleans, sallied out against them, and chased them even into their boulevards ; and did so much, that they killed and caused many to be drowned ; and the others fell into the ditches of their boulevards, which were then near the Grange of Cuyveret, and the Wine-Press of Ars, in the valley, which was there from ancient times. However, it became necessary for the French to abandon their skirmish, and return into the city, on account of the multitude of cannons, culverins, and other discharges which the English fired against them so thickly, and in such sort, that many in short were there killed on one side and on the other, and on their return one of the French fell into a well where he was killed.

In another direction the Pucelle and other lords and captains being with her, knew full well that the English amongst themselves despised and mocked her and her letter, having retained the herald who was bearer of the same. Wherefore they determined that they would march forward before their men at arms, provisions and artillery, and that they would pass by Sauloïgne, because the greatest power of the English was on the side of Beausse ; so that of this nothing was told to the Pucelle, whose intention was to go and to pass before them by force of arms. And in consequence she gave orders that all the men at war should *confess themselves,* and that they should leave behind them all their *silly women* and their baggage ; and thus they departed and proceeded in such sort, that they came unto a village named Checy, where they halted the ensuing night.

The next Friday, being the twenty-ninth of the same month, arrived the certain news in Orleans, how the king had sent by Sauloigne victuals, powder, cannon, and other necessaries for war, under the direction of the Pucelle. The which came on the part of our Lord, to victual and strengthen the city and cause the siege to be raised, whereat those of Orleans were mightily comforted. And because it was said that the English would use their endeavours to seize the provisions, it was ordered that every one should arm and be ready in the city, which was done accordingly. This day, also, there arrived fifty combatants on foot, habited and bearing javelins and other accoutrements for war, coming from the country of Gastinois, where they had been in garrison. On this same day was a very brisk skirmish, because the French wanted to appoint the place and the hour for the receiving of the provisions which were conducting to them. And to make the English believe that it was otherwise, they sallied forth in great force, and went running to skirmish before Saint Loup of Orleans. And no sooner did they approach than there were many killed, wounded, and taken prisoners on either side, so that the French transported within their city one of the standards of the English. And while this skirmish was taking place, the provisions and the artillery, which the Pucelle had escorted as far as Checy, entered into the city.   To meet the which, proceeded as far as the said village, the Bastard of Orleans, and other knights, esquires, and men at war, as well of Orleans as of other parts, mightily rejoicing at her coming, who all showed her great reverence, and there was fine feasting; and so did she to them.   And it was there concluded by all together that she should not enter into Orleans until the night, to escape the tumult of the people; and that the Marshal de Rays and Messire Ambrose de Loré, who, by the commandment of the king, had conducted her thither, should return to Blois, at which place lived many lords and French men at war, which was done accordingly.   For thus, about the eighth hour of the night, notwithstanding all the English, who raised every impediment, she entered completely armed and mounted upon a white horse, and caused her standard to be borne before her, which was white also, whereon there were two angels holding each a Fleur-de-lis in the hand, and at the tail was painted, like an Annunciation, which was the image of our Lady, having before her an Angel presenting to her a Lis.   She thus entering into Orleans, had at her left hand side the Bastard of Orleans, completely armed and mounted most richly.   And after came many other nobles and valiant lords, esquires, captains, and men at

war, besides many of the garrison, and also of the
citizens of Orleans, who had gone forth to meet her.
From another quarter there came to receive her
other men at war with citizens and their wives of
Orleans, bearing a great number of torches, and
testifying such joy as if they saw God descend
amongst them, and not without cause; for they had
much weariness, labours, and pains, and that which
is worse, great doubts of not being succoured and
losing both their bodies and their goods.   But they
now felt all comforted, and those besieged, by the
divine virtue, which they were told was in this
simple Pucelle, regarded her with much affection, as
well men and women as little children.   And there
was such a marvellous pressing in order to touch her,
or the horse upon which she rode, that one of them,
who was bearer of a torch, approached so near unto
her standard that the fire caught the tail thereof.
Wherefore she struck the horse with her spurs, and
turned it so dexterously towards the standard, of
which she extinguished the fire, as if she had for a
long time followed the wars; and this was by the
men at war esteemed a great marvel, as also by the
citizens of Orleans.   So they accompanied her the
length of their town and city, making great feasting,
and in great honour they all escorted her near unto
the gate Regnart to the hotel of James Boucher,
then treasurer of the duke of Orleans, where she
was received with great joy, with her two brothers,

and the two gentlemen and their valet, who had accompanied them from the country of Barrois.

The day following, which was Saturday, last day of the same month of April, sallied out La Hire, Messire Florent D'Illiers, with many other knights and esquires of the garrison, and a number of citizens, and charged with unfurled banners upon the force of the English, insomuch so, that they caused them to fall back and gained the spot where they had established the watch, which they then held at the place of Saint Povair, within two bow-shots of the city; in consequence whereof loud cries were heard the whole length of the town, at the which hour every one transported fire, straw and faggots, in order to kindle the fire in the lodgings of the English within their camp. But nothing was effected, on account of the English uttering forth dreadful cries, and that they arranged themselves in order for battle. And on this account the French returned; howsoever, before their coming, a very long and smart skirmish had taken place, during which the cannons, culverins, and bombs, fired marvellously, insomuch so, that many were killed, wounded, and taken prisoners on either side.

Towards night-fall, the Pucelle despatched two heralds to the English camp; requiring that they would send back the herald by whom she had forwarded her letters from Blois. And at the same time, the Bastard of Orleans made known unto

them, that in case he was not sent back, he would
cause to die by a bad death, all the English who
were then prisoners in Orleans ; together with all
such as by any English noblemen had been sent to
treat concerning the ransom of the others.   In
consequence of this, the chiefs of the host sent
back the heralds and the messengers of the Pucelle,
making known unto her by them, that they would
burn and cause her to perish by fire, and that she
was nothing more than a bunter, and that being
such she might return to keep the cows, whereat
she felt much ire.   And upon this occasion, on the
coming in of night, she repaired to the boulevard
of the beautiful cross upon the bridge ; and from
thence harangued Glacidas (Glasdale) and other
English being in the Tournelles, telling them on
the part of God, to surrender themselves up only
to save their lives whole.   But Glacidas (Glasdale)
and those of his band answered villanously, offering
her injuries and calling her cow-keeper as before,
and crying aloud that they would burn her if they
could catch her in their power.   At the which, she
was in no ways irritated, and answered them that
they lied ; and thus having said, she retreated into
the city.

The following Sunday, which was the first day of
May of this year one thousand four hundred twenty
and nine, departed from the city the Bastard of
Orleans, to repair to Blois in order to meet the

count de Clermont, the marshal of Saint Severe, the lord de Rays, and many other knights, esquires, and men at war. And this same day also, quitted the city the Pucelle, accompanied by sundry knights and esquires, because those of Orleans testified so great a wish to behold her, that they almost broke down the gates of the hotel wherein she was lodged; and for the seeing her, there were so many distinguished personages of the city along the streets where she went, that it was with great difficulty one could pass, for the populace could not solace themselves enough with beholding her. And unto all it appeared a great marvel, how she could hold herself as she did with such gentility on horseback. And in verity also, she maintained herself as nobly upon all occasions, as could have done a man at arms who had followed the wars from his youth upwards.

This same day again spoke the Pucelle to the English near unto the cross Morin; bidding them to surrender themselves only safe and alive, so that they might return by the will of God into England, or that she would irritate them. But they answered her with as villanous words as they had before done from the Tournelles; and she in consequence returned her way into Orleans.

Monday the second day of May, the Pucelle quitted Orleans, being on horseback, and immediately went to inspect the bastilles and the camp of

F

the English, after whom ran the people in very great crowds, taking much pleasure in seeing her and in surrounding her. And when she had reconnoitred and beheld at her pleasure the fortifications of the English, she returned to the church of the Saint Cross of Orleans within the city, where she heard the vespers.

On the Wednesday, fourth day of the said month of May, the Pucelle sallied forth into the fields, having in her company the lord de Villars, and Messires Fleurent D'Illiers, La Hire, Alain Giron, Jamet de Tilloy, and several other esquires and men at war, being in all five hundred combatants; and she went to the meeting of the Bastard of Orleans, of Messire de Rays, of the marshal of Saint Severe, of the baron of Colouces, and of several other knights and esquires, together with other men at war habited and with javelins, and bearing leaden mallets, who were conducting provisions, which those of Bourges, Angiers, Tours, and Blois, had despatched to those of Orleans; the same being received with very great joy into the city; which they entered in front of the bastille of the English, who did not dare come out at all, but kept themselves strongly upon their guard. And this same day, after twelve at noon, departed from the city the Pucelle and the Bastard of Orleans, conducting in their company a great number of nobles with about fifteen hundred combatants, and they went to attack the bastille of Saint Loup, where they experienced very great resistance. For the English, who had strongly fortified it, defended the same right valiantly during the space of three hours, which time the assault was carried on with great acrimony; in such a manner that at length the French took it by force, and killed an hundred and fourteen English, retaining and conducting forty prisoners within their city. But before this they beat down, burned and demolished the whole of this bastille, to the great rage, damage, and displeasure of the English; part of whom being in the bastille of Saint Pouvair, sallied forth with mighty power during this assault, desiring to give assistance to their people; whereof those of Orleans were advertised by means of the tocsin of the belfry, which sounded twice. Wherefore the marshal of Saint Severe, the lord of Graville, the baron de Colouces, and many other knights, esquires, men at war, and citizens, being in all six hundred combatants, sallied out hastily from Orleans, and marched to the fields in very good order for battle against the English; the which abandoned their enterprise and the succouring of their companions, when they beheld the manner of the French thus sallying forth in order for battle, and returned mourning and in rage within their bastille, from whence they had issued in very great haste. But notwithstanding their return, those of the bastille still defended themselves more and more. Yet in the end it was taken by the French, for thus it is said.

The Thursday ensuing, which was the Ascension of our Lord, a council was held by the Pucelle, the Bastard of Orleans, the marshal of Saint Severe, and de Rays, the lord de Graville, the baron de Colouces, the lord de Villars, the lord de Sainctes-trailles, the lord de Gaucourt, La Hire, the lord de Covraze, Messire Denis de Chailly, Thibaut de Termes, Jamet de Tilloy, and a Scottish captain called Canede, and other captains and chiefs of war, as also the citizens of Orleans, to advise and to conclude what ought to be decided upon in regard to the English, who held them in a state of siege. Wherefore it was agreed that the Tournelles and the boulevards at the end of the bridge should be assailed ; because the English had marvellously for-tified them with engines of defence, and a great number of persons well used to the art of war. And the captains therefore received command that each should hold himself in readiness on the morning of the following day, having all things necessary for the making an assault; the which orders were well obeyed. For by the night was so much diligence manifested, that all was ready by early morning, and announced unto the Pucelle ; the which sallied out of Orleans, having in her company the Bastard of Orleans, the marshals of Saint Severe, and de Rays, the lord of Graville, Messire Fleurend D'Illiers,

La Hire, and many other knights, esquires, and about four thousand combatants, and passed the river Loire between Saint Loup and the new tower; and *prima facie*, they took Saint John Le Blanc, which the English had repaired and fortified; and then retired upon a small island, which is to the right of Saint Aignan. And then the English of the Tournelles sallied out in great power, uttering loud cries, and came to charge them desperately and very near. But the Pucelle and La Hire, on all sides, joined together with their own people, and fought with such great force and hardihood against the English, that they obliged them to fall back to their boulevards and Tournelles. And immediately on coming up commenced such an assault upon the boulevard and the bastille near that spot, and fortified by the English on the ground where lately stood the church of the Augustins, that they took the same by force, delivering a great number of Frenchmen prisoners, and killing several English who were therein and had most obstinately defended the same, insomuch that many gallant feats of arms were performed upon either side. And the ensuing night the French commenced the siege before the Tournelles and the surrounding boulevards. Therefore, those of Orleans used great diligence in conveying, during the whole of the night, bread, wine, and other provisions, to the men at war carrying on the siege.

The day after, by the dawn of morning, which was

Saturday the sixth day of May, the French assailed
the boulevards and the Tournelles, even while the
English were engaged in fortifying them.   And
there took place a most marvellous assault, during
which were performed many gallant feats of arms,
as well by the assailants as those who defended,
because the English had great numbers of bold combatants, and were abundantly furnished with every
instrument of defence.   And well did they also
show it; for notwithstanding the French placed
their scaling ladders in divers places and very
thickly, and attacked in front the very highest of
their fortifications with such valour and hardihood,
that it seemed, from their bold array, that they would
fain be immortal; yet were they discomfited several
times, and hurled from the top to the bottom, as well
by cannon and other discharges, as by hatchets,
lances, javelins, leaden mallets, and even with their
own hands; so that many of the French were killed
and wounded, and among the others was there
wounded the Pucelle, being struck by an arrow
between the shoulder and the throat, so much in
front that it passed through.   At which all the
assailants were mightily doleful and in rage, and
more especially the Bastard of Orleans and other
captains, who advanced towards her, saying, that it
would be better to give up the assault until the
ensuing day.   But she consoled them by many fine
and hardy speeches, exhorting them to maintain

their courage; but they, not believing in her words, left off the assault, and retreated behind, wishing to carry back their artillery until the morrow : whereat she was very doleful, and bespake them :

" In the name of God, you will very briefly enter, " do not have a doubt; and the English will no " longer possess strength to oppose you. Where- " fore, if you halt a little, drink and eat."

Which they did forthwith, and it was a marvel that they obeyed her. So when they had drank, she said to them:

" On the part of God return to the assault imme- " diately; for without a doubt the English will no " longer have strength to defend themselves, and " their Tournelles and their boulevards will be taken."

And having spoken thus, she left her standard, and proceeded on horseback to a by-place to deliver her orison to the Lord; and said to a gentleman who chanced to be near,

" Take good heed, when the tail of my standard " shall be towards, or touch the boulevard."

Which he soon after told her was the case, exclaiming ; " Jeanne, the tail touches it ;" whereto she made answer : " All is yours, and now enter."

The which words were shortly after proved to be a prophecy; for when the valiant chiefs and men at arms, who had continued within Orleans, perceived that they wished to assault anew, many of them sallied forth from the city over the bridge. And in consequence of several arches being broken, they led with them a carpenter, and transported gutters and ladders, wherewith they formed planks; when, perceiving that they were not long enough to reach both extremities of one of the broken arches, they joined a small piece of wood to one of the longest gutters, so that it held fast. Over the which first passed, completely armed, a very valiant knight of the Order of Rhodes, called of Saint John of Jerusalem, named Brother Nicole de Giresme; and after his example several others also, which is since said to have been more a miracle of our Lord than any other thing, because the gutter was marvellously long and narrow, and high in the air, without having any support. The which having passed over, joined with their other companions in the assault, which had began shortly before; for, as soon as they had recommenced, the English lost all power of longer resisting; so that they could not re-enter the boulevard within the Tournelles, and in consequence very few were enabled to save themselves. For of four to five hundred combatants, who were there, the whole were either killed or drowned, excepting only a few who were retained prisoners, amongst the which there were no great lords; because Glacidas (William Glasdale), who was the captain and high renowned in feats of arms, the lord de Moulins (Moolins), the lord de Pommier (Poynings), the bailiff of Mente, and many other knights ban-

nerets, and English noblemen, were drowned; for in
endeavouring to save themselves, the bridge broke
under them, which proved a great shock to the
English host, and a considerable loss to the valiant
French, who, for their ransom, would have much increased their finances. Nevertheless they showed
great joy, and praised our Lord for this most signal
victory which had been accorded to them, as truly it
was their duty so to do. For, it is said, that this
assault, which lasted from the morning until the
setting of the sun, was so stoutly assailed and defended, that it was one of the most noble feats of arms
which had been achieved for a long time before.
And truly was there wrought a miracle of our Lord,
performed at the request of Saint Aignan and Saint
Euverte, anciently bishops and patrons of Orleans,
as it seemed to all appearance, according to common
opinion, and even by those persons who on the
same day were brought into Orleans; one of whom
certified that unto himself and to all the other
English of the Tournelles and the boulevards it
appeared, when they were assailed, as if they saw a
marvellous host of people, and that all the world
was there assembled. Wherefore the clergy and
the people of Orleans sung most devoutly *Te Deum
Laudamus*, and caused all the bells of the city to be
rang, most humbly returning thanks to our Lord and
the two Saints Confessors for this glorious and
divine consolation; and much rejoicing was there

testified on all sides, bestowing marvellous praises
on their valiant defenders, and especially, and above
all, unto Jeanne la Pucelle, who remained during this
night, as well as the lords, captains, and men at war
with her, in the midst of the fields, as well to guard
the Tournelles so valiantly conquered, as to ascertain
whether the English, on the side of Saint Lawrence,
would not issue forth, desirous of succouring or of
avenging their companions. But they testified no
such wish: wherefore upon the ensuing morning,
being the Sunday, and the seventh day of May, this
same year one thousand four hundred twenty and nine,
they retired from their bastille, as did also the English
of Saint Povair, and of other parts, and raising the
siege, placed themselves in battle array. Therefore
the Pucelle, the marshal of Saint Severe and of Rays,
the lord de Graville, the baron de Coulouces, Messire
Fleurent d'Illiers, the lord de Corraze, the lord de
Sainctes Trailles, La Hire, Alain Giron, Jamet du
Tilloy, and many other valiant men at war and
citizens, sallied forth from Orleans in great power,
and placed and ranged themselves in order of battle
before them. And in such manner they were very
near the one unto the other, during the space of one
hour, without touching each other. Which the
French endured most uneasily, in obedience to the
will of la Pucelle, who commanded and ordered them
from the very commencement, that for the love and
in honour of the Saint Sunday, they would not begin

the battle nor assail the English. But that in case the English should attack them, that they should defend themselves nobly and with hardihood, and that they should have no fear, for that they would be the masters. At the end of the hour did the English-men set forward, and proceeded on their way, well arranged and in good order, unto Meung on the Loire ; and raised and entirely abandoned the siege, which they had carried on before Orleans, from the twelfth day of October one thousand four hundred twenty and eight, until this same day. Neverthe-less, did they not go away nor carry in safety all their chattels; for an host from the city pursued them, and assailed the rear of their army in manifold assaults, in such sort, that they obtained from them several bombs, large cannons, bows, cross-bows, and other artillery. And upon this same day, an English Augustin confessor, belonging to the lord Talbot, had in his keeping a French prisoner, a very valiant man at arms of the name of Le Bourg de Bar, who was chained by the feet. And in the same manner he conducted him like the other English, holding him up by the arm the length of the way, because he could not otherwise proceed in conse-quence of his irons. The which, perceiving that he loitered very far behind, and well knowing, as being subtle in feats of war, that the English were going never to return, constrained by force this same Augustin, to convey him upon his shoulders even

unto Orleans, so that he escaped the payment of
his ransom; and therefore by means of this Augustin,
was much known concerning the proceedings of the
adversaries; for he was in very familiar friendship
with Talbot.   In another direction entered into Orleans the Pucelle, with other lords and men at arms,
to the very great exultation of all the clergy and of
the people, who altogether humbly returned thanks
unto our Lord, who well merited praises, for the very
great help and the victories which he had accorded
and sent to them against the English, the ancient
enemies of this kingdom.   And when the period
after mid-day had arrived, Messire Fleurent d'Illiers
took leave of the lords and captains and other men
at arms, as well as of the citizens of the city; and in
company with his men of war conducted thither by
him did he return unto Chasteaudun, of the which
place he was captain, carrying back with him great
praise and renown for the valiant feats of arms
achieved by himself and his followers in the defence
and the succour of Orleans.   And upon the following day, in like manner, departed the Pucelle,
and with her the lord de Rays, the baron de
Colouces, and many other knights, esquires, and
men at war, and proceeded towards the king to
convey unto him the news of this noble affair, and
also to lead him to put himself on his route, in order
to be crowned and consecrated at Rheims, even as
our Lord had commanded her.   But previous to this

she took her leave of those of Orleans, who all wept with joy, and right humbly thanked her, and offered up themselves and their goods unto her as well as their wishes; for the which, she thanked them most benignly, and then undertook the performance of her most saintly journey. For she had done and accomplished the first feat, which was to raise the siege of Orleans; during the which were enacted these manifold noble deeds of arms, skirmishings, and assaults, and then were found and used innumerable engines, novelties, and subtilties of war, and more than for a long period antecedent had been practised before any other city, town, nor castle of this kingdom; as was stated by all the personages knowing therein as well French as Englishmen, and who were there present to construct and to witness them. Upon this same day, and on the following also, were performed right beautiful and solemn processions by the fathers of the church, lords, captains, men at war, and citizens, being and residing within Orleans, and they visited the churches in mighty great devotion. And truly at the beginning, and before the laying of the siege, the citizens would not permit the men at war to enter into their city, misdoubting that they would pillage or too much maltreat them; nevertheless did they after suffer to enter as many as chose to come, when they had learned that they knew how to defend and right valiantly maintain them against their enemies, there-

fore they were very united in the defence of the city ;
and in consequence divided them between themselves in their hotels, and nourished them with such
things as God gave to them, just as familiarly as if
they had been their own children.

A short time after, the Bastard of Orleans, the
marshal of Saint Severe, the lord de Graville, the
lord de Courraze, Poton de Sainctes Trailles, and
divers other knights, esquires, and men at war, a
part of whom carrying javelins, had come from
Bourges, Tours, Angiers, Blois, and other good
cities of this kingdom, departed from Orleans, and
went unto Jargeau, where they performed several
skirmishes, which lasted upwards of three hours, to
ascertain if they could besiege the place; who then
found that they could accomplish nothing there, on
account of the water, which was risen high and had
filled up the fosses : and on this account did they
return in safety.   But the English sustained much
injury ; for a very valorous knight of England, called
Messire Henry Bisset, then captain of the city,
was there killed, whereat they performed great
mourning.

While these skirmishings were taking place, in such
sort acted the Pucelle, that she arrived where the
king was; before whom, as soon as she beheld him,
she kneeled herself down with much gentleness, and
embracing him round the legs, said unto him :

" *Gentil* Dauphin, come and receive your corona-

" tion at Rheims. I am mightily spurred that you
" should go ; and do not entertain a doubt that you
" will in that city receive your worthy inaugura-
" tion."

At the which the king performed marvellous grand
feasting, as did also all those of the court, taking
into consideration her virtuous life, and the great
feats, and marvels in arms, performed under her
conduct. Wherefore, shortly after, were the lords,
chieftains of war, captains, and other sage men of
the court, summoned by the king; and several
councils took place at Tours, in order to determine
what was requisite to be done concerning the request
of the Pucelle, who desired with so much affection
and with such instance, that he should retire to
Rheims, and be there consecrated. Upon the which
there were divers opinions, for some counselled that
he should previously go into Normandy, and others
that he should await the taking of some other principal places situated upon the banks of the Loire.
At length the king and three or four of his most
intimate princes, having retired apart, devising
among themselves in special secrecy, thought that it
would be expedient, for the greater surety, to learn
of the Pucelle what the voice said unto her, and
wherefore she thus gave them such firm assurances.
But they were in doubts as to requiring from her
the truth, fearing lest she should be ill pleased; the

which she knew by Divine Grace, wherefore she presented herself before them, and said unto the king :

" In the name of God, I know all that you think
" and wish to say respecting the voice that I have
" heard, in regard to your coronation ; and I will tell
" you.   I began to utter my orisons, as is my usual
" custom, making complaint because all that I said
" was not believed.   And then the voice said unto
" me : Girl, go, go, go ; I will be ready to assist
" thee : go ! And whensoever that voice comes, I
" am marvellously rejoiced, even beyond myself."
And while uttering these words, she raised her eyes
up to heaven, and testified a sign of great exultation.

These things being thus made known, the king
was immediately right joyous, and from thence was
it concluded that she should be believed, and that he
would go to Rheims ; but that he would not do so
before taking of some places upon the Loire.   And
that during the period which would be occupied in
reducing them, he would assemble together a great
power of princes, lords, men at war, and others
obedient unto him.   Wherefore he nominated, as his
lieutenant-general, John duke of Alençon, newly
delivered from captivity in England, where he had
continued a prisoner from the period of the battle of
Verneuil, since which time he had not returned
until the deposit was made of a portion of his

ransom pledges, with the hostages then remaining there in his stead, the which he briefly after acquitted, and in order so to do, sold a portion of his lands, thinking to recover others by assisting and succouring the king, his sovereign lord. Who, to do this, awarded to him a great number of men at arms and artillery, and gave to accompany him the Pucelle, expressly commanding him, that he should act and do entirely according to her counsel. And he conducted himself as one taking great delight to behold her in his company ; and in like manner did the people at arms, all conceiving and respecting her to be sent by our Lord, and so she was. Wherefore the duke of Alençon and she, and their men at arms, took leave of the king, and entered the plains, keeping themselves in good array. And in this manner did they shortly after enter into Orleans, at which place they were welcomed with great joy by all the citizens, and above the rest, the Pucelle in the gazing upon whom they were never sufficiently satisfied.

After the duke of Alençon, the Pucelle, the count de Vendosme, the Bastard of Orleans, the marshal of Saint Severe, La Hire, Messire Fleurent d'Illiers, Jamet de Tilloy, and a valiant gentleman very renowned of old, called Tudual de Carmoisen, sirnamed the Bourgois, of the nation of Brittany, with many other personages of war who had remained for a short period in Orleans, took their departure on

G

Saturday, being the eleventh day of June, comprising altogether about eight thousand combatants,
as well on horseback as on foot; of whom many
carried javelins, hatchets, cross-bows, and others
leaden mallets. And they caused to be transported
and taken a sufficient quantity of artillery, thus
departing in order to lay the siege before Jargeau,
then taking part with the English; in the which
place was Messire William de la Pole, earl of Suffolk,
and Messire John, Messire Alexander de la Pole
his brothers, and with them between six and seven
hundred English combatants, furnished with cannon
and other artillery, very valiant men in war; and even
so did they show it in many assaults and skirmishes,
which there took place during the said siege; the
which was half raised on account of the terrible
speeches of some, who said that it ought to be
abandoned for the purpose of proceeding to the encounter of Messire John Fascot (Fastolf) and other
chieftains of the adverse party, coming from Paris
and conveying provisions and artillery with full two
thousand English combatants, desirous of causing
the siege to be raised, or, at all events, of victualling
and affording succour to the city of Jargeau. And
immediately many departed, and so had all the rest
done, had it not been for the Pucelle and many
lords and captains, who with fine speeches caused
them to abide and made the others return; so that
the siege was recommenced in an instant, and they

began to skirmish against those of the city, who discharged marvellously from cannons and other engines, whereby many French were wounded; and among others, by a blow from one of their slings, was carried away the head of a gentleman of Anjou, who had taken his stand on the same spot from whence the duke of Alençon, by the advice of the Pucelle, who had showed to him the danger, had but that instant retired, so that he was not more than twelve feet distant from the spot. During the whole of this day and the ensuing night, the French discharged bombs and cannons against the city of Jargeau, in such sort, that it was much battered. For by means of three discharges from one of the bombs used at Orleans, and called *Bergerie* or *Bergere*, was battered down the greatest tower of the place. Therefore on the following day, which was Sunday the twelfth of June, the French men of war placed themselves within the ditches, having with them ladders and other implements necessary to carry on the assault, and those from within sallied forth marvellously, the which stoutly defended themselves with a large piece, and most virtuously. And in particular there was one of them upon the walls, who was very tall and lusty, and armed from head to foot, wearing an helmet upon his head, who conducted himself very ably, and threw outright marvellous large stones, continually hurling down ladders and the men upon them. The which was pointed out by the duke of Alençon to Master John the culverin gunner, in order that he might level at him his culverin ; with a ball from which he struck the Englishman upon the chest who had so stoutly showed himself to all, and thus killed him outright, so that he fell within the city. In another direction during this same assault, did the Pucelle descend into the fosse with her standard, and at the very spot where was the hottest resistance, and approached so nigh unto the wall, that an Englishman incontinent cast a great stone upon her head, and struck her so hard that she was obliged to seat herself upon the ground. And although the stone was very hard, it nevertheless brake into pieces without doing any great injury to the Pucelle ; who almost imme-diately arose, displaying virtuous courage, and then exhorted her people in the strongest manner, desiring that they would entertain no doubt ; for that the English had no longer any power to defend them-selves ; in uttering which she spake the truth : for instantly after these words, the French being all well assured, began to mount the walls with so much hardihood, that they entered into the city and took it by assault.

When the earl of Suffolk, and his two brothers, and many other English lords, perceived that they could no longer defend the walls, they retired upon the bridge ; but while retreating thither, was killed Messire Alexander, brother of the said earl. And

also soon after was this bridge surrendered by the
English, they knowing that it was too weak to be
retained, and seeing that they were also surprised.
Many valiant men at war pursued the English ; and
in particular there was a French gentleman named
Guillaume Regnault, who had strove hard to take
the earl of Suffolk ; so the earl demanded of him if
he was a gentleman ? to the which he answered,
Yea ; and then inquired if he was a knight ? and he
replied, Nay ; whereupon the said earl created him a
knight, and then surrendered himself up his prisoner.
And in like manner was there also taken prisoner
Messire John de la Pole, his brother, with many
other lords and men at war, of whom several were
that same evening conveyed prisoners by water,
and at night arrived at Orleans, fearful lest they
should be killed. For many others were massacred
upon the road, owing to a quarrel which took place
between some of the Frenchmen respecting the
division of the prisoners. And in regard to the city
of Jargeau, and even the church wherein was
stowed a great quantity of riches, the whole was
also pillaged. This same night returned the duke
of Alençon and the Pucelle, with many lords and
men at arms, into the city of Orleans, where they
were welcomed with the greatest joy. And from
thence they made known unto the king the taking
of Jargeau, and how the assault had lasted for the
space of four hours, in the course of which were

performed many rare feats of arms. And of the English were there killed from four to five hundred, without counting the prisoners, who were of great renown, as well for nobility as gallant achievements in war.

The duke of Alençon and the Pucelle sojourning some little time after this success within Orleans, at which place were already from six to seven thousand combatants, there came also to reinforce the army, many lords, knights, esquires, captains, and valiant men at arms; and among others was the lord de la Val, and his brother the lord de Lohiac, the lord de Chaivigny, of Berri; the lord de la Tour D'Auvergne, and Vidame of Chartres. At about this period came also the king unto Sully upon the Loire. And in truth his army augmented greatly; for there arrived from day to day persons from all parts of the kingdom obedient unto him. And then the duke of Alençon, as lieutenant-general of the army of the king, accompanied by the Pucelle, by Messire Loys de Bourbon, Count de Vendosme, and other lords, captains, and men at arms in great numbers, as well on foot as on horseback, quitted Orleans with large quantities of provisions, waggons, and artillery, on Wednesday the fifteenth of the said month of June, in order to commence the siege of Baugency, and in their way they attacked the bridge of Meung upon the Loire. So that notwithstanding the

English had fortified it, and well lined it with valiant men, thinking to defend the same, in despite of their resistance, it was at once taken by direct assault. From thence transporting their artillery, they departed early the following morning, and so gained the city of Baugency and entered therein; because the English had evacuated the same and retired to the castle and upon the bridge, which they had fortified against them. So that they did not continue there at all at their ease. For many of the English had placed themselves secretly within the houses and the old ruined places of the city, from whence they made a sudden sally upon the French, just as they were lodging themselves, and there commenced a very brisk skirmish; in the course of which, many were killed and wounded on either side. Nevertheless, in the end, the English were compelled to retire to the bridge and into the castle, which the French besieged on the side of Beausse, and planted their bombs and cannon. During this siege arrived Arthur count de Richemont, constable of France, and brother of the duke of Brittany; in company with whom was Jacques de Dignan, lord of Beau-manoir, brother to the lord of Chasteau-briant. And there did the said constable entreat the Pucelle, as also did the other lords out of love for him, that she would procure his peace with the king; and she promised him the same, upon this proviso, that he would swear, before herself and the

lords, that he would always serve the king with
loyalty.   And at the same time, the Pucelle also
required, that the duke of Alençon and the other
great lords, would ratify the obligation, and attest
the same with their seals; the which they performed, and by this means the constable continued
at the siege with the other lords.   And it was by
them resolved, that a part of their forces should
proceed to Sauloigne, in order that the English
might be besieged in every direction; but the bailiff
of Evreux, chief of the besieged, requested of the
Pucelle a parley and a truce, which were accorded
him; the termination of the same, it being about the
middle of the night of that day, was, that the English
should agree to surrender up the castle and the
bridge, and that they might depart on the ensuing
day, and carry with them their horses and their
harness, together with as much of their goods and
chattels, each one not amounting to more in value
than one mark in silver;   and that it should also
be sworn among them that they would not carry
arms until the expiration of ten days.   And upon
these conditions they departed that day and the
morrow, which was the eighteenth day of June, and
marched into Meung, and the French took possession of the castle, and reinforced it with troops
in order to guard it.   In another quarter, and on
the same night, when the agreement to give up
the castle and the bridge of Baugency was ratified,

came the lords Talbot and Escalles (lord Scales), and Messire John Fascot (Fastolf), who being informed of the taking of Jargeau, had left at Estampes the provisions and the artillery, which, in order to succour it, they had conveyed from Paris, and had advanced with great speed, thinking also to render aid to Baugency. And they had thought to cause the siege to be raised; but they could not enter, although they had four thousand combatants. For they found the French in such good order, that they gave up this enterprise, and returned to the bridge of Meung and attacked it with great animosity. But they were compelled to abandon every thing and enter into the city, on account of the avant-guard of the French; which came in great haste after the taking of Baugency, that day in the morning, being desirous of attacking them. Therefore, that same day did they evacuate the whole city of Meung, and began their march through the plains, in gallant array, with the intention of proceeding to Jenville. Wherefore, when the duke of Alençon, and the other French lords who arrived after their avant-guard, had learned the same, they hastened as much as in them lay, with their army, always keeping in good order, so that the English had no time to go as far as Jenville, but to a village in Beausse, named Pathay.

And because the Pucelle and several lords were not willing that the grand battle should be taken from their path, they chose La Hire, Poton, Jamet de Tilloy, Messire Ambrose de Lore, Thibaut de Termes, and other very valiant men at arms on horseback, as well as the people of the lord of Beaumanoir, together with others who joined in their company, to undertake the charge of scouring and skirmishing before the English, to prevent and guard them from seeking a retreat in any strong place, which they accordingly effected. And even more than that; for they entered and struck among them with so much hardihood, that although they were not more than from fourteen to fifteen hundred combatants, they routed and discomfited them, notwithstanding they had upwards of four thousand fighting men. Of the which there remained dead upon the field about two thousand two hundred, as well of English as of false Frenchmen, and the rest betook them to flight, in order to save themselves, proceeding towards Jenville; at which place the people of the city closed upon them their gates; wherefore it behoved them to fly elsewhere, at a mere hazard. And in consequence of this were many after killed and taken in the same manner as with those of the great battle, who, upon their discomfiture, had joined with the first who were put to flight. In the course of this day much was gained by the French; for the lord Talbot, the lord of Escales (Scales), Messire Thomas Rameston, and another captain named Hongnefort (Hungerford), were taken prisoners, together with many other lords and valiant men of England. And in another quarter those of Jenville were not the losers; to many of whom numbers of the English had confided the greater part of their money, when they had passed through that place, in order to go and succour Baugency. This same day surrendered themselves to the king, the inhabitants of Jenville; and there was a gentleman also named lieutenant to the captain, and the French were stationed within the great tower, to whom he tendered the oath to be good and loyal. And forthwith speeded unto the king the renown of this discomfiture, from the which many escaped by flight, and among others Messire John Fascot (Fastolf), who took refuge in Corbueil; and so greatly were affrighted the troops of the English garrisons in the country of Beausse, namely, at Mont-pipeau, Saint Sigismont, and other strong and fortified places, that they set fire thereto, and hastily took to flight. And on the contrary, the courage of the French increased, who from all sides assembled at Orleans, believing that the king was to proceed thither, to give orders concerning the journey for his coronation; which he did not perform; whereat those of the city, who had caused it to be hung and adorned, were very discontented, not taking into consideration the affairs of the king, who, in order to arrange concerning matters of state, sojourned at Sully, on the river Loire. And

thither went the duke of Alençon, and all the lords
and men at war, who had been present at the battle
of Pathay, and from thence they had retired to
Orleans.   And in particular the Pucelle, who spake
to him respecting the constable; displaying unto
him the good will which he showed towards him,
and the noble lords and valiant men at war, to the
number of fifteen hundred combatants, whom he
conducted with him; supplicating that he would
pardon his evil conduct.   The which was accorded
by the king at her request, as well as on account of
the love he bore to the lord de la Trimouille,
who possessed the greatest influence near his
person; but he would not permit him to be one
of the journey, nor present at his inauguration;
whereat the Pucelle was very much displeased, as
well as many other great lords, captains, and other
persons of the council, well knowing that he thereby
sent away many personages of worth and valiant
men.   But nevertheless they dared not to speak,
because they perceived that the king did all, in
every thing, as pleased unto the said lord de la
Trimouille, for whose satisfaction he would not
suffer that the constable should approach near unto
him.   Wherefore he bethought him to employ his
men at war in another direction, who were very
desirous to make use of their arms, and were willing
to go and besiege Marchesnoir, which is between
Blois and Orleans.   But when the English and

the Burgundians, who were garrisoned there, became acquainted therewith, they despatched under safe conduct some from among them to the duke of Alençon, who treated with them on the part of the king, and accorded them a lapse of ten days, to transport from thence their goods, and did so much that they promised to be good and loyal Frenchmen, and to surrender up the place into their king's hands, for the performance of which they sent hostages for the greater security. And for so doing, and on account of the same, the king was to grant them a pardon for all offences. After the said treaty, it was by the duke of Alençon made known to the constable, that he was no longer to proceed forwards; neither did he do so. But the traitors perjured themselves : for when they learned that the constable, misdoubting of whom they had ratified this treaty, was marched away, they so acted during the term of the ten days, that they took for security several of the people of the duke of Alençon, and imprisoned them within their town of Marchesnoir; in order that they might get back their hostages, and by this means did not surrender, but kept the place as they had before done.

Sunday, after the festival of Saint John the Baptist, this same year, one thousand four hundred twenty and nine, Bonny was surrendered up to Messire Loys de Culan, admiral of France, who had thither repaired to besiege it with a great power of people,

by order of the king ; the which had sent for his
wife the queen Mary, daughter of the deceased Loys,
king of Sicily, second of that name, because many
were of opinion, that he would conduct her to be
crowned with him at Rheims. And in a few days
after, was she conducted to him at Gien, at the
which place he assembled several councils, in order
to conclude the manner most convenient for the
performance of the journey for the inauguration.
At the conclusion of which council it was agreed,
that the king should send the queen back to
Bourges ; and that without besieging Cosne and
La Charité upon the Loire, it was the advice of
many, that it should be taken by storm, before his
departure and entering upon the route, which was
done accordingly. For the queen being sent back
to Bourges, the king began his journey to Rheims,
and took his departure from Gien on the festival of
Saint Peter, in the same month of June, accompanied by La Pucelle, the duke of Alençon, the
count de Clermont, afterwards duke de Bourbon,
the count de Vendosme, the lord de Laval, the
count de Boulogne, the Bastard of Orleans, the
lord de Lohiac, the marshals de Saint Severe and
de Rays, the admiral de Culan, and the lords de
Thouras, de Sully, de Chaumont, on the Loire, de
Prié de Chaivigny and de la Trimouille, de La Hire,
de Poton, de Jamet de Tilloy, surnamed Bourgois,
and of many other lords, nobles, valiant captains,

and gentlemen, together with about twelve thousand
combatants, all brave, hardy, valiant men, and of
singular great courage; as before, at the time present, and also afterwards, was manifested by their
feats and noble achievements; and in especial
during this same journey: in the progress of which
they traversed, in going thither, and repassed upon
their returning, frankly and fearing nothing, through
the lands and the countries, whereof the cities, the
castles, the bridges, and the passes, were manned
with the English and the Burgundians. And above
all did they arrive, still proceeding on their road, to
lay the siege and commence the assault of the city of
Auxere. And forthwith it appeared to the Pucelle,
and many other lords and captains, that it might
easily be taken by assault, and they were desirous of making the attempt. But the inhabitants of
the city gave in secret two thousand crowns to the
lord de la Trimouille, in order that he might prevent
it from being assaulted, and also delivered unto the
king's army great quantities of provisions, which
were very necessary. Wherefore, they did not
proffer any obedience, whereat were very mal-
content the greater part of the host, and even La
Pucelle; so that nothing more was done with them.
Nevertheless the king remained about the space of
three days, and then took his departure with all his
army, and proceeded towards Saint Florentine, which
was surrendered up to him peaceably; and from

thence he advanced as far as Troyes, where he
caused those of the city to be summoned, that they
might perform obedience unto him; whereof they
would do nothing, and therefore closed to their
gates, and prepared to defend themselves in case
they should be assailed. And there sallied forth
from five to six hundred English and Burgundians,
who were in garrison there, and they came and
skirmished against the army of the king, as soon as
it arrived and encamped around this city. But
they were compelled to re-enter in great haste and
in a mighty crowd by several valiant captains and
persons at arms of the king's army, who continued
there, holding as it were a siege, during the space of
five days, in the course of which those of the host
suffered many inconveniencies from the attacks of
hunger. For there were from five to six thousand,
who continued the space of eight days without
eating of bread. And in sooth many would have
died of famine, had it not been for the abundance
of beans which had been sown that year, owing to
the admonition of a Cordelier, named brother Richard, who, in the Advent of Christmas, as well as
before, had preached through the provinces of
France, in divers places, and had stated among
other things in his sermon:

" Sow, good people; sow beans in abundance;
" for he who ought to come will arrive briefly."

Wherefore, in consequence of this famine, and

also because the inhabitants of Troyes would not
tender their obedience, it was advised unto the
king, by many, that he should measure back his
steps, without passing onwards; considering that
the city of Chalons, and even that of Rheims, were
also in the hands of his adversaries : but even while
these things were treating of in the council before
the king, and that from the mouth of Master Regnaut de Chartres, then archbishop of Rheims, it
was required of many lords and captains that they
should now deliver their opinions ; and after the
greater part of them had demonstrated that on
account of the strength of the city of Troyes, and
in default of artillery and money, it were better to
return ; Master Robert le Maçon, who was a man
sage in counsel, and had previously been a knight,
stated thus, his opinion being asked, that it was
necessary the Pucelle should be expressly spoken
to, by whose advice this same journey had been
undertaken, and that perchance she would point out
a good expedient ; the which was accordingly done.
For, coming to this conclusion, she struck hard
upon the portal of the council chamber ; and when
she had entered, the chancellor briefly exposed to
her, in words and speech, the causes which had
prompted the king to undertake this expedition, as
well as those which led him to give up the same.
Upon the which she very sagely made answer,
and said, that if the king would yet continue, the

city of Troyes should be subjected to his obedience
within two or three days, either by love or by force.
And the chancellor said unto her, " Jeanne, if we
were certain that this should take place within six
days, we would willingly abide." To the which she
made answer immediately, that she did not entertain a doubt; wherefore, it was resolved that they
should remain. She then mounted upon a courser,
holding a stick in her hand, and caused all arrangements to be diligently made, to assail, and fire the
cannons, whereat the bishop and very many of the
city marvelled greatly. The which calling to mind
that the king was their rightful and sovereign liege
lord ; and also the enterprises and feats of the
Pucelle, and the report which was spread of her
being sent by God; they required a parley. And
then issued forth the bishop, with many wealthy
personages, as well men at arms as citizens, who
entered into agreement, that the men at war should
retire with their goods and chattels ; and that those
of the city should have a general amnesty. And
they required of the king, that those of the church
who held benefices under the title of Henry king of
England, should continue to abide firmly unto them ;
and that he should only annul new titles granted by
him. And upon these conditions, in the morning of
the following day, the king and the greater part of
the lords and captains, very richly attired, entered
into the city of Troyes, wherein there had previously

been kept many prisoners, whom those of the garrison were conducting with them in consequence of the treaty. But this the Pucelle would not suffer, when the period came for their departure. Wherefore they were ransomed by the king, who largely paid their masters.

On this same day did the king, upon his part, nominate captains and other officers of the city; and upon the following day, all those of his army entered into the same, who on the night before had remained in the open fields, under the command of Messire Ambrose de Loré. After this, the king, accompanied by all his forces, took his departure, according to the advice of the Pucelle, who much hastened him; and in such wise they acted, that they came unto Chalons, and there entered in great joy; for the bishop and the citizens went forth to meet him, and there performed full obedience. Therefore, upon his own part, did he place captains and officers, and then departed in the direction of Rheims. And in consequence of this city not being under his obedience, he lodged some four leagues distant, in a castle named Lepsaulx, belonging to the archbishop; whereat those of Rheims were much shocked, and in particular the lords of Chastillon on the Marne and of Saueuses, being therein garrisoned in behalf of the English and the Burgundians; who caused the citizens to be convened, and stated unto them, if they would hold out for the length of

six weeks, that they would bring them succour.
And afterwards with their consent did they take
their departure. The which not being yet gone very
far, a public council was held by the citizens, and
with the consent of all the inhabitants, were messengers despatched to the king, who granted unto
them all abolitions, and they delivered up unto him
the keys of the city. Into the which, this same
day in the morning, which was on a Saturday, the
archbishop proceeded and made his entrance; for
since he had been created archbishop, never yet had
he entered. And after the dinner hour, and towards
evening, the king entered, together with his whole
army, with whom was Jeanne la Pucelle, being much
regarded by all. And thither in like manner came
René, duc de Bar and of Lorraine, brother of the
king of Sicily, and also the lord de Commercy, well
accompanied by men at war, offering themselves for
his service.

The day ensuing, which was Sunday the seventh
day of July, of this same year one thousand four
hundred twenty and nine, the lords de Saint Severe
and de Rays, marshals of France, the lord de
Graville, and the lord de Culan, admiral of France,
were, according to ancient custom, despatched by
the king to Saint Remy in order to procure the
Saint Ampoulle. The which took the accustomed
oaths, whereby they promised to bring the same,
and to take it back again in surety; and very

devoutly and solemnly did the abbot bring the same, being clothed in the pontifical robes, having over his vestment a rich covering of gold, even unto the church of Saint Denys. And thither also repaired the archbishop, clothed, and accompanied by his canons, and there received and carried the same into the church, and placed it upon the grand altar of our Lady at Rheims, in front of which came the king, clothed as well befitted him. Unto whom the archbishop caused the accustomed oaths to be administered which were wont to be read unto the true kings of France when they received the holy oil. And immediately afterwards was the king made a knight, by the duke of Alençon, and this performed, he was anointed and crowned; the archbishop performing the ceremonies, and pronouncing the orisons, benedictions, and exhortations contained in the pontifical, always used at this holy inauguration; the which being accomplished, the king by an especial grant made him count of the lordship of Laval; and there did also the duke of Alençon and the count de Clermont raise many to the rank of knights. And the ceremony being ended, the Saint Ampoulle was restored and carried back in the same manner it had been brought. When the Pucelle saw that the king was consecrated and crowned, she fell upon her knees before him, all the lords being there present; and while embracing him round the legs, she thus addressed herself unto him, shedding warm tears :

" Gentle king, thus is accomplished the pleasure
" of God, whose will was, that the siege of Orleans
" should be raised, and that you should be con-
" ducted unto this city of Rheims to receive your
" holy inauguration ; thus to show, that you are the
" true king, and him unto whom the kingdom of
" France does by right appertain."

And much pity did she inspire into all those who beheld her. This same day, and the two days following, did the king sojourn at Rheims, and afterwards proceeded to Saint Marcoul, through whose intercession did the kings of France, by divine grace, obtain the power of healing the king's evil : and in consequence thereof, they should immediately repair thither after their coronation ; which the king did and accomplished accordingly. And being arrived there, he performed his orisons and presented his offerings ; from the which place he went into a small closed city, named Vailly, in the valley, and at four leagues from Soissons : the citizens of the which city of Soissons brought unto him the keys, as did also those of the city of Laon, to which he had sent his heralds to summon them to open their gates ; but, on quitting Vailly, he journeyed unto Soissons, at the which place he was welcomed with great joy by all those of the city, who much loved him and desired his coming. And there

arrived unto him the right and joyous tidings that
Chateau Thierry, Crecy en Brie, Provins, Coule-
miers, and many other cities, were subjected unto
his obedience. When the king had continued for a
space of time in this same saint city of Soissons,
he went his way and arrived at Chateau Thierry,
and from thence to Provins, at the which place he
continued three or four days, and ranged his army in
order of battle, and betook him unto the fields near
unto a place called La Motte de Maugis, awaiting
the coming of the duke of Bedford, who had issued
forth from Paris, and passing by Corbueil, arrived
at Melun, from whence he departed, having at the
most ten thousand combatants, stating that he
would give him battle. But he changed his tone
and returned to Paris, notwithstanding he had full
as great a force as the king : the which had many
in his company who so much desired to return
to the river of the Loire ; wherefore, in order to
satisfy them, he concluded so to do. But the
people of Bray, where he purposed to traverse the
Seine, and who had promised to yield him admittance, took into their city a great company of
English and of Burgundians, the night before he
was to pass the same ; whereat were mightily displeased the dukes of Bar and of Alençon, and the
counts of Vendosme and of Laval, with the other
captains and valiant men at war, against the will
of whom would the king fain think to return ; and

their opinion was, that he should undertake the
reconquest more and more, because the power of
the English had not dared to deliver him battle.
Wherefore, he caused them to return to Chateau
Thierry, and from thence to Cressy in Vallois, from
the which place he repaired and lodged his army
in the open fields near adjoining to Dampmartin in
Gonelle; when, in order to meet him, ran the
Frenchmen from all quarters, crying, " *Christmas!* "
and singing, " *Te Deum laudamus,*" with devout
anthems, verses, and responses ; keeping marvellous
feastings, and above all regarding much the Pucelle ;
the which, observing their conduct, wept most
amply, and turning herself aside, said unto the
count Dunois,

" In the name of God, there live here good and
" devout people, and I wish I might die in this
" country, when it is fitting I should die."

And then the said count demanded of her :
" Jeanne, do you know when you shall die, and
" in what place ? "

To the which she made answer :

" No, for every thing resteth with the will of
" God." And then continued, addressing herself to
him and the other lords :

" I have accomplished all that Messires com-
" manded me, which was to raise the siege of Or-
" leans, and cause the king to be crowned ; I wish
" it would now so please him, to cause me to return

" back unto my father and my mother, in order
" that I might watch over my sheep and my cattle,
" and do that which it behoveth me to do."

And then rendering up thanks unto the Lord, she raised her eyes with much humility unto heaven. By the which words that they knew to be true, and by her manner, did they firmly believe that she was the Saint Pucelle sent by God, and the which for a surety she was.

When the duke of Bedford, uncle and lieutenant-general of king Henry, and governing for him the cities, towns, and places, holding for him in the kingdom, knew that the king was in the plains in the vicinity of Dampmartin, he marched forth from Paris with a great number of men at war, and came and encamped near unto Nuctry, close to the said Dampmartin, and joined his army, which he ranged in good order of battle, and in an advantageous situation : the which was announced unto the king ; and he forthwith, in like manner, gave orders unto his people, with intention to await and receive the battle of his adversaries, or to advance and attack them, if they should encamp, or were to be found in a suitable situation. But the English showed no signs whatsoever of wishing to assail them ; but, on the contrary, they had occupied a ground very advantageous and well fortified ; as was perceived, and made known by La Hire and many other valiant captains and men at arms, who, upon this

same day, in order to behold their array, and if it
were right to attack them, proceeded in order to
give them a grand skirmish, in manifold places
and at sundry times, from the morning until night.
However, no injury was there done either on the
one side or on the other.   After the which skirmishes
the duke of Bedford returned with his army into
Paris : and the king approached unto Cressy in
Vallois, from whence he sent forward his heralds to
summon and require that those of Compiegne should
place themselves in obedience to him ; the which
sent for answer that they were right willing to do
the same.

At about this period proceeded many French
lords unto the city of Beauvais, whereof was
bishop and count Peter Cochon ; very much inclined
to the English party, notwithstanding he was a
native of the environs of Rheims.   But notwithstanding this, those of the city entered into full
obedience to the king, as soon as they beheld his
heralds bearing his arms ; and they all cried in great
joy, Long live Charles King of France ! and they
chanted *Te Deum*, and made great rejoicings.   And
this done, they permitted to go forth all those who
would not enter into such obedience, and suffered
them to depart peaceably with their goods and
chattels.

Some few days after, the duke of Bedford on a
sudden sallied forth from Paris, in order to march

to Senlis, his former army being augmented with four thousand English, which his uncle the cardinal of England had transported from thence by sea, under the pretext of marching them against the Bohemian heretics, but belying his promises, set them to work against the most Christian Frenchmen, although they had been subsidized with money of the church. The which came unto the knowledge of the king, who had entered on his route, marching his host for the city of Compiegne, and was lodged at a village named Barron, two leagues distant from the city of Senlis, the which held on the side of the English and the Burgundians. Wherefore orders were issued, that Messire Ambroise de Loré, after prevost of Paris, and the lord of Sainctes-trailles, should proceed well mounted towards Paris, or elsewhere, as should seem meet unto them, in order truly to survey the duke of Bedford and his army. The which, having with them many of their people mounted in the best manner, soon departed, and acted in such sort, as to approach so near unto the English host, that they saw and perceived upon the grand route, between Paris and Senlis, a great rising of dust: whereby knew they of their approach; so that they despatched one of their men in haste unto the king, signifying the coming of his adversaries. And notwithstanding this they awaited so long that they perceived, and ascertained for a truth, the whole army, and to what number it might amount,

and how its course was directed towards the said
city of Senlis ; wherefore, by another of their followers, did they forthwith send hastily unto the
king. And he issued orders for the ranging his
force in battle array, and advanced in all diligence
with his whole army, marching through the plains
towards Senlis ; taking his road between the river
which runs through Barron, and a mountain called
Mont Piloer. In another quarter, at the hour of
vesper chant, arrived the duke of Bedford with all
his army near unto Senlis, and proceeded to pass a
small river running from that city to Barron ; so
that the passage whereby he thus caused his army to
pass was so narrow that there might only go two
horses abreast at the same time. Therefore when
the lords of Loré and of Sainctes-trailles saw them
thus begin to enter this dangerous passage, they
returned with all the speed in their power unto the
king, and proved to him for a certainty what they
had seen ; whereat he was mighty joyful, and ordered
his battle, marching directly towards the English,
thinking to attack them at this same passage. And
in this manner did the two armies so nearly approach
that they perceived one another, and truly were they
distant but a very short league the one from the
other. And from either force, towards the setting
of the sun, departed many valiant lords and men at
war, who skirmished together at divers times, so
that many noble feats of arms were performed

Night causing them to cease, the English encamped themselves along the margin of the said river, and the French were encamped in the neighbourhood of Mont-piloer.

The following morning the king diligently commanded that his forces should be marshalled in battle array, the which he formed into three divisions; the first being the avant-guard, formed of the greatest number of men, the charge of which was given to the duke of Alençon and the count of Vendosme; of the second, which was in the middle, had the command René, then duke de Bar and of Lorraine, and after king of Sicily and duke of Anjou; and of the third, wherein were many lords and valiant men at arms, and which served as the arrière-guard, he willed himself to command; having with him the duke de Bourbon, and the lord de la Trimouille, with a great number of knights and esquires. Of the wings, consisting of three corps, the marshals of Saint Severe and of Rays took the charge, to the which were added many knights, esquires, and men at war, of all estates. And beyond these bodies was reserved in order to skirmish, reinforce, and assist the other divisions, being duly arranged, another battle of very valiant lords, captains, and other men at war, whereof were leaders, and had the charge, the Pucelle, the Bastard of Orleans, the count d'Alebret, and La Hire. And in respect to all the archers, the order of them was appointed to the lord de

Graville, and a knight of Limozin, called Messire John Faucot. The which corps thus arranged, the king several times proceeded a sufficient length of way from the three divisions towards the army of the English, of the which the duke of Bedford was chief, having in his company the Bastard of Saint Pole, with numerous Picards and Burgundians, and many other knights, esquires, and men at war, being ranged in order of battle near unto a village, and having at their back a great pool of water. The which, notwithstanding, had never ceased during the night, neither discontinued still to fortify themselves with great diligence, as well with palisades and stakes as with fosses. Wherefore, when the king, with the advice of all the princes of his blood, being there present, and other lords, knights, esquires, captains, and very valiant men at arms, had come to the determination to combat the English and their allies, if they would range themselves and were to be found on equal ground ; was advertised by many brave captains, and personages conversant with arms, the manner in which they held themselves, how they were encamped on a spot strong by nature, and had fortified themselves, and still continued so to do, with fosses and palisades ; he perceived right well that there was no appearance of being able to attack nor combat them, without too great danger unto his people. But notwithstanding this, he caused his forces to approach

within a distance of two cross-bow shots of the
English, and caused it to be signified unto them,
that he was ready to give them battle if they would
come forth from their park. The which they would
not do, and in consequence of this there took place
many smart and marvellous skirmishes. For many
valiant Frenchmen went frequently on foot as well
as on horseback, even unto the English fortification,
in order to move them to sally forth. So that a
great number of them issued from thence at sundry
times, and drove back the French. The which
being reinforced and succoured by many of theirs,
chased the English in turn; who again, aided by
others of their people, came forth anew, charging
upon the French, and caused them to fall back,
until new succours arriving from their great order of
battle which came and joined them, by whose force
and valour they once more regained the ground of
their enemies. And thus passed this day without
ceasing until near the hour of sunset. To these
sallies and skirmishes, so frequently renewed, must
needs go the lord de la Trimouille, the which being
mounted upon a very gallant courser, and grandly
caparisoned, holding his lance in the rest, pricked his
horse with his spurs, which by accident fell to the
ground and threw him off in the midst of his
enemies; by the which, he was in great danger of
being killed or taken prisoner; but to assist and
cause him to mount was great diligence used.

Wherefore he was with much difficulty reseated, for
at that hour there was a very hot skirmish.   So,
about the setting of the sun, many Frenchmen joined
together and came very valiantly to present themselves close to the fortification of the English; and
there fought with them, and skirmished hand to
hand for a long space of time, until several of them,
as well on foot as on horseback, issued forth in
great power from their park, and so caused them to
fall back.   Against the which, in like manner, advanced from the main body of the king's army, a
great number of very valiant lords, knights, esquires,
and other men at arms, and mingled with their own
people against the English.   And upon this occasion
was enacted the hottest and the most dangerous
skirmish of the whole day; and so nearly mingled
they together, that the dust rose in such thickness
amongst them, that they could neither know nor
discern the which were the French, and the which
English: and in so much so, that however the two
conflicts were near the one unto the other, yet could
they not discern one another.   This last skirmish
continued until dark night, when the French were
forced to go their ways from the English; of whom,
both upon the one part and on the other, there were,
on this day, many killed, wounded, and taken
prisoners.   The English retired and lodged altogether within their park and fortifications, as they had
done on the night before.   And the Frenchmen

assembled, went and lodged at half a league from them, nigh unto the Mont-piloer, as they had done upon the preceding night. And when the following morning dawned, the English began their march and went to Paris, and the king with his army returned to Crespy in Vallois.

The ensuing night, the king lodged in Crespy, and the day after went to Compiegne, at the which place he was greatly and honourably received by those of the city, who had recently placed themselves under his dominion. Wherefore he nominated his own officers, and in particular placed as captain a very valiant gentleman of the province of Picardy, called Guillaume de Flavy, who was descended of a noble house. And unto this city of Compiegne did those of Beauvais and of Senlis send fealty unto the king, the which departed from Compiegne towards the end of the month of August, and proceeded to Senlis; and when it was made known unto the duke of Bedford, he marched forth from Paris with a great power of men at war. And doubting that the king would wish to turn and reconquer Normandy, he marched thither, and left his people in divers places holding for the English, and stored them with provisions and artillery; leaving at Paris Messire Loys de Luxembourg, bishop of Therouenne, calling himself chancellor of France for king Henry, and with him Messire John

I

Ratelet, an English knight, and Messire Simon Morthier: the which had in their company two thousand combatants for the guard and the defence of Paris. In another quarter, the king having appointed officers and captains in his name at Senlis, departed from thence about the last day of the same month, and came unto the town of Saint Denis; the which was completely surrendered unto him, and he there continued for two days; in the course of which were performed many sallies and skirmishes by the French being there, against the English of Paris, and at which place were enacted many gallant feats of arms on either side. And upon the third day departed the Pucelle and the duke of Alençon, the duke de Bourbon, the count de Vendosme, the count de Laval, and the marshals de Saint Severe and de Rays, La Hire, Poton, and many other gallant knights, captains, and esquires, with a great number of valiant men at war, and went to lodge in a village called La Chapelle, which is in the grand route, and as it were mid-way between Paris and Saint Denis; and on the following day did they range themselves in order for fight in the Pig Market place before the gate of Saint Honoré, and conveyed several cannons which they discharged in many points and often within Paris; where the men at arms in garrison there were stationed, and also the people, and caused to be borne many standards

of divers colours, and manœuvred going and returning along the inside of the walls, among which flags
there was one very great, with a red cross. Some
French lords wished to approach nearer, and particularly the lord de Saint Vallier, of Dauphiny, who
did so much that he and his people went and set
fire to the boulevard and to the barrier of the gate
Saint Honoré. And although there were yet many
English to defend it, they found it necessary to
retreat by this portal, and enter again into Paris;
wherefore the French gained, and took by force, the
barrier and the boulevard. And because they
thought that the English would make a sally by the
gate of Saint Denis to surprise those French who
were before the gate Saint Honoré; the dukes of
Alençon and of Bourbon lay in ambuscade behind
the mountain, which is near and over against the
said market place for pigs, and nearer could they
not post themselves, fearful of the cannons, slingers,
and culverins, from which those of Paris fired incessantly. But they lost their labour; for the inhabitants did not dare come forth from the city. Wherefore the Pucelle, seeing their coward manner, bethought herself to attack them even to the very base
of their walls. And forthwith she went and presented herself before them to act accordingly, having
with her a great company of men at arms, and
several lords, among whom was the marshal de

Rays; who, for the purpose of keeping good order, proceeded on foot, and she descended into the first fosse, in the which, as there was water, she mounted the back of an ass, thence descending into the second ditch, and there planted her lance in divers places, feeling and trying what depth there might be of water and of mud, in the doing of which she occupied a great space of time. Insomuch so that a cross-bowman of Paris pierced her thigh through with an arrow. But, notwithstanding this, she would not depart, but used the greatest diligence in causing faggots and logs to be brought and thrown within the fosse, in order to fill it up, so that she and the men at war might proceed up to the walls; which did not then appear to be possible, because of the too great depth of the water, and that she had not a sufficient multitude of people to accomplish the same; and also on account of the night closing in. Yet notwithstanding this, she always kept at the fosse, and would not return or retreat on any account, neither for prayer and request which were made to her by many. At divers times did they go and require her to depart, and remonstrated with her that she ought to abandon this enterprise; until the duke of Alençon sent his request, and made her retreat and the whole army within the said village of La Villette; at which place they lodged that night, as they had done the night before. And upon the ensuing day, they all returned to Saint Denis. In the which town was highly praised the Pucelle, for the good will and the hardy courage by her displayed, in seeking to assault so strong a city, and so well garrisoned with men and artillery, as was the city of Paris. And for a certainty many have since said, that if matters had been better conducted, there was very great appearance that things had turned out according to her wish. For several notable personages being then within Paris, the which recognized king Charles, the seventh of that name, to be their sovereign lord, and the true inheritor of the kingdom of France; and how by great injury and by cruel vengeance they had been separated and cut off from his sovereignty and their allegiance, and placed in the hand of king Henry of England before his demise; and since continuing under king Henry his son, then usurping a great part of the kingdom; would have placed themselves, as they did, six years afterwards, when brought to obey their sovereign lord; and would have given him a free entrance into his principal city of Paris. The which, for this time, was not done for the cause above alleged. Wherefore the king, who then perceived that they did not manifest any signs of showing to him their allegiance, held many councils within the town of Saint Denis; at the termination of which, it was concluded

that, owing to the conduct of the inhabitants of the
city of Paris, the great power of the English and
the Burgundians stationed therein, and also that
they had not sufficient money, nor could they procure the same for the maintenance of so great an
army, that he should appoint the duke de Bourbon
his lieutenant-general. The which was done, and
he gave him command to repair to the cities, towns,
and places subjected to him on the other side of the
river Loire. And in order to place strong garrisons
therein, and to guard and defend them, he awarded
him a great number of men at arms, and abundance
of artillery. And besides this ordinance, he willed
and commanded that the count de Vendosme, and
admiral de Culan, should continue at Saint Denis,
where he also left many men at arms, in order that
they might hold the garrison. And this concluded,
he departed the twelfth day of September, and proceeded to Laigny on the Marne, which place he left
upon the following day ; and appointed there, as
his captain, Messire Ambrose de Loré, with whom
he also left Messire John Faucault with many men
at war ; and departed the next day to Provins, and
from thence to Bray upon the Seine, which the
inhabitants reduced to his allegiance. And then he
went before Sens, which showed no signs of opening
its gates ; but it became necessary to pass a little below at the ford of the river Yonne, and proceed in the

direction of Contrenay, and from thence he went to Chasteau Regnart, then to Montargis, and finally to Gien, where he awaited some days, thinking to come to terms with the duke of Burgundy, who had demanded of him, through the lord de Charnay, that he would cause him to enter Paris, and that he would come thither in person. And upon this occasion had the king despatched to him a safe-conduct in order that he might pass without impediment through the places and the passes, which were obedient unto him, and he did so accordingly. So that when he had arrived in Paris, the said duke abided by nothing which he had promised; but there made alliance with the duke of Bedford in opposition to the king, even much stronger than he had before done. And notwithstanding all this, in virtue of the safe-conduct, he passed securely and freely through all the countries, cities, and passes then obedient unto the king, and returned into his country of Picardy and of Flanders. And the king being made acquainted with the truth, passed the river Loire, and returned to Bourges, from whence he journeyed at the request and supplication of the Pucelle; the which had before told him all that happened concerning the raising of the siege of Orleans, and of his sacred coronation, as well as of his free return, according unto the revelation of our Lord. Offering thanks unto whom, and praising his grace, I end, by his divine grant, this present compendious treatise, intituled of the Siege of Orleans, by the English, and of the coming and the valiant feats of Jeanne la Pucelle; and how she made them depart, and caused to be crowned at Rheims, King Charles the Seventh, by grace divine, and by force of arms.

NOTES.

NOTES.

Page 1. *Thinking to take the city of Orleans.*

Orleans, anciently Cenabum or Genabum, one of the principal cities of the Carnules, is not far distant from Chartres and Dreux, the principal seat of the Druids, or philosophic priests of the Gauls. This city derives its origin from the most remote antiquity in the annals of the civilization of the Gauls or Celts, and under the sons of Clovis was the metropolis of a kingdom. It is surrounded by plains abundantly productive of wine, grains and fruits, watered by the Loire and various other streams, and from this current the department derives its name of Loiret, of which Orleans is the capital, containing a population of upwards of 40,000 souls. The cathedral is a very fine gothic structure, and there are still traces of the ramparts and towers which anciently protected the city from assailants.

Page 1. *Near one of the suburbs called Portereau.*

Portereau is a diminutive of the word *Port*, for in the ancient Latin records of Orleans, it is called *Porticellus*, a small gate or postern. It was near the suburbs of this portal that the English encamped at the opening of the siege of the city. According to Lemaire, Louis XI. in the ensuing reign, intended to enclose these outskirts with a wall; but he was deterred, on account of the frequent inundations of the river Loire to which it is exposed.

Page 2. *Nor construct any fortification against the city.*

" As soon as the inhabitants of Orleans had a knowledge of the intended siege, they began to raise soldiers on every side, causing quantities of arms, corn, and other provisions to be sent from all the surrounding towns and villages, to cleanse the moats, repair the boulevards and the walls of their city, to station good body-guards, and in brief, to make an ample provision of every thing necessary for maintaining an obstinate siege."—*Dubreton*, pp. 13, 14.

Page 2. *Stones that weighed one hundred and sixteen pounds.*

" The earl of Salisbury suddenly commenced his work in earnest, and having, with diligent captains, raised batteries on the highest and most commodious places, began to batter the city in ruins. The violence of these engines was so great, that not only the walls, but the houses, were thrown down as by a rude and furious tempest." . . . . " Those of Orleans had caused a fort to be erected beyond the Loire for the defence of the fortress which joins the bridge of the city; and which is commonly called Les Tournelles."—*Dubreton,* pp. 15, 16.

Page 2.   *Living near the Postern Chesneau.*

The designation of this *Postern* has varied according to different authors. Aldrevaldus, who flourished at the period of Louis the Fat, calls it the *Postern of Saint Benedict,* after the church dedicated to that saint which stands in the vicinity : *Posterula, quæ usque hodie Sancti Benedicti dicitur;* while in a diploma of the period of Philip I. anno 1080, it is named *Postica aglerii :* what the word *aglerii* means is, however, at present wholly unknown ; and lastly in our Diary the words *Postern Chesneau* are for the first time adopted to designate this gate.

Page 3.   *Placed in front of the Tournelles.*

This fort stood at the extremity of the old bridge, but was separated from the left bank of the river by a ravelin surrounded with water, over which was a small bridge. See *Polluche,* note 117, p. 147, and *Expilly,* 351. Villaret designates these forts and boulevart by the name of *Tourelles,* but the editor has preferred using the term *Tournelles,* which is adopted by ancient writers.

Opposite the Tournelles was the isle of the two *Mottes,* that divided the old bridge in two, which stood nearer the city than the suburb. That part of the island, situated east of the bridge, was called *La Motte Saint Antoine,* on which stood a chapel so called, while that to the west bore the name of *La Motte des Poissonniers.* In the

former was the almoury for strangers, otherwise called
the hospital of Saint Anthony; an edifice appropriated,
from remotest antiquity, for the reception of needy tra-
vellers. By an account of hospitals taken in 1625, it
appeared that these *Mottes* had been anciently given up
to the inhabitants of Orleans under the proviso, that
they should cause to be erected one or two chambers,
" To yield a shelter to poor pilgrims and other tra-
vellers, and afford them a resting place, and a covering
for the night only." We also learn from an account
bearing date from 1383 to 1386, that a female had
then the superintendence of this charity. " To Marguerite
la Chaumette, mistress of the Hotel Dieu upon the said
bridge, for the guardianship of the said Hotel Dieu, for
which she has a C sols a year, CIC sols." The hospital
being ruined during the siege, was rebuilt by order of
Louis XII. in 1501. This small island was destroyed on
the erection of the modern bridge.

Page 3.   *The Lord of Sainctes Trailles.*

Jean Poton de Saintrailles, grand seneschal of Limousin, born of a noble family of Gascony, greatly signalized
himself by his services under the respective reigns of
Charles VI. and VII.   He made the famous lord Talbot, earl of Shrewsbury, prisoner at the battle of Patay,
in 1429; as also the earl of Arundel at the conflict of
Gerberoy, in 1435: he equally pursued with the most
heroic ardour all the expeditions which conduced to
liberate the provinces of Normandy and Guienne from
the shackles of the English, and was presented with the

staff of marshal of France in 1454; of which he was, however, deprived in 1461, by Louis XI. the implacable enemy of the best and the most valiant supporters of his father Charles VII. Two months subsequent to this unjust treatment on the part of his sovereign, Poton de Saintrailles died at the castle of Trompette, of which he was the governor; his courage, in conformity with his chivalric character, was at once frank, noble, and decided.

Page 4. *The Tournelles from the end of the bridge.*

The ancient bridge at Orleans consisted of nineteen arches, and was divided in two about the centre by the island of the *Mottes* before described. This structure was nearly eleven hundred feet long, on which formerly stood the famous bronze monument erected in honour of the Pucelle, melted at the period of the Revolution, as well as a beautiful Cross of the same metal. During the troubles that occurred on the subject of religion, the Reformers destroyed the crucifix so frequently mentioned in the Diary, and which had been erected in 1407, while the more recent one had been placed there in 1578.

At the end of this bridge, on the left bank of the river, was a gate flanked with two towers, which were called the *Tourelles* or *Tournelles*, and fortified with a ravelin environed by water, over which was a small bridge communicating with this portal, called *Le Pont Jacquin*. It was customary every year to place a bird upon these Tourelles, at which a company, regularly in-stalled, used to shoot with their arquebuses at the festival

of Pentecost, and which, at a more remote period, used to
be placed on the tower of the church of Saint Aignan.

Page 5.   *The most renowned and dreaded of all the English.*

As the accounts of the death of this nobleman vary,
the following extracts from French and English chroniclers
may not prove devoid of interest.

" Tantost apres & durant le dit siege, le conte de Sal-
bery estoit en la tour et bastille de dessus le bout du
pont dudit Orleans, lesquelles avoient gaignees lesd
Anglois sur les François, et regardoit ledit conte par
une fenestre vers la dicte ville, et disoit on qu' ung de
ses capitaine nomme Glassidal lui disoit telles parolles
ou semblables : " Monseigneur, regardez vostre ville
vous la voyez dicy vient a plai." Et soubdainement vit
une pierre de canon de la dicte ville ferir contre ung des
costez de ladicte fenestre, tellement que ladicte fenestre
ferirent ledit comte parmy le visage en telle maniere que
trois ou quatre jours apres il alla de vie a trespas. Et
touteffois oncques homme de ladicte ville ne peut scavoir
qui avoit boute le feu ne tire icellui canon & nen scavoit
on riens en ladicte ville."—*Croniques de France dicte de
Saint Denys, Imprime a Paris, par Anthoine Verard*, 1493.
Vol. III. p. 143.

" Shortly after, and during the said siege, the earl of
Salisbury was in the tower and bastille above the end
of the bridge of the said Orleans, the which had the
said English gained of the French, and the said earl
looked through one of the windows towards the said
city ; and as it was said, one of his captains, named

Glassdal, (Glasdale) spake these or the like words to him : " My lord, look at your city, you see it well and at ease from here ;" and suddenly came a stone from a cannon of the said city, which struck against one of the sides of the said window, in such wise, that the said window assailed the said earl upon the face in such a manner, that three or four days afterwards he passed from life unto death. *And no man of the said city could learn who had set fire to nor discharged the said cannon, and nothing was known in the said city.*"

" In the tower that was taken at the bridge ende, as you before have heard, there was a high chamber, havyng a grate full of barres of yron, by the which a man might loke all the length of the bridge into the city ; at which grate, many of the chiefe capteynes stoode dyverse times, viewyng the citie, and devisyng in what place it was best assautable.   They within the citie perceyved well this totyng hole, and layde a piece of ordinaunce directly agaynst the windowe.   It so chaunced that the lix day after the siege layd before the citie, the erle of Salisbury, Sir Thomas Gargrave, and William Glasdale, and diverse other, went into the sayde tower, and so into the high chamber, and looked out at the grate ; and within a short space, the sonne of the maister goonner, perceyvyng men looke out at the chamber windowe, tooke his matche, as his father had taught him, which was gone downe to dinner, and fired the goon, which brake and shevered the yron barres of the grate, whereof one strake the erle so strongly on the hed, that it stroke away one of his eyes and the side of his cheeke ; Sir Thomas Gar-

K

grave was likewise stricken, so that he died within two dayes."—*Grafton*, p. 531.

" But sorowe it is to tell and doolfull to wryte, whyle one day the sayd good erle, Sir Thomas Montagu, rested hym at a bay wyndow, and beheld the compasse of the citie, and talked with his familiers, a gonne was leveyled out of the citie from a place unknowen, whiche brake the tymbre or stone of the wyndowe with such vyolence, that the peces therof all to quashed the face of the noble erle, in suche wyse that he dyed wythin thre dayes folowyng. Upon whose soule all christen Jesu have mercy. Amen.

" Thus after dyvers wryters was *initium malorum*, for after this myshape the Englyshmen loste rather then wanne, so that by lytell & lytell they loste all their pos- session in Fraunce. And albeit that somewhat they gate after, yet for one that they wane thei loste thre, as after shall appeare."—*Fabian's Chronicle*, fol. 376.

" It so chanced, that the 59th day after the siege was layd, the erle of Salisburie, Sir Thomas Gargrave, and William Glasdale, with divers other, went into the said tower and so unto the high chamber, and looked out at the grate, and within a short space, *the sonne of the master gunner perceiving men looking out at the window, tooke his match, as his father had taught him, who was gone downe to dinner, and fired the gunne,* the shot whereof brake and sheevered the iron barres of the grate, so that one of the same barres strake the earle so violently on the head, that it stroke away one of his eyes, and the syde of hys cheeke.

" Sir Thomas Gargrave was likewise striken, and dyed within two dayes." — *Holinshed*, vol. ii. p. 1240. Ed. 1577.

" For in like manner, as when you break off the point of an arrow, rendering the rest of the iron harmless ; so this chief (the earl of Salisbury) having been beaten down like the point of a sword, the courage of the English was overcome, insomuch so, that it rather seemed to have died with him than they to have lost it. For prior to his coming they had performed no very memorable war in France, nor any action worthy of praise, and at his death they did not signalize themselves by victories, but by losses and the misfortunes that attended them. So that it appears obvious, all the glory they had acquired in France was born and died with this great general of armies. His body having been opened and embalmed, was transported to England, and placed in the tomb of his ancestors. Many regarded this death as a blow from heaven and the effect of its wrath and vengeance, in consequence of his having broken the oath made to the duke of Orleans, a prisoner in England, that he would spare the cities subject to him ; whereas, he had besieged and battered into ruins the town of Orleans, as well as for his having pillaged with a sacrilegious hand the treasures of churches and religious houses, which had till then been carefully preserved ; and in particular, for robbing the church of our *Lady of Clery*, where, from a principle of avarice, he had melted down the plates and chalices, with other presents of gold and silver, which had been dedicated by the piety of the wealthy, for the service of him who punishes the sacrilegious and the robber. There were many other beautiful and sacred monuments of piety which princes and devout persons had bequeathed in testimony of their gratitude for the recovery of health, or the having miraculously escaped from perils, or on account of just victories gained over their enemies. This loss was sensibly felt by all good Catholics, and in particular by devout women, who were accustomed to carry their vows and their prayers to this beautiful church of our Lady so fruitful in grace and in miracles."—*Dubreton*, p. 25, &c.

Page 6. *John Bastard of Orleans.*

Jean d'Orleans, count de Dunois and de Longueville, was natural son of the lady de Cany and Louis duke of Orleans, which latter prince was assassinated by order of the duke of Burgundy. John the Bastard was born on the 23d of November, 1407, and such was afterwards the celebrity he acquired, that Valentine de Milan, duchess of Orleans, lamented she was not his mother, being in the habit of stating, after the phraseology of that period, " *Qu'il lui avait été* EMBLÉ:" (*derobé*) " *That he had been surreptitiously obtained from her.*"

The Bastard, when young, commenced his heroic career by the defeat of the earls of Warwick and of Suffolk, whom he pursued to the very walls of Paris. At the siege of Orleans he valiantly defended that place, as appears from this Diary, by which means sufficient time was afforded for Jeanne d'Arc to bring up her reinforcement. Upon the raising of the siege, the various subsequent successes on the part of the French were to be attributed to the bravery and unremitting perseverance of this gallant warrior, who finally succeeded in chasing his enemies from the provinces of Normandy and Guienne; to which he gave the finishing stroke at Chastillon, in 1451, after having taken from the English Blaie, Fronsac, Bordeaux, and Bayonne; to which belligerent exploits Charles VII. was indebted for the possession of his throne. Such signal services called forth the gratitude of the monarch, who was not famous for rewarding benefits conferred, wherefore he was honoured with the enviable epithet of " *Restaurateur de la Patrie*," Saviour of the Country. To the Bastard was also granted the title of count de Longueville, while he was further honoured with the charge of grand chamberlain of France. This count de Dunois was no less esteemed by Louis XI., under whose reign he entered into the league denominated " *Bien Public*," Public Good; of which he proved the very soul, from his excellent conduct and consummate experience. The Bastard Dunois died on the 24th November, 1468, aged sixty-one; being regarded as a second Du Guesclin, and as much feared by the enemies of the state, as he was idolized and respected by all good citizens for his courage, prudence, greatness of soul, and beneficence: in fine, for a concentration of all those virtues which constitute the great and the good man.

Speaking of this renowned warrior at the siege of Orleans, Grafton thus expresses himself: —

" Here muste I a little digresse, and declare to you, what

was this Bastard of Orleaunce, which was not onely now
capitayne of the citie, but also after by Charles the Sixt
made erle of Dunoys, and in great aucthoritie in Fraunce,
and extreme enemie to the Englishe nation, as by this
storie you shall apparantly perceyve, of whose line and
stem discended the dukes of Longuile, and the marques of
Rutylon.   Lewes duke of Orleaunce, murthered in Paris,
by John duke of Burgoyn, as you before have heard, was
owner of the castell of Concy, on the frontiers of Fraunce
towarde Arthoys, whereof he made constable the lord of
Cawny, a man not so wise as his wife was faire, and yet
she was not so faire, but she was as well beloved of the
duke of Orleaunce as of her husband ; betweene the duke
and her husband (I cannot tel who was father) she con-
ceyved a child, and brought forth a pretie boy called John,
which child being of the age of one yere,   the duke
disceased; and not long after the mother and the lorde
of Cawny ended their lyves.   The next of the kinne to my
lorde Cawny chalenged the enheritaunce, which was
worth foure thousand crownes a yere, alleging that the boy
was a bastard : and the kindred of the mother's side, for to
save her honesty, it plainely denied.   In conclusion, this
matter was in contention before the presidents of the parliament of Paris, and there hanged in controversie till the
chylde came to the age of eyght yeres olde.   At which
time it was demaunded of him openly whose sonne he
was : his friendes of his mother's side advertised him to
require a day, to be advised of so great an aunswere, which
he asked, and to him it was graunted.   In the meane
season his sayde friendes perswaded him to claime his in-
heritaunce, as sonne to the lorde of Cawny, which was an

honorable lyving, and an auncient patrimony, affirming
that if he sayde contrarie, he not onely slaundered his
mother, shamed himselfe, and steyned his blood, but also
should have no lyving nor any thing to take to. The
scholemaster thinking that his disciple had well learned
his lesson, and would reherse it according to his instruction, brought him before the judges at the day assigned,
and when this question was repeted to him agayne, he
boldly answered, My hart geveth me, and my noble
courage telleth me, that I am the sonne of the noble duke
of Orleaunce, more glad to be his bastard with a meane
lyving, than the lawful sonne of that coward cuckold
Cawny, with his foure thousand crownes. The justices much
marveyled at his bold answere, and his mother's cosyns
detested him for shaming of his mother, and his father's
supposed kinne rejoysed, in gaining the patrimonie and
possessions.   Charles, duke of Orleaunce, hering of this
judgement, tooke him into his family, and gave him great
offices and fees, which he well deserved, for (during his
captivitie) he defended his landes, expulsed the Englishmen, and in conclusion, procured his deliverance.

" This couragious Bastard, after the siege had continued
three weekes full, issued out of the gate of the bridge, and
fought with the Englishmen, but they receyved him with
so fierce and terrible strokes, that he was, with al his
company, compelled to retire and flie back into the citie :
but the Englishemen followed them so fast, in kylling and
taking of their enemies, that they entered with them the
bulwarke of the bridge : which, with a great towre standing at the ende of the same, was taken incontinent by the

English men.   In which conflict many Frenchmen were
taken, but mo were slain, and the keeping of the towre
and bulwarke was committed to Wylliam Glasdale esquire.
When he had gotten this bulwarke, he was sure that, by
that way neither man nor vitaile could pass or come.   After
that, he made certain bulwarkes round about the citie,
casting trenches betwene the one and the other, layeng
ordinaunce in every part, where he sawe that any battery
might be devised.   When they within perceyved that they
were environed with fortresses and ordinances, they laied
gonne against gonne, and fortefied towres agaynst bulwarkes, and within made new rampires, and buylded newe
mudwalles, to avoyde cracks and breches which might, by
violent shot, sudainly insue.   They appointed the Bastard
of Orleaunce and Stephen Veignold called the Heire, to see
the walles and watches kept, and the bishop saw the
inhabitants within the citie were put in good order, and
that vittailes were not wantonly consumed nor vainly
spent." — *Grafton, page* 529.

Page 6.   *Stephen de Vignolles, otherwise La Hire.*

Etienne (Stephen) de Vignolles, better known in history
by the name of La Hire, was a descendant from the illustrious house of the barons de Vignolles, who being driven
from their estates by the English, established themselves
in Languedoc.   This nobleman was one of the most
renowned French captains, during the reign of Charles
VII., that monarch being indebted to him for the raising
of the siege of Montargis, which had been invested

by the duke of Bedford; La Hire also accompanied Jeanne d'Arc to the siege of Orleans, as appears in the Diary, where all historians agree in stating that he performed prodigies of valour. This gallant captain terminated his brilliant career at Montauban, in 1447, and very deservedly holds the most distinguished rank among the number of those heroes, whose prowess greatly contributed to establish the tottering throne of Charles VII.

There is recorded in a very ancient volume of *bons mots*, and speeches of distinguished personages, the following anecdote of Etienne de Vignolles, introduced under the ensuing head: " *Paroles hardies de La Hire à Charles Sept.*" La Hire being despatched by the army of Charles VII., in order to set before him the real state of his affairs, and that, on account of the want of provisions, money, and other necessaries, the English had taken possession of several cities, while the French had lost many battles; the monarch, in order to display his familiarity towards La Hire, set before him those luxuries upon which his great delight was placed, namely, his courtesans, his banquetings, his balls, &c.; at the same time inquiring what he thought of them, to the which Vignolles bluntly made answer:

" *On n'a jamais vu roi, aussi gaîment que vous ;*
Se défaire de sa couronne, son royaume, et tout."

No monarch, like you, e'er acquired such renown,
In gayly surrend'ring his kingdom and crown.

Page 6. *Of which he died.*

Grafton thus describes the removal of the body of the earl of Salisbury, at page 531 :—

" The earl was conveyed to Meum upon Loyre, where he lay, beyng wounded, viii. days, and then died, whose bodie was conveyed into England, with all funerall pompe, and buried at Bissam by his progenitors, leaving behinde him an onely daughter named Alice, maryed to Richard Nevill, sonne to Raufe erle of Westmerland, of whom hereafter shall be made mention.   What detriment, what damage, and what losse succeeded to the Englishe publike wealth, by the sodeine death of this valiaunt capteyne, not long after his departure, manifestly appered.   For the high prosperitie and great glorie of the English nacion in the partes beyond the sea, began shortly to fall, and little and little to vanish away : which thing, although the Englishe people, like a valiaunt and strong bodie, at the first tyme did not perceyve ; yet, shortly after, they felt it growe like a pestilent humor, which successively a little and little corrupteth all the members, and destroyeth the bodie.   For, after the death of this noble man, fortune of warre beganne to change, and triumphaunt victorie beganne to be darkned.   Although the death of the erle were dolorous to all Englishmen, yet surely it was most dolorous to the duke of Bedford, regent of Fraunce, as he which had lost his right hande, or lacked his weapon, when he shoulde fight with his enemie.   But seeing that dead men cannot with sorowe be called againe, nor lamentation for dead bodies cannot remedie the chaunces of men lyving : he (like a prudent governor and a politike patrone) appoynted the erle of Suffolk to be his lieutenant, and captayn of the siege, and joyned with him the lord Scales, the lord Talbot, Sir John Fastolfe, and diverse other valiant knights and squires. These lordes caused bastiles to be made round about the citie, with the which they troubled their enemies, and assaulted the walles, and left nothing unattempted, which might be to them any advauntage, or hurtfull to their enemies."

Page 7. *Broken his promise to the duke of Orleans.*

The personage above alluded to was Charles duke of Orleans, half brother of the Bastard Dunois; he was born the twenty-sixth of May, 1391, of whom we are led to speak, on account of his poetical talents, altogether unknown, which possess an indescribable charm, breathing the innate effusions of the soul. It is, indeed, singular, that this most interesting versifier did not receive from the writers during the reign of Louis XIV., that justice which was so deservedly his due; and it is even more astonishing, that he continued unknown to the great Boileau. He married the widow of Richard II., of England, was taken prisoner at the battle of Agincourt, and conveyed to Britain, where he continued incarcerated for several years; he was the father of Louis XII., and uncle of Francis I. Obiit the eighth of January, 1466.

As a specimen of his poetical talent, exerted while in confinement, may be gratifying to the reader, I hereto subjoin a few lines, quoted from an original manuscript, preserved in the public library of Grenoble, as transcribed

by one Astezan, first secretary of the duke; the passage
being extracted from folio 78 of the volume in question.

" *Tempus quod regnat clamidem dimisit acerbam,*
  Ventorum nec non frigoris ac pluvie.
  Et comptas claris radiis solaribus atque
  Formosis.   Vestes induit inde novas
  Non est nunc ales ; non est nunc bellua, quæ non
  Cantet vel clamet more sonoque suo :
  Tempus quod regnat clamidem dimisit acerbam,
  Ventorum nec non frigoris ac pluvie."

Thus Anglicised.

" Old Time has cast his cloak away,
      Of wind and rain and nipping cold,
      And now is clad in burnish'd gold,
  Of smiling Sol's unclouded ray ;
  Nor beast, nor feather'd warbler gay,
      But in its strain or song hath told,
  That Time hath cast his cloak away.
  Stream, rivulet, and fountain's play,
      In beauty's guise are now enroll'd ;
      Gay glitt'ring jewels all unfold,
  Since each is deck'd in new array,
  For Time hath cast his cloak away."

Page 8.   *John Talbot, first baron of England.*

" John Talbot, earl of Shrewsbury, was born of a noble family in Herefordshire, and displayed great valour in the reduction of Ireland, where he was commander-in-chief for Henry V.   He afterwards went to France, serving under the duke of Bedford, where he was made prisoner at the battle of Patay, but not long after recovered his liberty, and then returned to Ireland; from which country he was once more recalled to France, where he gained several victories, and took some strong places; so that his name became a terror to the French until the period of his death; which occurred at the battle of Chastillon, where the great and valiant earl of Shrewsbury and his son were slain, in 1453." — *Rapin.*

Page 15.   *On the same day was to have been a pitched battle of six Frenchmen against six English, &c.*

Independent of the intended conflict above adverted to in our Diary, at a subsequent period of the siege, we find the following account delivered by Dubreton, at page 43, which is not mentioned in the manuscript of our work.

" Four days after took place a very memorable combat, worthy of this history, between four knights, being two from either side.   One of the French was named *Gasquet,* and the other *Vedille,* both of Gascony, and from the company of La Hire.   The defiance was such, that, if there were found among the English two knights so generous and loving of their country as to be willing to combat in her defence, they were to present themselves in the lists against the French, who, without any unfair play, would make an assay of their courage and address with them."

" This challenge being received and accepted, two Englishmen appeared at a spot environed on all sides with cords attached to posts, which was allotted for the combatants. In addition to this, it was lined with men on foot and on horseback in good array, of whom there were equal numbers on either side, to prevent any injury happening to such as entered the lists or came to behold the combat. This being done, they all four rushed upon each other with couched lances, meeting together with impetuous and unparalleled force : but, in the end, the greater glory of the battle remained with the French. For Vedille and his adversary having each pierced the other through the side armour, even to their shirts, without having done much injury ; and Gasquet having unhorsed his opponent with a blow of his lance, they were separated. This was done in order to prove that the contest was that of brave and courageous men, without any movement of hatred or choler having urged them to the rencounter."

Page 18.
And more especially there died an English lord.

The Editor's research has not enabled him to identify the name of the noble personage above adverted to, concerning whom Dubreton, at page 68, states as follows : —

" In this combat an Englishman of high quality and great reputation was killed. Some knights having dismounted, raised him up and transported him to the camp as he surrendered up his soul. He was extremely regretted by all the English, as well on account of the great proofs he had given of his courage in divers rencounters, as also from his being of considerable utility to them."

Page 20.

For he was their marshal, and a right valiant man.

Speaking of Lancelot de l'Isle, Dubreton, at page 71, inserts the following eulogium : —

" This death considerably elevated the courage of the Orleanese, and diminished their apprehension, as if the enemy's forces had been destroyed with this great captain, for he was one of the most redoubted of the English host. His counsel was fit to be executed, and his hand was never wanted. There was not an order to be issued, nor a watch, a review, nor a labour to be undertaken, or any act to be performed, that he would not accomplish with the most admirable patience and address. If God, by the hands of those of Orleans, had not taken from the world this wary, prompt, vigilant, bold, and generous enemy, it is not likely that the French would have easily escaped the threatening storm, nor extricated their necks from the yoke of servitude wherewith they were threatened by the English."

The English carried off the sticks, that is, vine stakes, from the vineyards.

The soil in the environs of Orleans has been for many centuries famous for its fecundity in producing the vine, and at the present period it is ranked the most prolific territory

in France for the growth of the grape. The space occupied
by the vineyards extends from ten to eleven leagues, upwards of thirty miles, comprising an extent of nearly thirty
parishes, between the towns of Jargeau and Beaugenci, of
which places mention is made in the course of the Diary.
According to the common computation, an ordinary year's
growth will produce an hundred thousand tuns of wine.
It is scarcely possible to picture a more gratifying spectacle than the numerous villages scattered through such an
extent of vine-land, while the countless country residences
of private individuals equally tend to diversify the rich
prospect. The environs of Orleans give two species of
wines, the white and the red, the former of which being the
produce of St. Mesmin, and called *Génetin*, is peculiar to
that country.

Page 22.

Bar, or *Barrois*, a considerable territory of France,
situated on either bank of the river Meuse, between Lorraine and Champaigne, is the country that gave birth to the
Pucelle of Orleans.

Domremy, a small village near Vaucouleurs, in Lorraine,
is situated in a barren soil, and was the natal place of
Jeanne d'Arc, who was the daughter of Jacques d'Arc and
his wife Elizabeth, or rather Isabella Romée.

Vaucouleurs, a small city, and formerly a provostship, is
very agreeably situated on the slope of a hill, at the base
of which is a meadow, watered by the river Meuse, which
stretches itself till lost in the distance. This place belonged
to the dukes of Lorraine, until Philip of Valois purchased

so important a key to the empire in 1335. Jeanne d'Arc being born in this provostship, the territory was, in consequence, highly favoured by Charles VII., who bestowed upon it great immunities and exemptions.

Page 23. *Narrated to him her visions.*

Numerous attempts have been made by French writers to prove that the mission of Jeanne d'Arc was the effect of celestial agency, which assertion is combated by Robertson, in his introduction to the history of Charles V. He therein examines the mission of the Pucelle in a political point of view, and while rendering justice to her wisdom and courage, deploring her untimely fate, and most eloquently inveighing against the superstition to which she was sacrificed, he nevertheless considers her as a mere instrument and a victim of party. This writer, however, is not the only one who has started objections against the heavenly mission of Jeanne; for we find that one Doctor Beaupere, who acted as an assessor during her trial, entertained an opinion, " *That her alleged visions and apparitions were rather the effects of human invention, than due to divine inspiration:*" and in the *Histoire Générale des Rois de France depuis Pharamond jusqu'à Charles Sept,* written by Bernard de Girard, lord de Haillan, first historian of France, and established genealogist of the Order of the Holy Ghost, by Henry III., appears the following statement, translated, as nearly as possible, verbatim : —

" Some say that Jeanne was the mistress of John Bastard of Orleans; others of the lord de Baudricourt, who

being wary and cunning, and seeing that the king knew no
longer what to do or to say, and the people, on account of
continual wars, so much oppressed as not to be able to
raise their courage, betook themselves to have recourse to
a miracle fabricated in false religion, being that which, of
all things, most elevates the heart; and makes men believe,
even the most simple, that which is not; and the people
were very proper to imbibe such superstitions.   Those
who believe she was a maid sent by God are not damned,
neither are those who did not believe.   Many esteem this
last assertion an heresy, but we will not dwell too much
upon it, neither too much on the contrary belief.   Wherefore these lords, for the space of some days, instructed her
in all she was to answer to the demands which should be
made of her by the king and themselves when in his
presence; for they were to interrogate her, and in order
that she might recognise the monarch when conducted into
his presence, they caused her every day to see, at various
times, his picture.   The day appointed on which she was
to be led to him in his chamber, which they had already
arranged, they did not fail to be present.   Being entered,
the first who asked her what she wanted, were the Bastard
of Orleans and Baudricourt, who demanded of her, her
business.   She replied she wanted to speak to the king.
They presented to her another of the lords who was there,
saying to her that he was the king; but she, instructed in
all which should be done and said, as well as what she was
to do and say, said, that it was not the king, and that he
was hid in the alcove, containing the bed.   This feigned
invention and appearance of religion, was of such profit to
the kingdom, that it raised the courage lost and beaten

down by despair * * * * * * * Wherefore the king caused to be given to her horses and arms, and an army with a good number of great captains, in company of whom she carried succour to those of Orleans."

Du Haillan, our informant, being first historiographer of France, and living but one hundred and forty years after the death of Jeanne, must, from the post he occupied, have possessed ample means of ascertaining the above facts, which, if true, set the matter at rest concerning any supernatural interposition in her favour; a circumstance that tends to exalt still more the noble disinterestedness of the heroic but unfortunate Maid of Orleans.

When speaking of the tree under which Jeanne is stated to have received her celestial commands, Dubreton says, at page 114, " That which the people of the country assert is greatly to be admired, namely, that the tree (it was a pear tree) beneath which she was seated, the first time that the voice from heaven commanded her to repair to the king, is neither subject to be worm-eaten, nor to the effects of age, neither to thunder, to hail, nor to any other injuries of time or the air."

In order to proceed to Blois.

Blois, capital of the department of Loire and Cher, is a very old but beautiful city, on the banks of the Loire, and is so renowned for the fertility of its soil, as to be surnamed *The Granary of France.* As the French court formerly resided in this place, it is highly reputed for having the best French spoken by its inhabitants.

Page 25.   *Messire John Fascot, &c. conducted about*
                 three hundred waggons, &c.

" In the Lent season, vittels and artillerie began to waxe
scant in the English campe, wherefore the earle of Suffolke
appointed Sir John Fastolfe, Sir Thomas Rampston, and
Sir Philip Hall, with their retinues, to ride to Paris, to the
lord regent, to informe him of their lacke, who incon-
tinentlie upon that information provided vittels, artillerie,
and munitions necessarie, and loded therewith many
chariots, carts, and horsses : and for the sure conveieng of
the same, he appointed Sir Simon Morhier, provost of
Paris, with the gard of the citie, and diverse of his owne
houshold-servants, to accompanie Sir John Fastolfe and
his complices to the armie lieng at the siege of Orleance.
They were in all to the number of fifteene hundred men,
of the which there were not past five or six hundred
Englishmen." — *Holinshed*, page 599.

Page 27.   *That no one should dismount.*

From this particular order, so strictly issued by the
count de Clermont, one might be led to infer, that the
armour worn at that period by the knights on horseback,
was particularly cumbersome ; and that, consequently,
danger was to be apprehended in the event of the riders
quitting their steeds. Shakspeare makes Richard the
Third, in his soliloquy, on the night prior to the battle of
Bosworth, use the following expression : " *The armourers
accomplishing the knights and closing rivets up,*" *&c.* by
which it should appear that the warriors were literally

rivetted into their iron trappings. Mezeray, the French historian, giving an account of a conflict, wherein some Italian knights were engaged and worsted, informs the reader that the victors, unable to uncase the vanquished, kindled a fire, whereon they placed the unfortunate warriors, who were thus roasted, like lobsters, within their shells.

Page 29.

Holinshed, speaking of this battle, and the loss sustained by the French and their confederates the Scots, says, at page 600 :—

" Wherefore Sir John Fastolfe set all his companie in good order of battell, and pitched stakes before everie archer, to breake the force of the horssemen. At their backes they set all the waggons and carriages, and within them they tied all their horses. In this manner stood they still, abiding the assault of their enemies. The Frenchmen, by reason of their great number, thinking themselves sure of the victorie, egerlie set on the Englishmen, which with great force them received, and themselves manfullie defended. At length, after long and cruell fight, the Englishmen drove backe and vanquished the proud Frenchmen, and compelled them to flee. In this conflict were slaine the lord William Steward, constable of Scotland, and his brother, the lord Dorvalle, the lord Chateaubrian, Sir John Basgot, and other Frenchmen and Scots, to the number of five and twentie hundred, and above eleven hundred taken prisoners, although the French writers affirme the number lesse."

Dubreton, at page 86, adverting to the deaths of John Stewart, constable of Scotland, and his brother, at the battle of Herrings, thus expresses himself :—

" Those two valliant brothers, as they were about to disengage themselves from their perilous situation, from the love they bore to each other, were killed, after having fought most bravely; and covered the error of their imprudence and inconsiderate ardor by the most signal proofs of their affection and their courage."

Page 30.

John Fastolff, knight, and knight banneret, was a general, a governor, and a nobleman, in France, under the several kings, Henry IV., V., and VI., of England, and was also a knight of the garter. Some have supposed this personage of French extraction, while others erroneously fixed his birth-place in Bedfordshire; whereas he was the descendant of an ancient and famous English family of the county of Norfolk, which had flourished there anterior to the conquest. As early as 1405, it appears that Sir John Fastolff accompanied Thomas of Lancaster, afterwards duke of Clarence, son of Henry IV., to Ireland ; the said Thomas being appointed lord lieutenant of that country; where Sir John Fastolff married a rich young widow named Milicent, lady Castlecomb, daughter of lord Tibetot, relict of Sir Stephen Scrope, knight. Upon the nomination of the English regency in France, Sir John was appointed to the command of some forces in that country, and he, in consequence, removed thither from his estate in Norfolk, and continued for many years on the Gallic soil ;

for, according to Caxton, in his edition of Tully's Offices, to use that printer's phraseology, when speaking of Fastolff, he states that, " *exercisyng the warrys in the royame of Fraunce and other countrees, &c., by fourty yeres enduryng.*" So that we see no reasonable pretence for supposing that the Sir John Falstaff of Shakspeare was intended as a representation of the character now under consideration; who, for his bravery, was made knight banneret on the field of battle, and on account of his discreet, valiant, chaste, and sober habits, was intrusted with the highest commands abroad; created also a baron in France, and knight of the garter in England, In 1428, Sir John Fastolff, with other approved captains, was despatched by William de la Pole, duke of Sffollk, to the regent at Paris, for supplies for the army besieging Orleans; who not only provided him plentifully, but appointed a strong guard at his return to secure the safe conveyance of the same. The French, being fully aware of the importance of this succour, united two armies to meet the convoy, but they were completely overthrown, their loss in slain being computed at more than Fastolff had under his command; which gallant victory was called the *battle of Herrings*. In the ensuing year, however, the tide of fortune was turned, for at the conflict at Patay Sir John Fastolff was obliged to fly to Corbeil, in order to escape being killed, with the lord Talbot, or made prisoner of war with lord Hungerford and Sir Thomas Rampston. In 1430 we find Fastolff named lieutenant of Caen, in Normandy; and in 1435, when the regent died at Rouen, he named Fastolff one of the executors of his will: after which, in 1440, Sir John made his final return to England, laden with the laurels acquired in France, and afterwards shining as bright upon his native soil. In 1459, having attained the venerable age of eighty years, he says of himself, that he was " in good remembrance, albeit I am greatly vexed with sicke-nesse, and thurgh age infebelyd." This great warrior and statesman lingered under an hectic fever and asthma for an hundred and forty-eight days, and died at his seat at Castre.

Having equally a great command of men at arms.

" After this fortunate victorie, John Fastolf and his com-panie, having lost no one man of any reputation, wyth all theyr caryages, vytail, and prysoners, marched forth and came to the English campe before Orleans, where they were joyfully receyved, and highly commended for theyr valiaunce and worthie prowes shewed in the battaile, the which, bycause most part of the caryage was *Herring* and *Lenten* stuffe, the Frenchmen call it the battaile of Her-rings."— *Holinshed*, vol. ii., p. 1241.   Ed. 1577.

Page 32.
About this period arrived at Chinon Jeanne la Pucelle.

Jeanne d'Arc was conducted by her uncle, Durand Lapart, to Vaucouleurs, where she was first presented to Robert de Baudricourt, governor of that town, but without making any impression upon his mind; notwithstanding which he afterwards went to the Pucelle, accompanied by the parish curate, arrayed in his stole, when the latter began by performing exorcisms upon Jeanne; *commanding her not to approach if she was wicked, but to come near him if she was good.* Upon this Jeanne was angry, and taxed the priest with being indiscreet, since he had been accustomed to hear her at confession. Baudricourt, after this interview, advised Lapart to conduct his niece back to her parents, yet thought it expedient to write to the king upon the subject, detailing the great promises made by Jeanne, and her assurances so frequently reiterated, that God would afford him succour before the middle of Lent.

Shortly after the above interview, the Pucelle returned to Vaucouleurs with her uncle, submitting to these delays with that violence of temper which formed a leading trait of her singular character. The duke of Lorraine being desirous to see her, she presented herself before him by means of a pass, wherewith she was furnished for that purpose : nothing, however, is detailed in history respecting the nature of their conference.

Jeanne at length became so anxious to see the king, that she resolved to set out on foot, when two gentlemen, chancing to be at Vaucouleurs, whose names were Jean de Novelompont, surnamed of Metz, and Bertrand de Poulangies, they introduced themselves to the Pucelle, and ultimately conducted her in safety to Chinon. During this tedious and perilous journey, through a country abounding with English and Burgundians, these gentlemen were filled with the greatest disquietude ; but Jeanne incessantly told them to apprehend nothing, as she was commanded to proceed ; that her brethren in Paradise had instructed her what was to be done ; and in this manner, after the expiration of eleven days, they arrived at Chinon, where the court then resided.

And all these feats they notified to the king.

Charles VII., surnamed the Victorious, succeeded his father, Charles VI., at the age of twenty, in the year 1422, and was crowned at Poictiers, whither he had removed his parliament, on the 6th November in the same year. The commencement of this king's reign was characterized by troubles and disorders fomented by Henry VI. of England, who was proclaimed king of France at Paris. Charles was a weak prince, formed to be governed by his mistresses and ministers; but the former were possessed of virtues, and the latter by no means deficient in talents. In 1428, the siege of Orleans was raised by the English, owing to the enthusiasm produced in the French army by the intrepid and glorious deeds of Jeanne d'Arc, surnamed the Maid of Orleans, and who ultimately conducted the king to Rheims, where he was crowned by the hands of the archbishop of Chartres. During the conflicts which succeeded, the English were almost uniformly discomfited, so that before the expiration of 1451 they were compelled to abandon France, retaining Calais only in their possession. Charles was espoused to Mary, daughter of Louis, the second duke of Anjou, by whom he had eleven children, four sons and seven daughters, of whom two sons only survived him, namely, Louis and Charles ; he had also three illegitimate children, according to Mezeray. In 1461, Charles died at Meun, in the province of Berry, in the sixtieth year of his age and the fortieth of his reign, having abstained from taking nourishment, under the apprehension of being poisoned,

through the machinations of his son, the dauphin, afterwards Louis XI.

Page 33. *And forthwith she spake there, and bowed
herself with reverence, &c.*

Jeanne d'Arc was presented to the king by the count
de Vendôme, and without hesitation recognized the
monarch at first sight, although there was nothing particular in his attire, or exterior appearance, and he was
indiscriminately mingled with the crowd; she immediately
made a profound reverence, and thus addressed him :
" *Gentil Dauphin, j'ai nom Jeanne la Pucelle, et vous
mande le Roi des cieux, par moi, que vous serez sacré et
couronné à Rheims; vous serez le lieutenant du Roi des
cieux qui est Roi de France.*"
" *Gentil Dauphin, I am named Jeanne la Pucelle, and the
King of heaven informs you, through me, that you shall be
consecrated and crowned at Rheims; you shall be lieutenant
of the King of heaven, who is King of France.*"
Charles, removing from those that surrounded him,
conversed with Jeanne in their presence, but without
being overheard; which conference lasted for some time,
and all the courtiers perceived that a degree of satisfaction was legibly depicted on the countenance of their
sovereign during this parley; who afterwards declared
to several personages, that a revelation which she had
made to him, of a secret known only to himself, gave
birth to the confidence with which she inspired him.
We are also informed from history, that prior to the
arrival of Jeanne d'Arc at Chinon, it had been predicted

to the king, that his realm as well as himself should
be greatly afflicted, but that a young maiden would
present herself, by whom their deliverance would be
accomplished.—See *Gerson, Pasquier, Hordal, Dupleix,&c.*

And to the above may be added, the English prophecies of Merlin, who is said to have foretold that we
should be banished by a maid from France.—*Hist. et
Antiq. de la Ville d'Orleans, par F. le Mair,* 1648. fol. 187.

Before definitively employing Jeanne, Charles was
determined to put her to the last proof; he was desirous
of ascertaining, if the purity of her conduct had always
answered to appearances ; wherefore she was confided to the
care of the queen of Sicily, his mother-in-law, and to the
ladies of her suite.   She was then visited in secret by
proper medical personages, after which a report was
made to the king by her Sicilian majesty, in presence of
Daulon, and many other individuals, purporting, that she
was " *entière et vraie pucelle;*" entirely and in every
respect a virgin.   Daulon, afterwards seneschal de Beaucaire, and whom the duke d'Alençon represented as the
most upright knight of his court, had the charge of
superintending the conduct and preservation of the
Pucelle.   It was the secret so revealed by Jeanne to
the monarch which afterwards prompted him to erect,
in 1458, the bronze effigies of the Virgin with the dead
Christ on her lap, together with himself and the Pucelle
kneeling, which were placed upon the ancient bridge at
Orleans.

Holinshed, describing this introduction of the Pucelle,
thus expresses himself :—

" In time of this siege at Orleance (French stories saie)

the first weeke of March 1428, unto Charles the dolphin,
at Chinon as he was in verie great care and studie how
to wrestle against the English nation, by one Peter Bad-
ricourt capteine of Vaucoulcur, (made after marshall of
France by the dolphin's creation) was caried a young
wench of an eighteene yeeres old, called Jone Arc, by
name of hir father (a sorie sheepheard) James of Arc,
and Isabell hir mother, brought up poorlie in their trade
of keeping cattell, borne at Domprin (therefore reported
by Bale, Jone Domprin) upon Meuse in Loraine within
the diocesse of Thoule. Of favour was she counted like-
some, of person stronglie made and manlie, of courage
great, hardie, and stout withall, an understander of
counsels though she were not at them, great semblance
of chastitie both of bodie and behaviour, the name of
Jesus in hir mouth about all hir businesses, humble,
obedient, and fasting diverse daies in the weeke. A
person (as their bookes make hir) raised up by power
divine, onlie for succour to the French estate then
deeplie in distresse, in whome, for planting a credit the
rather, first the companie that toward the dolphin did
conduct hir, through places all dangerous, as holden by
the English, where she never was afore, all the waie and
by nightertale safelie did she lead : then at the dolphin's
sending by hir assignement, from Saint Katharin's church
of Fierbois in Touraine (where she never had beene and
knew not) in a secret place there among old iron,
appointed she her sword to be sought out and brought
hir, that with five floure delices was graven on both sides,
wherewith she fought and did many slaughters by hir
owne hands. On warfar rode she in armour cap a pie

and mustered as a man, before her an ensigne all white,
wherin was Jesus Christ painted with a floure delice
in his hand.

" Unto the dolphin into his gallerie when first she
was brought, and he shadowing himselfe behind, setting
other gaie lords before him to trie hir cunning from all
the companie, with a salutation (that indeed marz all
the matter) she pickt him out alone, who thereupon had
hir to the end of the gallerie, where she held him an
houre in secret and private talke, that of his privie
chamber was thought verie long, and therefore would
have broken it off; but he made them a signe to let hir
saie on.   In which (among other) as likelie it was, she
set out unto him the singular feats (forsooth) given hir
to understand by revelation divine, that in virtue of that
sword she should atchive, which were, how with honor
and victorie shee would raise the siege at Orleance,
set him in state of the crowne of France, and drive the
English out the countrie, thereby he to inioie the kingdome
alone.   Heereupon he, hartened at full, appointed hir a
sufficient armie with absolute power to lead them, and
they obedientlie to doo as she bad them.   Then fell she
to worke, and first defeated indeed the siege at Orleance,
by and by encouraged him to crowne himselfe king of
France at Rheims, that a little before from the English
she had woone.   Thus after pursued she manie bold
enterprises to our great displeasure a two yeare togither,
for the time she kept in state untill she were taken and
for heresie and witcherie burned ; as in particularities
hereafter followeth.   But in hir prime time she, armed at
all points (like a jolie capteine) roade from Poictiers to

Blois, and there found men of warre, vittels, and muni-
tion, ready to be conveied to Orleance."

Page 34. *But the doctors found her so honest in appearance and so sage in her speech, &c.*

Bernard de Girard, lord de Haillan, historian of France
to Henry III., states, that upon the doctors presenting
themselves to Jeanne, by order of the king, for the purpose of ascertaining whether she was a virgin or not, she
expressed herself in these words :

" *Je le crois, je ne sais ni A ni B ; je viens de la part du
Roi du Ciel, pour faire lever le siège d'Orleans, et mener le
roi à Rheims."* — See *Laverdy*, CCCXII. and CCCLI.,
note 24.

" I believe it; I know neither A nor B; I come on the
part of the King of heaven, to cause the siege of Orleans
to be raised, and to conduct the king to Rheims."

Page 35. *And he also willed and commanded that she
should have a standard.*

Jeanne d'Arc caused a banner to be made at Blois
conformably to that which she stated to have been indicated to her in her visions; it was her chaplain who conducted this work, which represented our Saviour seated
upon clouds, and an angel holding in its hand a flower
de luce.

*The king being further desirous of giving her a beautiful
sword, &c.*

As soon as Charles was satisfied concerning the celestial mission of Jeanne d'Arc, he caused her to appear at
court caparisoned *cap à pie*, the weight of whose armour
did not however prevent her from remounting on horseback unassisted, which the most robust knights could with
difficulty accomplish.   The king being desirous of presenting her with a fine sword, she requested his majesty
to expedite a messenger to the church of Saint Catherine de Fiere Bois, in Touraine, stating, that he would
there find an old weapon, on whose blade were engraved
five crosses, and five fleurs de lys, with which it was
decreed that she should conquer the English.   Charles
inquiring if she had ever visited the said church, was
answered in the negative; and upon this, a person being
despatched brought back the sword indicated, and whereof
she made use during all her rencontres with the British.

Page 36.   *And he gave to accompany her, a very valiant
and sage gentleman named John Daulon, &c.*

On consulting the page of history for a description of
the Maid of Orleans, we find it stated, that the knight
Daulon, who was deputed to arm Jeanne d'Arc, affirmed,
that she was young, and rather lusty; that he had seen
her fine white bosom, while occupied in the performance
of his duty; that he lived with her for the space of one
year; during which period he states, in the most ex-

pressive terms, that she always pursued the same modest line of conduct; in which assertion he is supported by the testimony of the duke d'Alençon; who sometimes during the war slept in the same apartment as the Pucelle, *à la paillasse;* that is to say, " on a straw mattrass;" and who further attests, that her bosom, which he had seen by chance, was particularly beautiful.

All the pictorial representations upon which any reliance can be placed, as well as the written documents detailing Jeanne's external appearance, represent her as wearing a small green bonnet turned up round the brim, and adorned with an ample plume of feathers.

Whereat those of Orleans, seeing them depart, were not well content.

At the period when this dissatisfaction was testified by the people of Orleans, the Bastard Dunois, according to Dubreton, page 94, &c. delivered the following energetic speech, which merits well to be recorded.

" Gentlemen;

" I shall say nothing of the opinion of those who call a disgraceful servitude a very honourable agreement; and I think that they should neither be regarded as citizens nor admitted to the council of war. I have nothing to do with those whose advice is, that the city should be abandoned; it seems that your consent would only tend to preserve the recollection of their original valour. It is effeminate courage, and no generosity, not to be able to endure for a short period necessity and hunger. There are more found who will voluntarily brave death than of those who patiently endure misery. For myself, as

honour is dear to me, I should highly approve this advice, if I found that when put into execution, we had
nothing to lose but our lives.   Nevertheless, let us deliberate upon these things; place before yourselves,
gentlemen, your country exacting at your hands the
duty of good and loyal citizens, and conjuring you by
the soil of your birth, by the fidelity which you owe
to your legitimate prince, by the safety of your fathers,
your children, and your friends, as well as of yourselves.
Let me exhort you to fix your regard upon the whole
kingdom, whose sole dependence is placed on the preservation of your city.   You cannot, gentlemen, without
for ever dishonouring your name and your memory,
either deprive it of your succour by your own folly,
abandon it by your temerity, or subject it to per-
petual servitude by your want of courage.   For, to what
else do the English aspire, envious as they are of your
liberty and your glory, but to incarcerate in their cities,
and eternally enslave those amongst you, whom they
have found to be the most valiant and illustrious?   In all
the wars they have waged against you, they never had
any other aim or condition save that.   Cast your eyes
towards all the other cities of France, groaning under the
yoke of hard servitude, and suffering every thing that the
cruelty and the rage of tyrants are accustomed to exercise against towns that are oppressed.   There they ravish,
pillage, beat, wound, and murder with impunity, without
any respect of age, sex, or of dignity.   Daughters are
torn from the arms of their mothers, and cruelly violated
in their presence, and immolated at their feet like victims,
subject to the rage of soldiers.   Cities are daily sacked

that freely surrender; by night and by day, from every quarter resound the cries and the groans of desolated families.   Such being the case, consider, gentlemen, whether you prefer to protect your city with courage and with constancy; or, to betray and shamefully deliver it to a most avaricious and cruel enemy."

Page 38.   *The earl of Suffolk and the lords Talbot and Escalles (Scales) sent by a herald as a present to the Bastard of Orleans, a dish full of figs, raisins, and dates, &c.*

" At length, after sturdy blows being dealt on either side, the French were repulsed into the city; the Bastard of Orleans having acted worthily in this combat.   Upon this account the inhabitants had great confidence in him; for relying upon his valour and his prudence, they often made sallies, finding nothing hazardous or difficult under the order of this great captain.   So that it was no easy matter to discern whether he was most loved and obeyed by the soldiers, or by the citizens.   Upon the most important and perilous occasions there was no one more esteemed by the citizens as a leader than himself, nor did the soldiers ever fight with greater confidence and hardihood than when led to the field by the Bastard.   He was neither deficient on the score of courage in the midst of danger, nor of prudence during the conflict.   He was indefatigable of body, and his valour invincible in war.   He was abstemious in eating and in drinking, never yielding to voluptuousness, but following only the strict calls of nature.   Neither by day nor by night was any difference made by him in the

periods of watchfulness and of sleep, giving only that
time to repose which he could spare from the necessity of acting.   He was uniformly at the head of the foot
or the horse, always foremost in entering the battle, and the
last to retire.   Even his enemies admired his transcendent
virtues, openly avowing that he was endowed with all
the requisites appertaining to a great captain.   And
although he was mortally hated by their chiefs, whom
he had roughly handled in all the combats wherein he
had been engaged, and desirous as they were to possess
this city, they in consequence were jealous of his fame :
nevertheless the earls of Suffolk, and the lords Talbot
and Scales, one day sent him by an herald a basket full of
figs, grapes, and dates, begging him to remit them from
the city some skins wherewith to line their robes.   This messenger, having been welcomed most humanely, was sent
back to the camp with the skins required, together with
other presents, being a very rare and signal example of
the liberality of this captain."—*Dubreton*, pp. 117, &c.

*And the current was so strong and so rapid that it was
difficult to believe, &c.*

The sources of the river Loire take their rise in Upper
Vivarais in Languedoc, and at the base of Mount Gerbier-
le-joux, and after running through an extent of country
the river becomes navigable at the small town of Saint
Rambert, above Roanne ; it then waters the Bourbonnois, which it separates from Burgundy, and after entering
the province of Orleans, continues its current through
Blaisois, Touraine, Anjou, and a portion of Brittany, and
at length empties itself into the ocean, after a course

extending more than an hundred and fifty leagues, at twelve leagues below Nantes.

The overflowings of this river are recorded by the devastations they have occasioned at different periods ; and in particular, the country situated between the Loire and the Loiret, appear to have been visited by the most extraordinary floods.   There is still to be seen in the parish of Saint-Nicolas Saint Mesmin, a stone on the gable end of the church, behind the door, upon which appears this inscription :

> *L'an mil cinq cent soixante-sept,*
> *Du mois de Mai le dix-sept,*
> *En cette place et endroit,*
> *Se trouvera Loire et Loiret.*

These inundations are occasioned by the thawing of the snows of the mountains of Forez and Auvergnac ; from very remote periods every means has been adopted to prevent, or at least, render those overflowings less frequent, since we find that so early as the reign of Charlemagne, banks were constructed to retain the Loire within her boundaries, and the successors of that prince have uniformly kept those works in repair.   Except in times of inundation and high tides, the Loire pursues a very tranquil course.

Page 39.   *Of which five was the lord de Grey, nephew of the defunct earl of Salisbury, &c.*

The Editor has not been able to ascertain who was the personage designated in the above lines.

Page 40.   *And drove the French until very near the boule-*
           vard of Banier Gate, &c.

Banier Gate is at the northern extremity of Orleans,
communicating with the square of the citadel. This
portal, like the others, had two towers, which are no
longer standing, having been demolished in 1754.

Wherefore the tocsin was sounded from the belfry, &c.

Before the tower was raised on which is now placed
the large city clock, the tower of Saint Pierre Empont
served as the belfry. From thence the couvre-feu (the
curfew), public rejoicings, alarms, &c. were sounded, as
we find by an order of the parliament of Paris, bearing
date the tenth of April 1323.

From thence also, during the night, was rung the setting, continuance, and breaking up of the watches; the
bell used upon those occasions being named *La Trompille
de la Guette,* otherwise *Chasse-ribault.*

Page 41.   *A ball which killed a lord of England, for whom
            the English performed great mourning.*

The name of the nobleman here alluded to, as being
killed, does not appear in any of the chronicles.

Page 42.   *The following day, which was Wednesday, and
            no Frenchman being there found, was an hole nearly pierced
            through the wall of the almonry, &c.*

When detailing this occurrence, Dubreton, at page 130,
states: " The keeper of the almonry, fearful of being

suspected, would not await the fury of the people, but ran away as soon as he found the affair was known. Under the same apprehension, the soldiers, one after another, disappeared without procuring a pass, and secretly absconded from the city. In consequence of which, the Bastard of Orleans, to hold out an example for others, and prevent them, through fear of punishment, from committing a similar fault, having surprised two light horsemen, of the company of Villiers, who were proceeding without leave, caused them to be seized for deserters, and condemned as guilty of *leze majesty*."

Page 46. *This same day the Pucelle being at Blois, &c.*

Grafton, speaking of the Pucelle from the period of her interview with the king at Chinon to her arrival at Blois, thus expresses himself, at page 534 : —

" There came to him, beyng at Chynon, a mayde of the age of xx yeres, and in mannes apparell, named Jone, borne in Burgoyne, in a towne called Droymy besyde Vancolour, which was a greate space a chamberlein in a common hostrey, and was a rampe of such boldnesse, that she would course horses, and ride them to water, and do thinges, that other yong maydens both abhorred and were ashamed to do: yet as some say, whether it were because of her foule face, that no man would desire it, either because she had made a vowe to live chaste, she kept her maydenhed, and preserved her virginitie. She (as a monster) was sent to the dolphyn, by Sir Robert Bandrencort capteyne of Vancolour, to whom she declared, that she was sent from God, both to ayde the miserable citie of Orleaunce, and also to restore him to the possession of his realme, out of the which he was expulsed and overcommed : rehersyng to him visions, traunces, and fables, full of blasphemie, superstition, and hypocrisye, that I marveyle much that wise men dyd beleeve her, and learned clerkes would write such phantasyes, what should I reherse, howe they say, she knewe and called him her king, whome she never sawe before : that she had by revelation a sworde, to her appoynted in the church of Saint Katheryn of Fierboys in Torayne, where she never had bene ; that she declared such privie messeges from God, our ladie, and other saints, to the dolphyn, that she made the teares ronne downe from his eyes ; so was he deluded, so was he blinded, and so was he deceved by the devilles meanes which suffered her to begin her race, and in conclusion rewarded her with a shamefull fal.   But in the meane season, such credence was given to her, that she was honored as a saint of the religious, and beleved as one sent from God of the temporalitie, insomuch that she (armed at all poyntes) rode from Poyters to Bloys, and there founde men of warre, vitaile, and municions, readic to be conveyed to Orleaunce."

Page 48.

To the duke of Bedford, calling himself regent, &c.

John, duke of Bedford, third son of Henry IV. and uncle of Henry VI., in 1422, had the command of the English forces in France, and the same year was nominated regent of that country by his nephew, Henry VI.

whom he caused to be proclaimed at Paris. He defeated the French fleet near Southampton, and made himself master of Cotoi, entered Paris at the head of his army, and beat the duke d'Alençon, having thus rendered himself conqueror of France. He died at Rouen, 1435, where a sumptuous monument was erected to his memory, which one of the courtiers of Charles VIII. advised that monarch to destroy, who, we are informed, made the following reply: "No; let *him* rest in peace now dead, who, while living, made all Frenchmen tremble." It is to be regretted that the duke of Bedford, as renowned in the field as consummate in the cabinet, should have completely tarnished his fame by pursuing a line of conduct towards the youthful and heroic Jeanne d'Arc, which would have degraded the most ignoble of the human race. We cannot account for the conduct of this nobleman towards La Pucelle, whom destiny had placed in his power; she nobly combated to emancipate her country from a foreign yoke, and whatsoever might have been the effect produced on vulgar minds from the idea of her supernatural mission, it is scarcely to be believed that the regent of France gave credit to the tales of sorcery and infernal agency attributed to the Maid of Orleans; in which case his mind could only have been swayed by the basest of all human passions; the gratification of a dark and cowardly revenge towards an heroic victim whom fate had placed at his mercy.

Page 51. *And upon the same day was a smart skirmish delivered by the pages of the French and those of the English between the two islands of Saint Lawrence, they having no shields excepting small wicker baskets, &c.*

Nothing can more forcibly display the rooted animosity that subsisted between the French and the English in the neighbourhood of Orleans, than the hostile rencounters described in this and the ensuing pages of our Diary, from which it appears, that the youth of either country harboured a hatred as implacable as that wherewith the bosoms of veteran soldiers were inspired.

Page 55. *To the which would not acquiesce in any sort, to either of them, the duke of Bedford.*

Upon the duke of Burgundy making the above application to the regent, Dubreton, at page 102, states as follows : —

" The duke of Bedford, puffed up with his victories and the prosperity of his king, having already begun to despise the duke of Burgundy with proud and brutal insolence, made this answer, ' *That having beaten the bushes, it was not just that any one else should possess the birds.*' The duke of Burgundy, offended and incensed to the quick at these words replete with ostentation and disdain, forthwith sent by his herald a command to all such as owed him obedience, forthwith to quit the English camp, under pain of death."

Page 59.   *And in consequence she gave orders that all the*
men at war should confess themselves, and that they
should leave behind them all their silly women, and
their baggage, &c.

Whether Jeanne ever wielded her sword, we cannot
take upon ourselves to determine; the following very
curious extract will, however, afford sufficient proof of
the rooted animosity entertained by the Maid of Arc
towards females who pursued a vicious course of life;
and, as the annotator has never before found this
incident quoted, which is handed down by a contemporary writer, it may not prove uninteresting to the
lovers of historical facts.

" Et pourcé quen la compaignie avoit plusiers femmes
diffamées, qui empeschoiēt aucuns gens d'armes d'aller
avant, la dicte Jehanne la Pucelle feist crier qu'elles
s'en departissent. Apres le cry fait chascun se meit à
aller avant. Et pourcé que la dicte Jehanne, qui estoit
à cheval, en rencontra deux ou trois en sa voye, elle
tira son espée pour les batre, et frappa sur l'une d'elles du
plat de son espée si grand coup qu'elle rōpit sa dicte espee,
dont le roy fut fort deplaisant quant il le sceut, et luy dist
qu'elle devoit prendre ung baston pour les frapper, sans
habandonner sa dicte espée, qui luy avoit revelée de par
Dieu."—*Annales de France, par Maistre Nicole Gille Con-*
treroleur du Tresor de Louis XI.

" And as there were in the company several women
of loose morals, who prevented the men at arms from
advancing, the said maiden Jeanne, in an elevated voice,

commanded them to begone. After this exclamation, every one prepared to march forward ; and as Jeanne, who was on horseback, met two or three of these females on the road, she drew her sword to strike them, and beat one with the flat side of her weapon with such lusty strokes, that she broke her said sword, which caused the king great displeasure when he heard it, who said to her, that she ought to have taken a stick to beat them, and not the sword which had been revealed to her by God."

This sword was the same which the above author announces in the following manner during the interview of Jeanne with Charles VII., at Chinon.

" Apres ces choses, ladicte Jehanne pria au roy qu'il luy envoyast querir par ung de ses armuriers une espée qui luy avoit esté denoncée estre en certain lieu en l'eglise Saincte Katherine de Fierboys, en laquelle avoit pour empraincte de chascun costé trois fleur-de-lys, et estoit entres plusieurs autres espées rouillées. Si luy demanda le roy si elle avoit autres fois este en la dicte eglise de Saincte Katherine, laquelle dit que non, et qu'elle le sçavoit par revelation divine, et qu' avec d' icelle espée elle devoit expeller ses ennemys, et le mener sacrer a Reims. Si y envoya le roy ung de ses sommeliers d'armeures, qui la trouva au lieu, et ainsi que la dicte Jehanne le luy avoit dit, et la luy apporta."

" After these things, the said Jeanne begged that the king would send one of his armourers to fetch a sword which had been announced to her in a certain place in the church of St. Katherine de Fierboys, upon both sides of which was the print of three fleur-de-lys, and the which was among many other rusty swords. The king then asked her whether she had before been in the said church of St. Katherine, who answered no; for that she knew it by divine revelation, and that with the said sword she was to expel his enemies, and conduct him to be crowned at Rheims. So the king sent one of his purveyors of arms, who found it at the place mentioned by the said Jeanne, and brought it unto her."

After this statement, it is not to be wondered at, that the king should express his displeasure at the sacred weapon in question being broken on the back of a prostitute by the person to whom it was apparently delegated for such ostensible purposes.

Page 60. *The which* (Jeanne) *came on the part of our Lord, to victual and strengthen the city, and cause the siege to be raised, whereat those of Orleans were mightily comforted.*

In the *Recueil Historique sur Jeanne d'Arc*, by M. Chaussard, vol. i. p. 20, we find that " Jeanne était attendue avec impatience dans cette ville; les habitans, réduits à la dernière extrémité, étaient instruits qu'il avait passé à Gien, une fille qui se disait envoyée de Dieu, pour les délivrer. L'effet que cette nouvelle avait produit fut si grand, que le comte de Dunois, qu'on appelait alors le Bâtard d'Orléans, et qui commandait dans la ville, avait envoyé à Charles VII., le sieur de Villers, sénéchal de Beaucaire, et le sieur de Tollay devenu depuis bailli de

Vermandois, pour s'informer de la vérité de cette singulière
nouvelle. Ils avaient rapporté à leur retour, et dit aux
habitans, qu'ils avaient vu cette fille aupres du roi, et
qu'elle allait venir avec des secours."

" Jeanne was expected with impatience in the city; the
inhabitants, reduced to the last extremity, had learned,
that a girl had arrived at Gien, stating that she was sent
by God for their deliverance. The effect produced by this
news was so great, that the count de Dunois, then called
the Bastard of Orleans, and who commanded within the
city, had sent to Charles VII. the lord de Villers, seneschal
of Beaucaire, and the lord de Tollay, who was subsequently
bailiff of Vermandois, to ascertain the truth of this singular
news. Upon their return they acquainted the inhabitants
that they had seen the maid with the king, and that she
was on the eve of coming to their succour."

Such was the astonishing influence produced by the presence of Jeanne, that Dunois stated, according to Laverdy,
page 354, note 31, " Asserit quod Anglici qui 200 priùs
fugabant 800 aut 1000 de exercitu regis, à post et tunc
400 aut 500 armatorum pugnabant in conflictu contra
totam potestatem Anglicorum," &c. While other contemporary writers affirm that, " before her arrival two hundred English would put to flight, in skirmishes, five
hundred Frenchmen; but, that after her coming, two
hundred Frenchmen drove four hundred Englishmen
before them."— *Histoire de la Pucelle*, p. 510.

Page 62. *And there was such a marvellous pressing in order to touch her* (Jeanne) *or the horse upon which she rode, that one of them who was bearer of a torch, approached so near unto her standard, that the fire caught the tail thereof.*

" The Pucelle entered the city in good array about eight o'clock at night, without the army of the enemy, which was very numerous, showing any desire to oppose her reception.   Armed, therefore, as she was, *cap à pic*, except an helmet, and mounted on a white horse well barbed and very beautiful, she was received, as it were, in triumph with great magnificence, and a joy scarcely to be believed, by all the people.   There was carried behind* her a white flag, whereon was painted the image of our lady, with that of an angel presenting to her a fleur-de-lys. The Bastard of Orleans, richly caparisoned and nobly mounted, followed by many lords, proceeded at her left side, not to protect, but to honour her."

* In the Diary it is stated that the standard was borne before her, of which there can be little doubt, as it is not to be supposed she would suffer what was regarded as an holy banner to be carried in her rear; added to which, the circumstance of the standard catching fire, and being extinguished by Jeanne, who immediately perceived the accident, fully coroborates the statement made in the journal.

So they accompanied her the length of this town and city,
making great feasting, and in great honour they all
escorted her unto the gate Regnart, to the hotel of James
Bouchier, then treasurer of the duke of Orleans, &c.

While the Pucelle resided at Orleans, she continued at
the hotel of Jacques Bouchier, treasurer of the duke of
Orleans, situated near to Renard or Regnard Gate,
which mansion was afterwards called Maison de l'Annonciade, wherein was used to be shown the apartment
occupied by that courageous woman.

Two circumstances relative to Jeanne, while a resident in
this dwelling, and which have been handed down, are well
worthy being recorded, as they testify her extreme sobriety,
and the strict attention she uniformly paid to remove from
herself every thing like a shadow of suspicion, that might
tend to cast any taint upon the rigid tenor of her conduct.
An historian records : " that the treasurer Bouchier had
given orders for an excellent supper to be placed before
her, with all becoming honours ; whereas she only caused
some wine to be brought in a silver cup, to which she added
half water, with five or six pieces of bread sopped in the
same, which she ate ; taking nothing else to eat or to drink
during the day (yet she had been the whole of the day on
horseback); when she retired to rest in the chamber which
had been prepared for her, and in her company was the
wife and the daughter of the said treasurer, the which girl
slept with the said Jeanne."

Page 64. *And at the same time the Bastard of Orleans made known unto them, that in case he was not sent back, he would cause to die, by a bad death, all the English who were then prisoners in Orleans.*

" This same day, La Pucelle, having advanced towards night to the foot of the beautiful cross, held conference with Glasdale and some other English captains. She began by complaining of their tyranny and their injustice in having laid siege to the city of Orleans, and in seeking to expel Charles from his kingdom, and from the throne of his progenitors. In fine, the termination of this interview was, her offering them terms of a very just and reasonable peace, if, after the first summons sent, they abandoned France and marched away their army; the which, if they performed, she would injure no one : such being the only and the last condition of peace. But if, on the contrary, under the belief that they were sanctioned in violating the rights of others, and aspired to occupy the kingdom ; and that, under such hope, they thought to make a longer stay, she would use all her efforts, and put every expedient she possessed in full force, to drive them before her sword in hand, and would never be satisfied until the fulfilment of that enterprise. That there still existed great courage in France, as well as mighty troops of foot and of horse ; and, finally, that God declared himself in favour of this invincible people, of this great and truly Christian realm, as well as of this beautiful city, and would assist to repel the injustice and the power of these usurpers. To all which, the only reply made by the

English, was, her being a strumpet and a cow-keeper,
menacing, that they would cause her to be burned,
and uttering all that calumny could suggest, which the
Pucelle listened to without emotion, or uttering a word
by way of resentment, and thus withdrawing with the
same calmness of aspect which she had displayed on
arriving."—*Dubreton*, pp. 166, &c.

But Glasidas (Glasdale) *and those of his band answered
villanously, offering her injuries, and calling her cow-
keeper, &c.*

Dubreton, speaking of this abuse towards Jeanne d'Arc,
thus expresses himself, at page 165, &c. : —

" Notwithstanding, news was brought into the city of the
laugh and the disdain expressed by the English, respecting
the intentions of the Pucelle, as well as the opprobrious
terms vomited forth by those insolent men, who called
her a cow-keeper, a strumpet, and a magician. These
epithets, which wounded her in the most delicate and
sensible part of her soul, caused her to entertain towards
them the most implacable hatred, and to meditate singular
vengeance; but more especially for having retained and
put her herald into irons, a calling uniformly held inviolable and sacred among men. This crime, haughtily
committed against the laws and customs of war, she determined not to submit to in prejudice of her honour. Therefore she despatched an herald to the camp, proclaiming,
that if they did not forthwith restore to liberty the man
they had imprisoned, she would cause to be put to death
every English prisoner within the city, together with those

who had been deputed to negotiate respecting the ransom of their companions. The English, therefore, fearful lest she should execute this threat, immediately liberated her herald, making him the bearer of a thousand terms of disdain, menace, and indignation."

Page 65. *Because those of Orleans testified so great a wish to behold her, that they almost broke down the gates of the hotel wherein she was lodged, &c.*

" The Pucelle, in order to show herself to the people, who burned with desire and impatience to give her the most satisfactory proofs of their joy and their affection, accompanied by many of the leading and most qualified personages, proceeded on horseback through the city. At the noise of her coming forth, and this review, so great a multitude got together from all quarters, that many of the crowd were well nigh suffocated. All the workmen quitted their instruments and their toils, preferring the honour and the content of beholding her, to the necessity of their own occupations. Each admired her comely appearance, her winning grace, her action and general demeanour. Nor was there truly any thing about her, but denoted a girl of illustrious birth ; her soul being so well regulated, and her mind so truly exalted. But that which, above all, caused her to be looked upon and extolled, was, her noble carriage on horseback, in which estate she supported the helmet, the shield, and the cuirass, with so much grace and address, that it might be said, she had never done any other thing from her

infancy, and that her heart had been always addicted to
arms, encounters, and battles."—*Dubreton*, p. 169, &c.

*And unto all it appeared a great marvel, how she could
hold herself, as she did, with such gentility on horseback, &c.*

This description of our heroine is strictly correct;
for by referring to Monstrelet, we find that Jeanne d' Arc
" *montait chevaux à poil, et fesait apertises qu'autres filles
n'ont point coutume de faire.*"
Jeanne's expertness in wielding the lance is proved by
an ocular witness, according to the statement of Philippe,
and the duke of Alençon indirectly confirms the same:
" For no sooner had he learned the arrival of Jeanne at
Chinon, than he forthwith repaired to St. Florent, and on
the following day beheld her pass, *une lance à la main,
qu'elle portait et faisait mouvoir avec beaucoup de grace;
et alors il lui fit don d'un beau cheval:* bearing a lance in
her hand, which she carried and wielded with much grace;
and then he made her a present of a fine horse."

Page 66.   *Where she heard the vespers.*

Jeanne, from this epoch, directed nearly all the attacks
which were made; and early on the morning of the ensuing
day, awaking suddenly from her sleep, with a start, she
forthwith summoned Daulon, exclaiming, to use her own
words, as handed down to us by the historians of her
time: " *En nom de Dieu, mon conseil m'a dit que je vaisse*

contre les Anglais ; où sont ceux qui me doivent armer ?
Car le sang de nos gens coule par terre." " In the name of
God, my counsel has told me, that I should go against
the English; where are those that should arm me? For
the blood of our people flows on the ground."

Page 69.　*And immediately on coming up commenced such*
an assault upon the boulevard and the bastille near that
spot, and fortified by the English, on the ground where
lately stood the church of the Augustines, that they took
the same by force, &c.

In speaking of the capture of this boulevard, without
having recourse to any of the marvellous statements of
Jeanne's historians, who conceived that she would acquire
more reputation if held forth in the light of an inspired
woman, than an intrepid warrior; we find, according to
the narrative handed down by the Bastard Dunois: " *Et*
Joanna posuit se super bordum fossati, et instante, ibi ipsâ
existente, Anglici tremuerunt et effecti sunt pavidi; armati
verò regis resumpserunt animum et ceperunt ascendere . . . . .
Bollevardum fuit captum," &c. — Laverdy, pp. 361, 362.

Page 71.
And their Tournelles and their boulevards will be taken, &c.

The innate love for war that animated Jeanne d'Arc
is testified in history, where it is recorded, that in
preparing for a *coup de guerre*, and when the soldiers
were ranged in order for battle, the Pucelle by her
harangues knew how to inspire and invigorate their spirits

for action; and that, whensoever the cry was TO ARMS,
" *elle étoit la première et la plus diligente, fut à pied ou à*
cheval: that she was the foremost and the most active,
whether on foot or on horseback."   In addition to which,
a contemporary historian, speaking of her equestrian
prowess, asserts: " *A principio ætatis suæ . . . . . pascendo*
pecora . . . . . sæpius cursum exercebat ; et modo huc atque illuc
illi frequens cursus erat ; et aliquando currendo hastam ut fortis
eques manu capiebat et arborum truncos . . . . . percutiebat,"
&c.— *Phillipe de Bergame,* in *Hordal,* p. 40, who, according
to Moreri, under the head *Foresti,* was born in 1434.

Page 73.   *And many other knights, bannerets, and English*
                noblemen, were drowned.

It is a curious fact, that in confirmation of this circumstance, when the new bridge was building at Orleans, a
number of helmets, breast-plates, &c. were dragged up
from the bed of the river at this very spot.

And truly was there wrought a miracle of our Lord,
    performed at the request of Saint Aignan and Saint
    Euverte, &c.

After Jeanne and the Bastard had taken the bastille,
Dubreton, at page 203, gives the following marvellous
narrative.   " This great victory was signalized by a still
more wonderful miracle; which was, that two young
men, armed in a different manner from the other combatants, perfectly beautiful and well-grown, were seen in
the air upon two white horses; and that the cries of a
great army, accompanied by the clangour of trumpets,

were heard during the hottest period of the battle. It was commonly believed, that these two young men were Saints Aignan and Euverte, whom the inhabitants of Orleans firmly believe their patrons, and their tutelar divinities in all mischances that may chance to threaten them."

Superstition, which might very justly be termed an epidemic disorder among the people at that period, was fully called into action upon the subject of Jeanne d'Arc's exploits; and a few instances will be sufficient to demonstrate how far this weakness predominated, even with writers and studious personages, whose pursuits were calculated to dispel such chimeras from the brain. In the history of the Abbey of Saint Dennis, which was translated by Le Laboureur, in a chapter where he treats of an eclipse of the sun, he seriously remarks that—" The astrologers, judging from a natural science of effects from causes, prognosticated that extraordinary accidents would ensue, and which happened accordingly."—*Laboureur*, p. 548.

From Juvenal des Ursins, archbishop of Rheims, we learn " that sometimes the image of a certain saint had suddenly turned its back upon a soldier who sought to purloin the same, and who, in consequence, lost his wits, while the rest of his comrades turned devotees,"—(page 50.) * * * * Sometimes priests, by means of invocations, raised the devil; and such was the confidence placed in them, that the council of Charles VI. enacted, that they should offer up their prayers in order to effect the king's recovery. — (Page 192.) * * * * In another place, the thunder entered the hotel of the dauphin, killed a child, and wounded others; in which strain he continues, —

" Until a sprinkling of holy water in the chamber and about the dwelling, expelled the thunder no one knew whither."—(Page 206.)

While we are occupied upon the subject of visions and revelations, this same Juvenal des Ursins testifies, that the most illustrious persons were not less superstitious than the poor. A Mathurin, a Carmelite, and others of the University, assembled in 1413, to *imagine* what would be the termination of the Burgundian government, and they in consequence entreated Juvenal de Treignel, father of the archbishop, and one of the most eminent characters in the state, to join them. They in consequence deliberated, and came to a determination that it was requisite to consult studious and religious persons; when the latter communicated their visions. . . . . The one having seen three suns; another three different periods; a third the king of England at the top of the towers of Notre Dame. . . . . . . Upon which these grave and sapient doctors decided, that there might be a change in the government of the kingdom. *(Juvenal, p. 316.)* Seven years afterwards, the archbishop of Rheims, who was then occupied in writing his history, having occasion to speak of the treaty of Troyes, did not forget to call to mind *Ces visions vues par bonnes creatures* * * * * * *de trois soleils:* these visions seen by good creatures . . . . of three suns; for, continues he gravely—" There were three kings in France, namely, the English monarch, and monseigneur le dauphin :" *(Juvenal,* page 477.) In short, his mother had equally visions of the same wonderful force.—See also *Voltaire's Essai sur les Mœurs,* ch. lxxix., note 16.

Page 74. *And much rejoicing was there testified on all sides, &c. unto Jeanne la Pucelle, who remained during this night, as well as the lords, captains, and men at war with her, in the midst of the fields, &c.*

" This strong fortress of the English having been captured, and the whole garrison either put to the sword, or drowned, although the French army was very much exhausted and harassed, and that night was fast approaching, the Pucelle, nevertheless, would not suffer the same to re-enter the city to seek refreshment, but caused the forces to remain without; arranging the troops during the whole night to keep watch as with a camp in a state of siege, for the purpose of holding the place which had been gained. This combat ended, all the people assembled in the churches to offer thanks to God for this signal victory, so advantageous to their city and the whole kingdom, as well as to supplicate for a continuance of his favour and assistance. The Pucelle, great and illustrious even prior to this combat, began to wax greater and more illustrious in the general opinion after this victory, accomplished by her wise conduct and her generous devotedness in battle. The soldiers and the citizens extolled her to the skies ; and the English, changing their contumely into respect and their vile abuse into admiration, were in greater dread of her than is customary in respect to a mortal creature. Briefly, all the French and their enemies began really to apprehend that there was something divine in her, and that a wiser head and a stronger arm than that of man fought in the person of

this excellent and incomparable girl." —— *Dubreton,*
pp. 204, &c.

Page 75.
At the end of the hour did the Englishmen set forward, &c.

When speaking of the English raising the siege of
Orleans, Holinshed, at page 601, thus expresses himself.

" The Frenchmen, puffed up with this good lucke, fetched
a compasse about, and in good order of battell marched
toward the bastile, which was in the keeping of the lord
Talbot : the which upon the enimies approch, like a
capteine without all feare or dread of that great multitude, issued foorth against them, and gave them so sharpe
an incounter, that they not able to withstand his puis-
sance, fled (like sheepe before the wolfe) againe into the
citie, with great losse of men and small artillerie. Of
Englishmen were lost in the two bastiles, to the number
of six hundred persons, or thereabout, though the French
writers multiplie this number of hundreds to thousands,
as their manner is.

" The earle of Suffolke, the lord Talbot, the lord
Scales, and other capteins, assembled togither in councell,
and after causes shewed to and fro, it was amongst them
determined to leave their fortresses and bastiles, and to
assemble in the plaine field, and there to abide all the
daie, to see if the Frenchmen would issue foorth to fight
with them. This conclusion taken was accordinglie executed : but when the Frenchmen durst not once come
forth to shew their heads, the Englishmen set fire of
their lodgings, and departed in good order of battell

from Orleance. The next date, which was the eight daie of Maie, the earle of Suffolke rode to Jargeaux with foure hundred Englishmen, and the lord Talbot with another companie returned to Mehun. And after he had fortified that towne, he went to the towne of Lavall, and woone it, together with the castell, sore punishing the townsmen for their cankered obstinacie against them."

Page 76.

In another direction entered into Orleans the Pucelle, &c.

" The enemy driven away and routed, the Pucelle and the other captains, well satisfied and covered with glory, returned to the city with their victorious army. All the people issued forth in crowds to meet the conquerors, to admire the chiefs, and in particular the Pucelle. The regards of every one were fixed upon her; they had no eyes but to behold her, nor tongues but to utter benedictions and praises; contemplating her as a maid really sent from heaven, and as victory herself; showing her extraordinary and almost divine honours; affirming her to be the saviour of France, and the performer of greater actions than men for its re-establishment and lasting duration; while her valour combating with her virtue had got the better of a cruel and almost invincible necessity: in fine, that the fortunate result of so great and so perilous an enterprise had acquired her immortal glory. Wherefore, that the remembrance of this great and admirable service should never die, it was resolved throughout the city, that from thenceforth this glorious day should be annually solemnized by actions of grace, of joy, and of gratitude."—*Dubreton*, pp. 210, &c.

Page 77.
Were performed right beautiful and solemn processions.

On the eighth of May an annual ceremony takes place at Orleans, to consecrate the memory of the heroine who caused the siege of the city to be raised. Upon this occasion, early in the morning, all the authorities of the place repair in procession to the Cathedral, where a discourse is delivered in honour of Jeanne d'Arc; at the conclusion of which all the persons assembled, together with the principal citizens of the town, proceed from the cathedral to the church of the Augustins. Upon their return the procession passes before the monument of the Maid of Orleans, in the midst of which assembly is a young lad, habited in an ancient costume, displaying the colours of the city, bearing in his hand a flag, while before him is carried a banner; the youth in question being intended to represent Jeanne la Pucelle.

Page 78. *Gentil Dauphin.*

Until after the coronation of Charles VII. at Rheims, he was only regarded by the generality of the people as the inheritor of the throne; Jeanne herself, prior to that epoch, never addressed him as king, but only as the dauphin.

Page 80. *Wherefore he nominated as his lieutenant-general*
John duke of Alençon.

Grafton, speaking of this prince and his ransom at
page 523, thus expresses himself :

" The regent of Fraunce thus beying in England, meanes
was made by the duke of Burgoyn, for the deliverie of the
duke of Alanson, which was taken prisoner at the battaile
of Vernoyle the last yere. So he for the somme of two
hundred thousand crownes, was delivered and set at
large : but neither for the release of all, or abatement of
part of his ransome, he would in no wise acknowlege
the king of England to be his liege and sovereigne lord ;
such affection bare he to the dolphyn, and such truth
shewed he to his naturall countrie."

The duke of Alençon obtained his freedom in 1427, by
leaving hostages for a portion of his ransom. Those he
set at liberty by the sale of lands to the duke of Brittany, which took place in December 1428 and April 1429,
as well as by the aid received from Charles VII. who, in
1427 and 1428, assisted him with twenty thousand
crowns. Finally, the duke of Bedford declared him to be
fully exonerated, even, *de ses foi et promesse* (from his
faith and promise) which occurred on the 21st of May
1429. See the acts quoted in the history of the duchy
of Alençon, by Bry, 1620, page 320.

Page 81. *That he (the duke of Alençon) should act and*
do entirely according to her counsel.

When we find Charles delivering an injunction like the

foregoing, to such a powerful prince and captain as the duke of Alençon; it cannot be doubted for a moment, that Jeanne d'Arc had acquired great credit at court, and that, be her mission what it might, the most sanguine hopes were entertained by the monarch as to the final result of her intervention.

Page 85. *Whereupon the said earl created him a knight, and then surrendered himself up his prisoner.*

This chivalric and truly noble conduct on the part of the earl of Suffolk is thus detailed by Dubreton at page 237. " In this flight the earl of Suffolk, followed by a French gentleman named Renault, he honoured him with the order of knighthood, and then surrendered himself at discretion, having seen him act most worthily upon this occasion. For the dignity of knight, which is not acquired through favour during a cowardly and voluptuous life, but by brilliant acts of courage in the midst of the hazards of war, is calculated to ennoble the most lowly, and to elevate them to the highest dignities of the state."

Of whom several were that same evening conveyed prisoners by water, fearful lest they should be killed.

Grafton, at page 536, gives the following statement:
" After that the Englishmen were thus retired from the siege of Orleaunce, and severed themselves in dyvers townes and fortresses, holding on their parte : the duke of Alaunson, the Bastard of Orleaunce, Jone the Puzell, the lorde of Glancort and divers other Frenchmen, came

before the towne of Jargeaux, where the erle of Suffolke
and his two brethren sojourned, the twelve day of June,
and gave to the towne a great and terrible assault, which
the Englishmen (being but a handefull) manfully defended on three partes of the same. Poyton of Sentrailles,
perceyving one part of the towne to be undefended, scaled
the walles on that part: and without any difficultie tooke
the towne, and slue Sir Alexander Pole brother to the
erle, and many other, to the number of two hundred: but
they not much gayned, for they lost three hundred good
men and more. Of the English men were taken xl.
beside his brother John. After thys gayne and good
luck, the Frenchmen returning towarde Orleaunce, fell
in contention and debate, for their captives and prisoners,
and slue them all, saving the erle and his brother."

*And even the church, wherein was stowed a great quantity
of riches, the whole was also pillaged.*

At the commencement of the Diary the writer states
that the death of the earl of Salisbury was supposed
by the devout to be an ordinance of the Divinity on
account of his breaking his word to the duke of Orleans,
as well as for having pillaged churches and monasteries,
" and in particular the church of our Lady of Clery."
Our historian, however, does not think fit to comment
upon a similar mode of conduct pursued by those of his
own party: so true is it, according to the scriptural
adage, that " we can see the moat in our brother's eye
without perceiving the beam in our own."

Page 87.

During this siege arrived Arthur, count de Richemont, &c.

Artus III., duke of Brittany, surnamed the Judge, formerly count de Richemont and constable of France, was born in 1393, being the son of John, duke of Brittany. He was small of stature, but possessed of undaunted courage, and greatly contributed in restoring Charles VII. to his throne; he signalized himself at the battle of Agincourt, where he was made prisoner, and in order to recover his liberty was compelled to serve under the king of England. Richemont afterwards overcame the English in Normandy and in Poitou, gaining the battle of Patay, in Beauce, in 1429, and that of Formigni in 1451. His nephew, Peter, called the Simple, dying in 1456 without children, he succeeded to the dukedom of Brittany; from which period he always caused two naked swords to be carried before him; the one as duke of Brittany, and the other as constable. He enjoyed his reign but fifteen months, and died without heirs in his sixty-sixth year, A. D. 1458, regretted by his subjects, whom he governed with mildness, and by whom he was esteemed, though hated by the courtiers and troops, because he suppressed the plunderings of both with as much haughtiness as severity.

The favourites of Charles VII. were not spared by Artus, when he had charge of the affairs of that prince; for having perceived that Giac, one of the king's minions, placed to his own account sums destined for the army, he caused him to be seized in his bed, and after some slight formalities of justice, ordered him to be thrown into the

river. Camus Beaulieu, another favourite, no less rapacious than Giac, was assassinated in a street of Poitiers by
marshal de Boussac, charged with the constable's orders,
the deed being committed almost under the king's own
eyes; and La Trimouille was also committed to prison
upon another occasion, although Charles VII. regarded
him less in the light of a courtier than that of a friend.

And there did the said constable entreat the Pucelle.

In the Memoirs of the constable Richemont, we find,
that, upon his first introducton to Jeanne d'Arc, he exclaimed: " *Viens-tu de par Dieu, ou de par le diable?
Si c'est de par Dieu, je ne te crains guère ; si c'est de par
le diable, je te crains encore moins.*" " If thou comest on
the part of God, I little fear thee; if it is on the part of the
devil, I fear thee still less." It was, notwithstanding, this
same warrior, so superior, on account of his rare qualifications, to the age in which he flourished, who took honour
to himself for having, when in Brittany, caused to be
burnt, all those whom he met reputed to be adepts in
sorcery and witchcraft; and of such he states the having
found instances at every step. As a further proof of
the superstition of that period, when the physicians
despaired of curing the malady of king Charles VI., a
magician was sent for, in whose suite were several
monks of St. Augustine's order, together with a company
of sorcerers, the least skilful of whom were burnt. See
Essai sur l'Histoire générale du Règne de Charles VI.

" During this siege (of Beaugency) Artus, count de
Richemont, constable of France, and brother of the duke

of Brittany, went to the Pucelle and made offer, that if the king would restore him to his good graces, and continue him in the first rank of honour which he held in his kingdom, he would render unto his majesty, in that unfortunate season, his first duties and ancient fidelity; that he would unite with his army one thousand five hundred horse which accompanied him; and that he would proceed every where she might judge expedient, and for the benefit of his affairs. To the which the duke of Alençon, and the other chiefs, having become guarantees for this lord, the Pucelle retained and assured him, that, by her prayers, she would secure the grace of the king and the entire forgiveness of his inconsiderate revolt." — *Dubreton*, p. 244.

It appears obvious from the above statement, that Jeanne must have acquired very high consideration, when a prince so powerful as the count de Richemont should have thought it expedient to apply to her in order to become his peace-maker with the king; while the Pucelle's undertaking to ensure his pardon, is no trifling proof of the internal conviction she had of her power in directing the counsels of Charles VII.

Page 90. *In the course of this day much was gained by the French, &c.*

Speaking of the unfortunate conflict at Pathay, Grafton gives the following narrative, at page 536 :—

" The Englishe men coming forward perceyved the horsemen, and imagining to deceyve their enemies, commaunded the footemen to environe and enclose themselves

about with their stakes ; but the French horsemen came on
so fiercely, that the archers had no leysure to set themselves in aray. There was no remedie, but to fight at
adventure. This battayle continued by the space of three
long hours. And although the Englishe men were over-
pressed with the number of their adversaries, yet they
never fled back one foote, till their captayne, the lorde
Talbot, was sore wounded at the backe, and so was taken.
Then their hartes began to faint, and they fled, in which
flight there were slayne above twelve hundred, and taken
xl., whereof the lorde Talbot, the lorde Scales, the lorde
Hungerford, and Sir Thomas Rampstone, were the chief :
howbeit divers archers, which had shot all their arrowes,
having onely their swordes, defendyng themselves, and
with the helpe of some of the horsemen, came safe to
Meum."

Grafton, at page 526, gives the following testimony of
the glorious achievements and character of the lord
Talbot : —

" After this, the lord Talbot was made governor of
Aniow and Mayn : and Sir John Fastolfe was assigned
to another place ; which lord Talbot, being both of noble
birth, and haute courage, after his coming into Fraunce,
obteyned so many glorious victories of hys enemies,
that his onely name was, and yet is, dreadfull to the
French nacion, and much renouned amongst all other
people."

Page 91. *And among others Messire John Fascot,*
(Fastolf), *who took refuge in Corbueil.*

As some statements tending to vilify the character of
Sir John Fastolff, have appeared in French histories of
that time, which crept into the English chronicles, we
subjoin the following extract from Grafton, page 537,
being one of the reports in question; whereto we have
subjoined some historical facts, to disprove these aspersions
on one of the bravest captains the English had to boast,
during the period of our possessing sovereign sway in the
realm of France.

" When the fame was blowen abroade, that the lorde
Talbot was taken, all the Frenchmen not a little rejoysed,
thinking surely that nowe the rule of the Englishemen
should shortly assuage and waxe faynt: for feare whereof,
the townes of Jenevile, Meum, Fort, and dyvers other,
returned from the Englishe parte, and became French, to
the great displeasure of the regent. From this battayle
departed without any stroke striken, Syr John Fastolffe,
the same yere for hys valyauntnesse elected into the order of
the garter. For which cause the duke of Bedford, in a great
anger, toke from hym the image of St. George and his
garter : but afterward, by meane of friends, and ap-
paraunte causes of good excuse by him alledged, he was
restored to the order agayne, agaynst the minde of the
lorde Talbot."

Soon after the famous battle of Herrings, whereby Sir

John Fastolff acquired so much renown, he received a check at the battle of Pathay, that took place in June, 1429, upon which occasion many English, who were of the most experienced and approved valour, seeing themselves so very unequal, and the onset of the French so unexpected, that nothing but inevitable ruin would prove the consequence of a rash resistance, and that all must be lost, effected the best retreat in their power; and among those who saved themselves, as it is said, was Sir John Fastolff, who, with such as could escape, retired to Corbueil; thus avoiding being killed, or, with the great lord Talbot, &c. made prisoner.

Thus terminate the French accounts, which some English historians have credited, whereas they contradict themselves; for, after having made the regent, most improbably, and without any examination or defence, divest Fastolff of his honours, they no less suddenly restore him to them, for, as they phrase it, *" apparent causes of good excuse, though against the mind of the lord Talbot;"* between whom there had been, it seems, some emulous contests, and therefore it is no wonder that Fastolff found him, on this occasion, an adversary. It is not reasonable to suppose that the regent ever conceived any displeasure at this conduct, because Fastolff was not only continued in military and civil employments of the greatest magnitude, but seems to have been more in favour with the regent after the battle of Pathay than before.

Page 92.   *Supplicating that he* (the king) *would pardon his*
(the count de Richemont's) *evil conduct.*

Dubreton, at page 255, thus expresses himself upon this
subject : —

" For as the Pucelle most humbly beseeched his majesty
to extend his pardon to this lord, the king took her by the
hand, desiring her to cease her prayers, protesting in the
middle of his council, that her virtue and her services had
acquired him such a degree of power, that for the love of
her, he, with a willing heart, suppressed all his vindictiveness, and freely forgot all the injuries done to himself and
to the kingdom.   However, he would not permit him to
join in the journey to Rheims, fearing that his presence
would be offensive, and appear ill, in the sight of La
Trimouille, who then held the greatest influence over his
good graces.   The which gave great displeasure to the
Pucelle, because he might have very usefully served the
king, as well by his advice as his forces in prosecuting the
war.   In regard to the constable, he dissembled and stifled
his dissatisfaction, perceiving well that the king had not
refused him this honour from any animosity entertained
towards him; but only for the purpose of gratifying his
favourite."

The which was accorded by the king at her request, as
well as on account of the love he bore to the lord de
la Trimouille, &c.

None of the favourites of Charles usurped a greater

influence over his mind than the lord Trimouille, who appears from history to have cared very little about the French monarchy, provided he could augment his power at court, accumulate riches, and sow the seeds of discord among the best friends of his sovereign. Indeed, to such a pitch did he carry his abuse of princely favour, that many zealous royalists, and even princes of the blood, declared themselves against the king, and took possession of Bourges when that city was his capital. It has been equally affirmed by some historians, and with every appearance of probability, that the shameful abandonment of Jeanne d'Arc, after she had been made prisoner, originated in the jealousy of Trimouille, who could not bear a rival in his monarch's favour.

But he would not permit him to be one of the journey, nor present at his inauguration.

The dissatisfaction evinced by Jeanne and the nobles at this conduct of the king is little to be wondered at, when it is considered that the count de Richemont was a most powerful prince ; his friendship and succour being of the very last importance to the king, whose overweening fondness for his favourite Trimouille might, by incensing Richemont, have completely turned the tide of fortune against him.

Page 95. *But the inhabitants of the city gave in secret two thousand crowns to the lord de la Trimouille, &c.*

From this conduct on the part of Trimouille, it is evident, that no treasonable practice was worthy consideration, if gold was the price at which his honour was to be compromised.

Page 99. *And then departed in the direction of Rheims.*

Rheims, formerly the capital of Champaigne, now of the department of the Marne, is computed to contain upwards of thirty thousand inhabitants. The principal church, a most magnificent Gothic structure, dedicated to the Virgin, was built prior to the year 406, the principal portal of which stands unrivalled, as a specimen of grand and costly architecture of the remote period when it was erected. Behind the high altar of the church of Saint Remy were formerly preserved the relics of that archbishop, which were deposited in a sumptuous shrine; in the same temple was also kept *la Sainte Ampoule,* being a reddish liquor contained in a phial, which was in former ages supposed to have been brought from heaven, and was always used at the coronation of the French monarchs, who were successively inaugurated at Rheims; because Clovis, who founded the French monarchy, on being converted from paganism, was baptized in the cathedral of Rheims in the year 496. This city is situated north-east of Paris, from whence it is distant about seventy-five miles.

Page 100. *And after the dinner hour and towards evening, the king entered (Rheims) together with his whole army.*

" The inhabitants (of Rheims) then despatched towards Charles, the principal from among them to present him

the keys of the city, and to inform him that they confided their goods and their lives to his faith and power.
Charles having welcomed them with his accustomed
clemency, the churchmen and the magistrates in a body
went to welcome him under a canopy, and received him
in their city, with a degree of pomp and magnificence
suitable to his grandeur and the dignity of his person:
the streets through which his majesty was to pass, were
covered with flowers; and the exterior of the houses
adorned with beautiful and rich tapestry and choicest hang-
ings, &c. . . . . Nevertheless they equally regarded
the Pucelle with avidity and pleasure; for independent
of the particular reverence which this people naturally
entertained towards their king, it was scarcely credible,
with how much tenderness of heart, and love, respect and
admiration, they welcomed her, in consequence of the
wisdom of God and the strength of his hand having been
visible throughout all her enterprises."—*Dubreton*, pages
278, &c.

Upon this occasion, as was customary at all public
rejoicings in those days, a very grand mystery is said to
have been performed by the inhabitants of Rheims.
Concerning this species of amusement the editor is in
possession of some very curious matter connected with
the reigns of Charles VI. and Charles VII. of France;
as well as relating to earlier and subsequent periods;
most of which bears reference to the monarchs of both
or of either country. As some account therefore of these
singular representations may tend to illustrate the page
of history as regards pageants, shows, &c. the editor has
ventured to subjoin the accompanying note, the interest

of which, it is presumed, will compensate for the space it necessarily occupies.

The Mysteries derived their origin from the pilgrimages so universally performed in ancient times to the Holy Land, or such sanctified places as Saint James of Compostella, the saintly Baume of Provence; La Sainte Reine of Mount Saint Michael; Notre Dame du Puy, &c. &c. Upon these occasions the pilgrims frequently composed rude pieces of poetry descriptive of their journeys, whereto they subjoined the records of the martyrdom of the Saint, at whose shrine they had offered up their vows. In the second book of the history of the city of Paris, page 523, it is stated, that, in 1313, Philip le Bel gave the most sumptuous entertainment in that city ever remembered, to which Edward II. of England, whom he had invited, together with his queen Isabel of France, and a great retinue of nobility, repaired, crossing the channel for that express purpose. Every thing shone (says the historian) with the magnificence of the costumes, the variety of the amusements, and the splendour of the banquetings. During the space of eight days, the princes and the lords changed their garments three times a day; and the populace on their side represented divers spectacles: sometimes *La Gloire des Bienheureux* (The Glory of the Blessed); at others, *La Peine des Damnés* (The Torments of the Damned); together with various sorts of animals; which last spectacle was called *La Procession du Renard* (The Procession of the fox).

Le Mistere de la Passion de Notre Seigneur (The Mystery of the Passion of our Lord), was done to the life as it is figured round the choir of Notre Dame at Paris; being performed at the entrance of the kings of France and of England into Paris, the first day of December 1420, in the street called Kalende, before the palace, on a raised scaffolding about one hundred paces in length, reaching from the said street unto the wall of the palace.

Le Mistere de la Conception, Passion, et Resurrection (The Mystery of the Conception, Passion, and Resurrection), appeared in the reign of Charles VI., being performed at the Bourg de Saint Maur, about five miles from Paris ; the edict to perform the same having been accorded by that monarch on the fourth of December, 1402. The writer of this piece was Jean Michel, who died in 1447. In this mystery of the passion, &c. we find in the *dramatis personæ*, God the Father, Jesus Christ, the Holy Ghost, the Virgin Mary, together with archangels, cherubims, seraphims, &c. as also Lucifer, Beelzebub, Astaroth, Belial, &c. But in order to convey an idea of the manner in which sacred matters were handled in this composition, under the thirty-first head is, *Le doubte de Joseph touchant l'Incarnacion du Filz de Dieu* (Joseph's doubt respecting the Incarnation of the Son of God) ; in which, after expressing himself pretty freely to Mary, he is made to retire and go to sleep, when God the Father seeing the trouble and agitation of Mary and Joseph, and being very desirous that they should not remain in a state of uncertainty, commands the angel Gabriel to go and inform Joseph in a dream, that Mary is pregnant of Christ, that he must not entertain any further doubts in regard to her virginity, as the whole operation has been performed by the Holy Ghost : which commission Gabriel punctually executes ; so that, when Joseph awakes, he is ashamed of the suspicions he had previously harboured, and asks pardon of the Divinity for the same.

Under the head denominated, *De la Nativité de Jésus*, (Of the Birth of Jesus), the Almighty, foreseeing the moment when his Son shall come into the world, de-patches his angels to attend upon Mary during that night, who is made to express herself in the following terms:

> *O ! doulx Dieu, de moi te souvienne,*
> *Comme y a parfaite crédence.*
> *A ta haulte magnificence*
> *Et clere illumination,*
> *O riche tresor de clemence !*
> *O divine incarnation !*
> *Bien doy en exaltacion,*
> *En virtu de devotion.*
> *Honnorer ce mistere en moy,*
> *Quant sous quelque vexation,*
> *Sans fracture, ne corruption,*
> *Le fruit de mon ventre reçoy.*

The conception, or the first day's performance, being ended, under head the fifth, which represents the mys-tery of the passion, Saint John thus addresses Christ, who demands of him the performance of the baptismal ceremony.

> *Pas requerir ne me devés,*
> *Car mon cher Seigneur, vous sçavés*
> *Qu'il n'affuret pas a ma nature,*
>   *Je suis creature,*
>   *Et pour facture,*
>   *De simple stature,*
>   *Humble viateur :*

Ce servit laydure,
Et chose trop dure,
Laver en eaüe pure
Mon hault Créateur.
Tu és precepteur,
Je suis serviteur ;
Tu es le pasteur,
Je suis l'auditeur ;
Tu es le ducteur,
Moy consecuteur,
Sans qui rien ne puis, &c.

And under the same head, God the Father is made to commence a speech in the following manner:

Hic est Filius meus dilectus,
In quo mihi bene complacui.
Cestuy cy, c'est mon Fils amé Jesus,
Qui bien me plaist, ma plaisance est en luy, &c.

During the representation of the fourth day, after Jesus is crucified on the stage, under the head, *La quarte Parolle de Jesus en Croix,* Christ is thus made to express himself;—

Hely, hely, lama zabatani :
Deus meus ut quid me dereliquisti?
Mon Dieu, mon pere de lassus,
Comme quoy ma tu lessé cy ?
J'en souffre tant que je n'en puis plus ;
Et d'apre douleur suis transi :
Je ne reconfort de milli,
Non plus qu'ung poure homme oublyé,
Recoy la douleur de celuy,
Que tu voys tant humilié.

Another mystery of equal consequence with the fore-going,—was *Le Mistere des Actes des Apostres* (Mystery of the Acts of the Apostles); partly composed by Arnoul Greban, a canon of Mans, and born at Compiegne in 1450. Simon Greban, native of the same place, a monk of Saint Richier in Ponthieu, and brother to the former, being also secretary of Charles duke of Anjou, earl of Maine, and a doctor of theology, living under Charles VII., completed the manuscript which Arnoul had left unfinished. This mystery was first performed at Bourges in 1536, and continued for the space of forty days; which plays, says Jean Chaumau, in his history of Berri, " were less labourious, never having before been divided into acts and scenes, or so well and excellently plaid by grave men who knew well by signs and gesticulations to feign the personages they represented, insomuch so, that the spectators judged the matter to be true and not feigned; the theatre consisting of two stories, surpassing every thing in solemnity, covered above with a spread curtain to protect the audience from the intemperance and ardor of the sun, being excellently painted in gold and azure, and other rich colours, impossible to be by words expressed."

This mystery was afterwards represented at various periods at Mans, Angers, Tours, and Paris. In this piece, God the Father, Jesus Christ, the Holy Ghost, the twelve apostles, &c. are introduced; it was published in black letter in 1541, occupying two folio volumes, the first containing five, and the second four books.

On the entrance of the duke of Bedford, regent of France, into Paris, on the eighth of September, 1424, *Le*

Mistere du Vieil Testament et du Nouvel (The Mystery of the Old Testament and the New), was represented by the young people of Paris, without speaking or singing, as if they were images raised against a wall.

Le Mistere depuis la Conception de Notre Dame jusque Joseph la mena en Egipte (The Mystery from the Conception of our Lady till Joseph conducted her into Egypt), represented on a scaffolding before the Trinity, which erection reached from beyond Saint Saviour's to the end of the street named Ernetal; upon the entrance of Henry VI. of England, king of France and Eu, into Paris, the first Sunday in Advent, being the second of December 1431.

Le Mistere de la Sainte Hostie (The Mystery of the Sacred Host) was played by twenty-six persons, and commenced with these lines :—

> *Lisez ce fait, grand et petit,*
> *Comment un faux et maudit Juif*
> *Lapida moult cruellement*
> *De l'Autel le tres Saint Sacrement.*

In *Le Mistere du Juif* (The Mystery of the Jew), being a continuation of the foregoing, the Jew appeared in a chariot, having before him the holy gospels, as if he was being conducted to be burnt; after whom marched Justice, his wife and his children. Along the streets were two scaffoldings whereon were enacted most piteous mysteries. This procession being made, the fifteenth day of May, 1444, on a Friday, the bishops of Paris and of Beauvais, with two abbés, carried the body of our Lord from Saint John in Greve upon their shoulders, and from thence proceeded to the street of Les Billettes to fetch the knife wherewith the false Jew had dissected the flesh of our Lord, and from thence it was carried with the holy cross and other relics, to Saint Catherine du Val of the students; and this procession was performed, because great hope was entertained that a peace would be concluded between the kings of France and of England.

In 1491, appeared a mystery entitled, *Vengeance de la Mort de Notre Seigneur Jesus Christ, et Destruction de la Ville de Jerusalem par l'Empereur Vespasian et Titus;* (Mystery of Vengeance for the Death of our Lord Jesus Christ, and the Destruction of the City of Jerusalem by the Emperors Vespasian and Titus;) written in verse, and performed before Charles VIII. In this piece figured all the sacred personages of Scripture.

Le Mistere de la Passion de Saint George (The Mystery of the Passion of Saint George), was performed in the hotel of Belle, by the Parisians, during the festival of the Pentecost, which occurred upon the last day of May, in order that they might show their love to the king of England, his queen, and the nobles of the said country.

In 1478, *La Patience de Job* (The Patience of Job), was represented by forty-nine persons; and, *The Assumption of the glorious Virgin Mary,* by thirty-eight performers.

Le Mistere du Vieil Testament (Mystery of the Old Testament), was printed about 1500, occupying one thick volume in folio, and contains no less than twenty-three mysteries.

In the first, God creates heaven; the angels precipitate

Lucifer and his rebellious cohorts into hell; then are created the day, the night, sun, moon, &c.; this mystery terminating with the formation of Adam and Eve.

In the second is the marriage of Cain and Abel, &c. During the sixth mystery, the Almighty, indignant on beholding the sins of Sodom, will not listen to the prayers of *Mercy* therein personified, and to whom the Divinity is thus made to express himself;

——— *Sans tenir plet* *
Leur peché si fort me deplest,
Veu qu'il n'y a raison ne rime,
Qu'ils descendront tous en abime.

In the eighteenth mystery, when the angel Raguel seeks to console Sarah on account of her barrenness; in reply to this question;

Comment va, fille?

Sarah answers,

————— *Toute esplorée;*
En moi n'y a ne jeux ne ris.
Vous sçavez, que tous mes maris
Sont morts la premiere nuite :
Je ne suis en rien viollée :
Et si fort je m'en desconforte,
Que bref, je voudrois être morte.

In mystery the twentieth, Susannah, going to the bath, speaks as follows to the damsel who accompanies her.

Et pourtant une fille sage
Se doit montrer douce et honnête,
Sans souffrir qu'on la tate ou baise ;
Car baiser attrait autre chose.

* *Sans disputer davantage.*

P

And in mystery the twenty-first, when the valet of Holofernes has undressed him, and is retiring for the purpose of conducting Judith to his presence, he is made to say,

> *Un beau petit Holopherne*
> *Ferez cette nuit.*

HOLOPHERNE.

— — — — — *point n'en doubte.*

Le Mistere du Chevalier qui donne sa Femme au Diable (Mystery of the Knight who gives his Wife to the Devil) was performed in 1505, by ten persons; the singular subject of which runs as follows:

A dissipated knight being reduced to wretchedness from his profligacy, the Devil appears to him with offers of making him far richer than ever, if he will convey his wife over to him: a proposition acceded to by the knight after some dispute; when a promise is regularly drawn out and signed with the blood of the knight, wherein it is stipulated that, after the lapse of seven years, his wife is to become the property of the fiend. Not satisfied however with this, the Devil further exacts, that he must deny his God also, which proposition, after some difficulty, is equally acceded to; Satan, however, anxious to make the best bargain possible, requires also of the knight that he shall deny the blessed Virgin Mary, but this is most resolutely refused; wherefore, the Devil is obliged to rest satisfied with the bargain already concluded. The allotted term of seven years is then supposed to transpire, when Lucifer makes his appearance, and claims of the knight the performance of the engagement. Upon this the latter, resolved to keep his word, commands his wife to follow him to a certain spot; when, chancing in their way to see a church, she begs permission of her husband to enter the sanctuary for the purpose of prayer: this being agreed to, while she is offering up her devotions, the Virgin Mary assuming the form of the wife, presents herself before the knight, who fully believes her to be such; whereas the Devil, who recognizes the Virgin, upbraids the knight for deceiving him, when the latter, in reply, asserts his total ignorance of the whole affair. Upon this Mary tells Lucifer, that she has assumed that form, in order to rescue two souls from his gripe, and then commands him to give up the promise signed with the knight's blood, which the Devil is compelled to do, and so runs away. The Virgin, in conclusion, exhorts the knight to live a better life in future, restores to him his partner, and thus concludes the mystery.

We shall now terminate with an extract from a chronicle entitled *De Metz Veritable,* in manuscript, the author of which subscribes himself curate of Saint Euchaire, of the said city.

" On the third of July 1437, was performed *The Play of the Passion of our Lord,* in the plain of Veximiel, * where was built a park of a very noble kind, for it was nine tiers in height; all around and behind, were great and long seats for the lords and the ladies; and he who re-

---

* On the seventeenth of September of the same year, they played on the same spot the Mystery of the Vengeance of our Lord Jesus Christ.

presented God was called the lord Nicolle, * baron of Neufchastel in Lorraine, being curate of Saint Victor, of Metz. This same Nicolle would have died when upon the cross, if he had not received help, and agreed that another priest should be fixed to the same, in order to personify the act of the crucifixion. On this and the following day, the said curate of Saint Victor personated the Resurrection, and carried himself right nobly during the said plays. And another priest, named Messire Jean de Nicey, who was chaplain of Metrange, acted the part of Judas, who was also well nigh killed, for his heart failed him, so he was hastily taken down and borne away. And there was displayed the jaws of hell, very well executed, for they opened and closed as the devils wished to go in and come out, and there were two large *evix* † of steel. One of the seven clerks of war, of Metz, named Fourcelle, was master of the said play, and author and original manager of all that was done for this time. A multitude of strange lords and ladies came into the said city of Metz, whose names I have under enumerated.

" First, my lord bishop of Metz, Sire Conrad Bayer.

" The count de Vaudemont, lord Baudouin de Fleville, abbé of Gorze.

" The countess of Sallebruche.

" And the council of the duchy of Bar, and of Lorraine ; Mr. Heney d'Encay, and his two brothers, the baron de Saulx, Charles de Leruolles, Henry de la Tour, and many

* This same lord Nicolle represented Titus in the mystery of *Vengeance.*

† This word *evix* does not appear in any glossary of the old French language.

other lords and ladies of Germany, and other countries, whose names are unknown to me.

" And lanterns were caused to be hung in the windows during the whole continuance of the said plays."

The Lords de Saint Severe and de Rays, &c. were, according to ancient custom, despatched by the king to Saint Remy, in order to procure the Saint Ampoulle.

Holy oil, or *la Sainte Ampoulle*, is said to have been a present sent down from heaven to king Clovis, upon his embracing Christianity at the solicitation of his wife Saint Clotilda, and, we are told, was brought from on high in the beak of a dove. One might be led to doubt the veracity of this assertion (says my authority gravely), were it not that all historians attach faith to the relation, and that the continued miracle of this Ampoulle always furnishing a sufficient quantity of unction for the purposes of the coronation of each succeeding monarch, did not attest the singular interposition of Heaven and the puissant effect of Divine Providence. As this prodigy was accorded to France in the time of Saint Remy, archbishop of Rheims, the precious treasure was confided to him and his successors, who were always to perform the ceremony of the coronation.

Page 101.

When the Pucelle saw that the king was consecrated, &c.

Upon the coronation of Charles VII. a contemporary historian states :

" *Au dit sacre fut toujours près et presente la dicte
Jehanne la Pucelle, tout armée à blanc, et tenant son estan-
dard en le main, et bien y devoit estre, comme celle qui
estait principallement cause de l'ordonnance et volunte de
Dieu d'icelluy sacre.*"

" At the said inauguration was always near and present
the said Jeanne la Pucelle, completely armed in polished
steel, and holding her standard in her hand, as by good
right, she having been the principal cause of the order
and will of God concerning the said coronation."

Page 102.   *She (Jeanne) thus addressed herself unto him
(the king), shedding warm tears.*

After the coronation of Charles, Dubreton, at page 282,
thus narrates the conduct of Jeanne:

" That done, the Pucelle, whom all the world listened
to, looked at and admired, as if an angel spake from
God, having in the presence of all the princes knelt down
at the king's feet, told him : ' That she had rendered to
him and to his kingdom her first duties ; and exhorted him
to reign as wisely and as virtuously as he had been
legitimately summoned to the crown.' "

Page 104.

I have accomplished all that MESSIRES *commanded me.*

By this term *Messires* (sirs or gentlemen) Jeanne im-
plied those saints who had visited her from heaven ; being
a term which appears very singular to apply to celestial
emissaries, at the present period of time.

Page 105.   *When the duke of Bedford, &c. knew that the king was in the plains in the vicinity of Dampmartin, &c.*

Grafton, at pages 538 and 539, when describing the then situation of affairs between the regent duke of Bedford, and Charles VII., gives the ensuing statement, which by no means coincides with the text of the Diary, from whence it should seem that the English were averse to give battle to the French, the direct opposite of which is asserted by our chronicler : —

" The duke of Bedford, hearing that these townes had returned to the part of his adversaries, and that Charles, late dolphin, had taken upon him the name and estate of the king of Fraunce, and also seeing that daylie cities and townes returned from the English part, and became French, as though the Englishe men had nowe lost all their hardie chiefetaynes and valyaunt men of warre, espied and evidently perceived that the last and uttermost point of recovery, was driven onely to overcome by battayle, and to subdue by force. By which victorie (as he put his confidence in God) he trusted not onely to scourge and plague the cities, which were so sodainely chaungeable, but also to asswage and caulme the haute courage of the newe sacred French king and his companions. Wherefore he having together ten thousand good Englishe men (besides Normans), departed out of Paris in warlike fashion, and passed through Brie to Monstrell Faultyow, and there sent by Bedford his herault letters to the French king, alleging to him that he, contrary to the laws of God and man, yea, and contrary to the finall conclusion taken, concorded, and agreed betweene his noble brother king Henry V. and king Charles VI., father to the sayde now usurper, leavyng all humaine reason and honest communication (which sometime appeaseth debates and pacefyeth strifes) onely allured and entysed by a devilish witch, and a fanaticall enchaunteresse, had not onely falsely and craftely taken upon him the name, title, and dignity of the king of France ; but also had, by murder, stealing, craft, and deceitfull meanes, violently gotten, and wrongfully kept, divers cities and townes belonging to the king of England, his most best beloved lorde, and most deerest nephew.   For proof whereof, he was come downe from Paris with his armie, into the countrie of Brye, by dent of sword, and stroke of battayle, to prove his wryting and cause true, willing his enemie to chose the place, and he in the same would give him battayle.

" The newe French king, departyng from his solempne ceremonies at Reins, and removing from thence to Dampmartine, studiyng howe to compasse the Parisians, either with money, or with promise, was somewhat troubled with this message ; howbeit, he made a good countenance and a French bragge, aunswering to the herault, that he would sooner seeke hys master the duke, than that the duke should pursue him.   The duke of Bedford, hering his aunswere, marched toward him, and pitched his field in a strong place, and sent out divers of his ramgers, to provoke the Frenche men to come forward.   The French king was in manner determined to abide the battayle, but when he heard saye by his espialles, that the power and number of the Englishe men were to his army equall in power, he determined that it was more for his profite to abstaine from battayle without daunger, then to enter into the conflict with jeopardie : fearing least that with a rashe courage he might overthrowe all his affayres, which so effectuously proceeded. And so well advised, he turned with his armie a little out of the way. The duke of Bedford perceyving his faint courage, followed him by mountaynes and dales, till he came to a towne in Barre, not farre from Senlis, where he found the French king and his army. Wherefore he ordered his battayle, lyke a man expert in marciall science, setting the archers before, and himselfe with the noble men in the mayne battayle, and put the Normans on both sides for the wings. The French king also ordered hys battayles, according to the devise of his capitaynes. Thus these two armies, without any great doing (except a fewe skirmishes, in the which the duke's light horse men did very valyauntly,) laye eche in sight of other, by the space of two dayes and two nightes. But when the French king sawe, and perceyved, how glad, howe diligent and couragious the Englishe men were to fight and geve battayle, he imagined that by his taryeng, one of these two things must nedes chaunce ; that is to say, eyther he should fight against his will, or lye still like a coward, to his great rebuke and infamie. Wherefore in the dead of the night (as prively as he could) he brake up his campe and fled to Bray. When this flight was perceyved in the morning, the regent could scarce refraine his people, from folowyng the French army, calling them cowardes, dastardes, and loutes ; and therefore, he perceyving that by no meanes he could allure the newe French king to abide battayle, mistrusting the Parisians, and *giving no great credite to their fayre, swete, and flattering wordes*, returned agayne to Paris, to assemble together a greater power, and so to prosecute his enemies."

Page 106.   *At about this period, proceeded many French lords unto the city of Beauvais.*

The city of Beauvais is of great antiquity, and the principal town of the Oise; being celebrated for the siege it sustained in 1472, under Jeanne Hachette, who headed the women of the place, against the duke of Burgundy, commanding eighty thousand men.   The inhabitants, to the present moment, pride themselves on their city's never having been taken.   One curious circumstance appertaining to Beauvais it may not be amiss to record, which was, that, on the fourteenth of January, annually, was celebrated the Ass's festival, or holiday, being a representation of the Virgin's flight into Egypt.   Upon this solemn occasion, all the clergy of the city being assembled in the cathedral, a beautiful damsel was presented to them, placed upon an ass most sumptuously caparisoned; and thus conducted from the principal church to that of Saint Stephen, into the chancel of which the maid and her bearer were escorted, and stationed on the right side of the altar.   During the service which followed, the whole congregation at intervals imitated the brayings of a jack-ass; and at the conclusion of the mass, the deacon, in lieu of repeating the *ita missa est*, articulated three stentorian brays, whereto his auditors gave the loudest nasal responses. The whole of this ceremony, together with a hymn in Latin, sung upon the occasion, have been preserved by Charles du Cange, the French antiquary, who transcribed the same from a manuscript five hundred years old.

Page 107. *Under the pretext of marching them against the Bohemian heretics, &c.*

Grafton, at page 539, thus explains this affair.

" In this season, the Bohemians (which belike had espyed the usurped authoritie of the bishop of Rome) began to rebell against his sea. Wherefore, Martin the fift, bishop of Rome, wrote unto them to absteyne from warre, and to be reconciled by reason, from their damnable opinions. But they (beying perswaded to the contrary) neyther gave eare unto him, nor yet obeyed his voyce. Wherefore the bishop of Rome wrote to the princes of Germanie, to invade the realme of Beame, as the den of heretykes. Beside this, he appoynted Henry bishop of Winchester, and cardinall of Saint Eusebie, a man very well borne (as you have heard) but no better borne then high stomacked, to be his legate in this great iourney, and to bring out men from the realme of England, into the countrie of Beame. And because the war touched religion, he licenced the sayd cardinall to take the tenth part of every spiritual dignitie, benefice and promocion. This matter was declared in open parliament in England, and not dissented, but gladly assented to ; wherefore the bishop gathered the money, and assembled foure thousand men, and mo, not without great grudge of the people, which daily were with tallages and aydes weried and sore burdened. And when men, municions, and money were redie for his high enterprise, he with all his people came to the sea strond at Dover, redie to pass over the sea into Flaundyrs.

" But in the meane season, the duke of Bedford, consideryng how townes dayly were gotten, and countries hourely wonne in the realme of Fraunce, for lacke of sufficient defence and number of men of warre, wrote to his brother the duke of Gloucester, to relieve him wythe ayde, in that tempestuous tyme and troubleous season. When this letter was brought into England, the duke of Gloucester was not a little amazed, because he had no armie redie to sende at that tyme: for by the reason of the crewe sent into Beame, he could not suddeinly rayse a new armie. But because the matter was of such importance, and might neyther be from day to day differred, nor yet long delayed, he wrote to the bishop of Winchester, to passe with all his armie toward the duke of Bedford, which at that tyme had both nede of men and assistaunce, consideryng that nowe all stood upon losse or gaine: which thing done, and to his honor achieved, he might performe his iourney agaynst the Bohemians. Although the cardinall was somewhat moved with this countermaund, yet least he should be noted, not to ayde the regent of Fraunce in so great a cause, and so necessary an enterprise, he bowed from his former iourney, and passed the sea with all his companie, and brought them to his cousin, to the citie of Parys."

Page 112. *Wherefore he was with much difficulty reseated.*

This appears to confirm a former suggestion hazarded in regard to the unwieldy armour with which the knights in the fifteenth century were wont to be accoutred.

Page 113. *And when it was made known unto the duke of Bedford, he marched forth from Paris, with a great power of men at war.*

Holinshed, in his quaint manner, at page 602, describes the proceedings of the regent of France in the following manner; which refutes the statements of the writer of our Diary, who plainly wishes to have it inferred, that, the English were uniformly averse to deliver battle to the French king.

" The duke of Bedford, advertised of all these dooings, assembled his power about him, and having togither ten thousand good Englishmen (beside Normans) departed out of Paris in warlike fashion, and passing thorough Brie to Monstreau fault Yonne, sent by his herald Bedford, letters to the French king, signifieng to him; that where he had (contrarie to the finall conclusion accorded betweene his noble brother k. Henrie the fift, and king Charles the sixt, father to him that was the usurper) by allurement of a divelish witch, taken upon him the name, title, and dignitie of the king of France; and further had by murther, stealing, craft, and deceitfull meanes, violentlie gotten, and wrongfullie kept diverse cities and townes belonging to the king of England his nephue; for proofe thereof he was come downe from Paris with his armie, into the countrie of Brie, by dint of sword and stroke of battell to proove his writing and cause true, willing his enimie to choose the place, and in the same he would give him battell.

" The new French king being come from Reimes to Dampmartine, studieng how to compasse them of Paris, was halfe abashed at this message. But yet to set a good countenance on the matter, he answered the herald, that he would sooner seeke his maister, than his maister should need to pursue him. The duke of Bedford, hearing this answer, marched toward the king, and pitched his field in a strong place. The French king, though at the first he meant to have abidden battell; yet when he understood that the duke was equall to him in number of people, he changed his purpose, and turned with his armie a little out of the waie. The duke of Bedford, perceiving his faint courage, followed him by the hils and dales, till he came to a town not far from Senlis, where he found the French king and his armie lodged; wherefore he ordered his battels like an expert cheeffteine in martiall science, setting the archers before, and himselfe with the noble-men in the maine battell, and put the Normans on both sides for wings. The French king also ordered his battels with the advise of his capteins."

Page 116. *Insomuch so that a cross-bowman of Paris pierced her thigh through with an arrow.*

" The following day, as the Pucelle possessed an excellent mind in foretelling events and admirable diligence in executing her purposes; she caused an attack to be made

on the boulevard and the barrier of the gate of Saint
Honoré. And the French having suddenly entered with
great courage, and chased the garrison, they became
masters of the same. The English at this were greatly
affrighted, seeing that the enemy, immediately upon
arriving, had seized this place before their eyes, and
ere the city had time to afford any assistance. But
shortly after, as the Pucelle valiantly descended into
the moat, and exhorted the others to transport the things
necessary to fill it up in order to approach the wall,
she received a wound in the thigh from an arrow, which
being extracted, a quantity of blood issued forth. Upon
this occasion the soldiers were greatly affrighted, believing her hurt to be more dangerous than it was in
reality. Jeanne, on the contrary, without changing colour,
ordered the flowing of the blood to be stopped, and that
the wound should be bound up. She then continued for
a long space before the standards, having either dissembled or got the better of the anguish she endured,
when the blood, which the means adopted had for some
time stopped, began to reflow in greater abundance; while
the wound being recent, not having inflicted its utmost
pain then increased in acuteness, and the part swelled
most dreadfully. At that juncture the courage and the
legs of this generous girl began to fail her, so that those
nearest received and supported her to the camp. This
mishap the duke of Alençon regretted greatly ; and, fearful lest the wound of the leader should be followed by
the defeat of the whole army, caused the retreat to be
sounded. There was in the courage of the Pucelle a
certain confidence rather supported by a supernatural

agency than any human interposition; in such sort, that she contemned all those dangers which make others turn pale, as if she believed not only that the Parisians would unite their forces to hers, but also that God visibly favoured her by his assistance. Nevertheless this hope, however conceived with temerity, would not have been deceitful, if, upon the point of executing her bold enterprise of so arduous a feat, the French had forwarded forces equal to the courage which was manifested on this occasion."—*Dubreton*, pages 308, &c.

Grafton, at page 542, relates this affair in the following manner.

" While the duke of Bedford was thus enterteinyng and encouragyng the Normans, Charles the newe French king, beyng of his departure advertised, longyng and thirstyng for to obteyne Paris, the chiefe citie and principall place of resort within the whole realme of Fraunce, departed from the towne of Senlis wel accompanied, and came to the towne of Saint Denise, which he found desolate, and abandoned of all garrison and good governance. Wherefore, without force and small damage, he entered into the voyd towne and lodged his armie at Mountmartir, and Abbervilliers, nere adioinyng and liyng to the citie of Parys. And from thence sent John duke of Alanson and his sorceresse Joan (called the Mayde sent from God), in whom his whole affiaunce then consisted, with three thousand light horsemen, to get againe the citie of Paris, eyther by force, or by fayre flatteryng, or reasonable treatie; and after them, he without delay or deferryng of tyme, with all hys power, came betwene

Mountmartir and Parys, and sodeinly approched the gate of Saint Honore, settyng up ladders to the walles, and castyng faggots into the ditches, as though he would with a French brag, sodeinly have gotten the fayre citie. But the Englishe capteynes, every one keppyng his warde and place assigned, so manfully and fiercely, with a noble courage, defended themselves, their walles and towers, with the assistence of the Parisiens, that they rebutted and drave away the Frenchmen, and threw downe Jone, their great goddesse, into the botome of the towne ditche, where shee lay behinde the backe of an asse, sore hurt, till the tyme that she, all filthie with mire and durt, was drawen out by Guyschard of Thienbrone, servaunt to the duke of Alaunson."

Page 117. *For several notable personages being then within Paris, the which recognised king Charles to be their sovereign lord, &c.*

As the Parisians uniformly proved themselves a treacherous race, the duke of Bedford was well aware that nothing but vigorous measures could keep them under subjection, and upon this account a very numerous garrison was maintained in the city of Paris. At other times, however, a different line of conduct became necessary, as will appear in the following extract taken from Grafton, page 543: the regent being compelled to have recourse to flattery, as, in consequence of the defection of so many places in favour of Charles VII., every expedient became necessary to prevent a commotion against the English in

Q

the capital of the kingdom, and more particularly so, as the victorious claimant had marched to its very gates.

" The duke of Bedford, beyng in Normandie, and heryng of this sodain attempt, lost no time, nor spared no travaile, till he came to Parys.   Where he not onely thanked the capteynes, and praysed the citizens for their assured fidelitie and good will towarde their king and sovereigne lorde, but also extolled their hardinesse and manly doynges above the starres and highe elementes; promisyng to them honour, fame, and great advauncementes.   Which gentle exhortacion so incoraged and inflamed the heartes of the Parisians, that they sware, promised, and concluded, to be friendes ever to the king of England and his friendes, and enemies always to his foes and adversaryes, makyng proclamation by this stile : Friendes to king Henrie, friendes to the Parisians, enemyes to England, enemies to Parys. But if they spake it with their hearts, eyther for feare, that Charles, the French king, should not punishe them, if he once obteyned the superioritie over their citie and towne, or that they flattered the Englishemen, to put themselves in credite with the chiefe capteines, you shall plainely perceive, by the sequele of their actes."

Page 118. *And this concluded, he departed the twelfth day of September, and proceeded to Laigny on the Marne, &c.*

As mention is made of the town of Laigny in our Diary, the editor cannot refrain from inserting the following extract from Holinshed, page 603, who, when speaking of the siege of that town by the English, in 1430, relates an anecdote of Jeanne d'Arc, which, if correct, not only belies the French historians, who pretend that the Pucelle never used her sword in battle, but displays her in a point of view not very favourable to her character as a magnanimous and noble-minded woman.

"In the moneth of Maie, 1430, with a valiant man in feats of armes on the duke of Burgognions side, one Franquet and his band of three hundred souldiers, making all towards the maintenance of the siege, the Pucell Jone and a foure hundred with hir did meet. In great courage and force did she and hir people sundrie times assaile him, but he with his, (though much under in number) by meanes of his archers in good order set, did so hardilie withstand them, that for the first and second push she rather lost than wan. Whereat this captinesse, stricken into a fretting chafe, called out in all bast the garrison of Laignie, and from other the forts thereabout, who thicke and threefold came downe with might and maine, in armour and number so far exceeding Franquet's, that though they had done hir much hurt in hir horsemen, yet by the verie multitude were they oppressed, most in hir furie put to the sword; and as for to Franquet that worthie capteine himselfe, hir rage not appeased, till out of hand she had his head stroken off: contrarie to all manhood (but she was a woman, if she were that) and contrarie to common right and law of armes. The man for his merits was verie much lamented, and she by hir malice then found of what spirit she was."

Page 119.   *So that when he had arrived in Paris, the said
     duke abided by nothing which he had promised.*

Grafton, speaking of the duke of Burgundy's visit to
Paris, at page 543, states as under : —

" Sone after these doynges, came to Parys with a great
companie Philip, duke of Burgoyn, which was of the
regent, and the ladie his wife, honourably receyved, and
highly feasted.   And after long consultation had, for the
recoveryng of the townes, lately by the French king stollen
and taken, it was agreed, that the duke of Bedford should
raise an armie, for the recoverie of the sayde fortresses,
and that the duke of Burgoyn should be his deputie,
and tary at Parys, for the defence of the same."

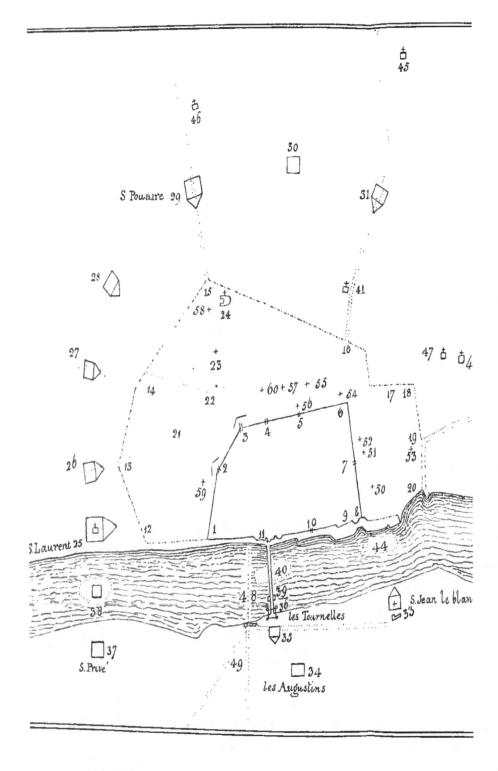

S Pouaire 29

30

31

46

45

28

15
58 +   24

41

27

23

14

22

21

60 + 57 + 55

56

3   4   5   6

54

52
51

7

50

53
19

47   4

17   18

20

26

13

2

59

12

1

44

40

S.Laurent 25

39
38
36

les Tournelles

S.Jean le blan

33

38

37
S. Privé

49

35

34
les Augustins

9 8

10

11

44

4 8

THE

CHART OF ORLEANS,

WITH

ITS WALLS, BOULEVARDS, TOURNELLES, &c.

EXPLAINED:

BEING A DELINEATION OF THAT CITY AND ITS FORTIFICATIONS,
AS THEY APPEARED DURING THE SIEGE IN 1428.

THE CHART.

THE method adopted in order to furnish the following account, has, in some instances, led to the discovery of facts of which no trace whatsoever is to be found in the details of modern historians, or the existence of which but ill accorded with their narrations; this having more particularly been the case as regards the siege of Orleans, which certainly ranks as an era in the history of France, as well as of England, of sufficient consequence to render it an object worthy of the most minute investigation; and the more so, as there was no paucity of materials to work upon, in the progress of such inquiry. Independent of all the accounts furnished by the chroniclers respecting this siege, recourse might be had to the depositions made by several witnesses during the process instituted for the justification of Jeanne d'Arc; in short, the ancient history of the Pucelle, and the journal of Tripaut, evidently corrected and arranged by ocular witnesses, abound in the most curious and interesting recitals.

It must nevertheless be allowed, that if the mine was stored with riches, the labour of extracting the ore was attended by numerous difficulties. The witnesses and the

recorders of such journals, answering or writing for con-
temporaries or fellow citizens, paid little attention to the
elucidating those periods and localities of which we now
stand in need, in order to comprehend clearly their several
statements. Independent of this, the manuscripts of such
journals underwent, prior to publication, many alterations,
either owing to the effects of time, or resulting from the
negligence, as well as the ignorance, of the original editors.
For example, that chronicle which, for its perspicuity
and the impartial statements it contains, merits the most
attention, although, perhaps, prolix from its scrupulous
exactitude, nevertheless, to all appearance, frequently
presents a confusion in the dates : in that work, for
instance, the business of an entire week is twice recorded ;
or, to speak more comprehensively, seven days contain the
business transacted in the course of fourteen ; added to
which, the days, either of the week or the month, are
constantly misplaced, &c.   The statements, however,
which are subjoined, will furnish a much better idea of
the difficulty experienced by modern historians, which has
not, perhaps, unfrequently prompted them to imitate the
Abbé Vertot, *by writing the siege themselves.* In combining
all the details with the geographical charts, the topo-
graphical descriptions, together with the voyages and
various chronologies, we have been obliged to compose : —
first, a chart of the fortifications of the city, and of the besiegers : secondly, a complete calendar from the commencement of October, 1428, that is to say, from the march of
the English army towards Orleans, until the end of the
month of May 1430 , at which period the capture of

Jeanne d'Arc took place : and, thirdly, to examine, with the greatest exactitude, all these accounts, comparing them at the same time with the plan and the calendar. Notwithstanding this, if the scrutiny proved extremely long and tedious, we were amply compensated by the result of the labour bestowed ; for, with the exception of some circumstances of little or no interest, almost every thing that has been handed down to us relating to the siege of Orleans, and the exploits of Jeanne d'Arc, is found to be completely developed.

Another source of embarrassment and error to the modern historian, has been, that the year during the fourteenth and fifteenth centuries commenced at Easter, and consequently was incessantly varying, since that festival is never found to occur twice upon the same days. In consequence, if the strictest attention is not paid to this circumstance, how can it be accounted for that the ratification of a particular treaty in the month of October, 1416, should be anterior to the death of a prince which took place on the fifth of April in that year; or that a battle fought on the twentieth or the twenty-first of March should be the identical conflict recorded by one chronicler as occurring on the twentieth of March 1420, and by another on the twenty-first of March 1421. There are very few writers who have not been led into error by such variations in the calendar, and this the more easily, because those writers who preceded them were very faulty in their statements on the score of chronology.

By the following table extracted from *L'Art de Vérifier les Dates* (The Art of Verifying Dates), edit. of 1750

and 1770, will be found the first days of the several years
during which the events took place, forming the subject
matter of our volume.

Years.	EASTER.		Years.	EASTER.	
	March.	April.		March.	April.
1401	—	3	1416	—	19
1402	26	—	1417	—	11
1403	—	15	1418	27	—
1404	30	—	1419	—	16
1405	—	19	1420	—	7
1406	—	11	1421	23	—
1407	27	—	1422	—	12
1408	—	15	1423	—	4
1409	—	7	1424	—	17
1410	23	—	1425	—	8
1411	—	12	1426	31	—
1412	—	3	1427	—	20
1413	—	23	1428	—	4
1414	—	8	1429	27	—
1415	31	—	1430	—	16
			1431	—	1

If the examination of the Paschal Calendar is indispen-
sably requisite, that also of the festivals of the saints is of
great utility in discovering the dates of events, because the
old writers frequently contented themselves, (a practice
still in use among artisans and labouring men on the
continent in particular,) with indicating these same festivals;
to which circumstance we have likewise paid attention in
the progress of our researches.

No. 1.   *Observations.*

Having explained the plan pursued in the formation of this chart, we must add that the scale accompanying the same, if not *strictly* correct, will serve to elucidate every thing stated in the Diary of the Siege of Orleans, as well as the various other accounts of that event, which have been recorded by writers of the period.

No. 2.   *Bastilles.*

The positions of several of these bulwarks could not be accurately determined.   The name of that numbered 31 in the Chart, is placed at that point, because it is positively affirmed in the History of the Pucelle, pages 500 and 501 of Godfroy's Collections, &c. &c. that the English established bastilles on all the public roads.*   The same incertitude exists in regard to another bastille, which must, however, have been Nos. 28 or 30 on the chart; there is also some reason for conjecture, that the bastille of the wooden cross was situated near to No. 26.   In regard to that called Colombier, it is very probable that it stood at No. 27, because the English, by whom it was garrisoned, made frequent sallies, and gave battle to the

* According to Tripaut, from pp. 83 to 85, the English at first lodged in the environs of the Cross of Fleury (No. 45 in the Chart), and that several days after, the French advanced as far as that cross in order to protect some merchants journeying to Orleans, whose progress was resisted by the English; a convincing proof that the latter afterwards established themselves between that cross and Orleans.

Orleanese in the environs of Colombier Turpin, which, according to an observation of Miquellus of the ensuing century, (see *Aureliæ Obsidio*, &c. p. 26. ed. 1560), occupied the spot which now forms the street Colombier.

The uncertainty attending the positions of these several fortresses is owing to the history already quoted not having designated them in their regular order. With respect to the other bastilles, there is very little doubt of their having occupied the stations assigned to them upon the chart.

No. 3.   *Designations.*

At the explanation, No. 5, will be found the various edifices, forts, &c. delineated upon the Chart. Being compelled to form the plan upon a very circumscribed scale, we have been under the necessity of noting only those objects which were of utility in recording the history of the siege of Orleans.

No. 4.   *Churches burnt.*

The following are the names of the religious edifices burnt by the Orleanese. Saint Aignan, No. 50 on the Chart. Saint Michael, No. 51. Saint Aux, or Saint Avit (now the seminary, see *Polluche*, 127), No. 54. The chapel of Martroy, No. 55. Saint Victor, in the suburb of Burgundy Gate, No. 52. Saint Michael, on the fosses, No. 56. The Cordeliers, afterwards the Recollets, No. 60. The Jacobins, No. 57. The Carmelites, No. 59. Saint Mathurin, No. 23. The Almonry of Saint Povaire, No. 58.

Saint Lawrence, No. 25. Saint Loup, No. 32. Saint Mark, No. 42. Saint Euverte, No. 18. The chapel of Saint Aignan, No. 53. Saint Vincent of the Vines, No. 41. Saint Ladre or Saint Lazarus, No. 46. Saint Povaire or Saint Paterne, No. 24. The Magdalen, No. 27. Saint Gervais, afterwards Saint Phalier, No. 47. Vide *Polluche*, p. 19 and 153.

No. 5. *Explanation of the Numbers on the Chart.*

1, 2, 3, 4, 5, 6, 7, 8, 9, 10, and 11, boundaries of Orleans at the period of the siege.

12, 13, 14, 15, 16, 17, 18, 19, 20; 8, 9, 10, 11, and 1, boundaries of the city at the present period.

1. Notre Dame de Recouvrance.
2. The Gate and Boulevard Renard.
3. The ancient Gate and Boulevard Banier.
4. Postern Saint Samson.
5. Paris Gate.
6. The Bishop's Palace.
7. Anciently Burgundy Gate.
8. The New Tower Postern.
9. The New Tower.
10. Postern Chesneau.
11. Anciently the Chatelet and Bridge Gate.
12. The City Garden, formerly Saint Lawrence Gate.
13. Gate and suburbs of Magdalen.
14. Gate and suburbs of Saint John.
15. Banier Gate, still standing.
16. Saint Vincent's Gate, also standing.
17. Saint Euverte Gate, since walled up.

18. Saint Euverte.

19. Burgundy Gate, now standing at the extremity of the ancient suburb; near to which is Notre Dame Duchemin, which was formerly the Chapel Saint Aignan. Vide *Erpilly*, 345; *Polluche*, 121.

20. Tower de la Brebis.

21. Moriri Cross.

22. Colombier Street.

23. The Visitation, formerly Saint Mathurin.

24. Saint Paterne, anciently called Saint Povaire.*

25. The Bastille of Saint Lawrence.

26 and 27. Bastilles of the wooden Cross and Colombier.

28 and 30. At one of these points there was a Bastille, name unknown.

29. The Bastille of Saint Povaire.

31. At this point there was also a Bastille.

32. The Bastille of Saint Loup.

33. ——— —— of Saint John le Blanc.

34. ————— of the Augustins.

35. Boulevard of the Tournelles.

36. The Tournelles.

37. Bastille of Saint Privé field.

38. ——— of Charlemaine island.

39. Boulevard of the beautiful Cross on the old bridge.

40. Mounds of the fishermen of Saint Anthony.†

---

* The English forming the garrison of Saint Povaire held their watch near this church.

† This island, as before stated in the notes to the Diary, was destroyed at the erection of the present bridge.

41. Parish and suburbs of Saint Vincent of the Vines.
42. Parish of Saint Mark.
43. L'Orbette.*
44. The island which was in front of Saint Aignan.
45. The cross of Fleury.
46. The Cistercians, formerly St. Lazarus or St. Ladre.
47. Saint Phallier, formerly Saint Gervais.
48. The bridge now existing.
49. The three suburbs of Portereau.
50. Saint Aignan.
51. Saint Michael.
52. Saint Victor, in the suburb of Burgundy Gate.
53. The Chapel of Saint Aignan.
54. Saint Aux, or Saint Avit.
55. The Chapel of Martroi.
56. Saint Michael on the Fosses.
57. The Jacobins.
58. The Almonry of Saint Pouvaire.
59. The Carmelites.
60. The Cordeliers, afterwards the Recollets.

* The English forming the garrison of Saint Loup, held their watches at L'Orbette. Vide *Tripaut*, 80 : *Guyon, Hist. of the Diocese of Orleans*, p. 216.

END OF THE FIRST VOLUME.

LONDON:
PRINTED BY J. MOYES, GREVILLE STREET.

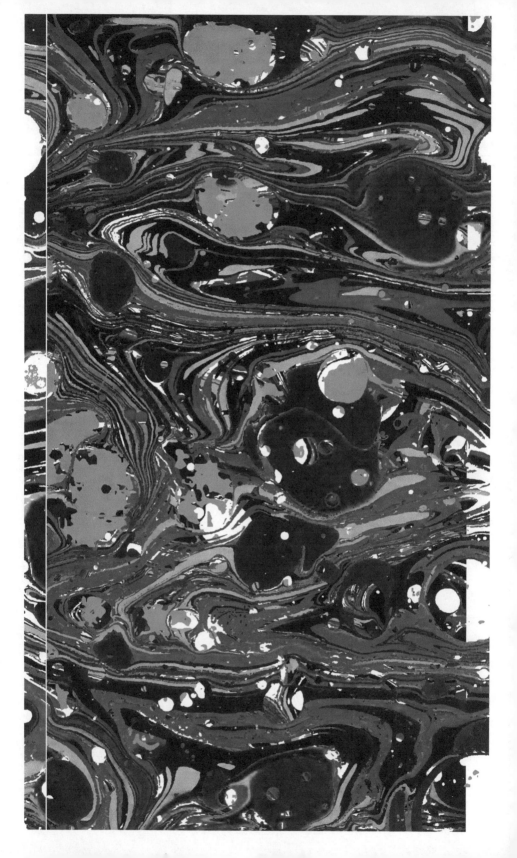

SD - #0014 - 130123 - C0 - 229/152/24 - PB - 9781314714081 - Gloss Lamination